D1298043

MILITARY RESUMES
AND COVER LETTERS

Military career transition books authored by Carl S. Savino and Ronald L. Krannich

From Air Force Blue to Corporate Gray

From Army Green to Corporate Gray

From Navy Blue to Corporate Gray

Military Resumes and Cover Letters

Resumes and Job Search Letters For Transitioning Military Personnel

MILITARY RESUMES AND COVER LETTERS

Carl S. Savino, USAR (Ret.)
Ronald L. Krannich, Ph.D.

IMPACT PUBLICATIONS
Manassas Park, VA

MILITARY RESUMES AND COVER LETTERS

Liability/Warranty: The authors and publisher have made every attempt to provide the reader with accurate, timely, and useful information. This information is presented for reference purposes only. The authors and publisher make no claims that using this information will guarantee the reader a job. The authors and publisher shall not be liable for any loss or damages incurred in the process of following the advice presented in this book.

Library of Congress Cataloguing-in-Publication Data

Savino, Carl S., 1955-
    Military resumes and cover letters / Carl S. Savino, Ronald L. Krannich
        p.   cm.
    ISBN 1-57023-159-1
        1. Veterans–Employment–United States. 2. Retired military personnel–Employment–United States. 3 Resumes (Employment)–United States. 4. Applications for positions. 5. Cover letters–United States. 6. United States–Armed Forces–Job descriptions. 7. United States–Armed Forces–Records and correspondence. I. Krannich, Ronald L. II. Title.

UB357.S28 2001
355.1'1–dc21   00-054153

Publisher: For information on Impact Publications, including current and forthcoming publications, authors, press kits, online bookstore, and submission requirements, visit Impact's website: *www.impactpublications.com*

Publicity/Rights: For information on publicity, author interviews, and subsidiary rights, contact the Media Relations Department: Tel. 703-361-7300, Fax 703-361-7300, or email: *military@impactpublications.com*.

Sales/Distribution: All bookstore sales are handled through Impact's trade distributor: National Book Network, 15200 NBN Way, Blue Ridge Summit, PA 17214, Tel. 1-800-462-6420. All other sales and distribution inquiries should be directed to the publisher: Sales Department, IMPACT PUBLICATIONS, 9104 Manassas Drive, Suite N, Manassas Park, VA 20111-5211, Tel. 703-361-7300, Fax 703-335-9486, or email: *sales@impactpublications.com*

Contents

v

MILITARY RESUMES
AND COVER LETTERS

1

Show Me Your Resume

I T'S SHOW-AND-TELL TIME. YOU HAVE LOTS OF VALUABLE
military experience which you hope will be readily marketable in the
civilian job world. Your skills and accomplishments, if properly organized and communicated to employers, should attract the attention of many
employers. If you're lucky, you may receive multiple job offers. At least that's
the plan—get an exciting new job which fully utilizes your many talents and
which also is well compensated. If all goes well, you will soon start a new job
that should lead to renewed career success.

Employers Have Expectations

Let's assume we're a civilian employer who may be interested in your talents.
Since we're trying to screen for the perfect candidate, we want to see your
resume—along with a cover letter, salary history, and salary requirements—
before we see you in person. Yes, if you want to apply for a job with our
company, you need to immediately send us this information via email, fax, or
mail. We have many candidates, some with military experience, whom we will
be interviewing during the next two weeks.

So what are you going to do when you get this standard message from
civilian employers? Are you prepared for us and others who want to first see
your credentials on paper, or electronically, before inviting you to the critical
job interview?

It Has Been a Long Time Coming

When was the last time you looked for a job in the civilian world? Did your job search involve writing a resume and crafting various types of job search letters? How effective was your writing? Did you get the response you expected? If you used a resume to find a job, did you mail it in response to vacancy announcements, pass it around as part of your networking activities, or attach it to completed application forms? Do you know how to put together an outstanding resume that clearly communicates your qualifications to employers in today's job market? Can you succinctly state your career objective and summarize your experience in one to two pages? Are you prepared to write different types of job search letters for different job search audiences? Can you translate your military experience into the language of civilian employers and then present it in a proper resume format?

Employers Want to See Your Resume

Let's not beat around the bush. It's time to speak truth about your future. Your resume writing skills are probably either nonexistent or very rusty. Accordingly, you may be at a disadvantage in today's highly competitive civilian job market because you may not know how to write dynamite resumes and letters that command the attention of civilian employers.

> *Does your resume incorporate the right language for the civilian work world or it is filled with lots of military jargon only fellow service members understand?*

If you are like many other members of the military, chances are your first real job, and career, was with the military. You've probably never had to look for a job outside the military. If you did conduct a job search, perhaps you only completed applications rather than wrote and distributed resumes and job search letters. And if you once wrote a resume, chances are it is now dated, doesn't incorporate your most recent experiences, and may be inappropriate for today's new job market which requires three types of resumes—conventional, scannable, and electronic.

To most employers, you are a stranger who has military work experience that may or may not relate to their specific needs. Before inviting you to an interview, employers want to see your qualifications summarized on a one or two-page resume. Based on their evaluation of your resume, they may want to invite you to an interview. But they first want to see you on paper before seeing you in person.

Whatever your past experience in navigating the civilian job market, today you're approaching a different job market. It's a very competitive job market where individuals market their skills in exchange for position and money. If you want to be successful in this job market, you must have a well crafted resume. When an employer asks you to send a resume, what exactly will you send? Does your resume incorporate the right language for the civilian work world, or it is filled with lots of military jargon only fellow service members understand? Does it best state your career goals as well as represent your major strengths? Will an employer in 30 seconds or less understand exactly what it is you can do, will do, and want to do?

Special Challenges for Special People

As you transition from the military to the civilian work world, you face special challenges in communicating your military background to civilian employers. One of the best ways to deal with these challenges is to begin writing a resume designed for your new civilian job or career. This resume writing exercise will help you pull together what it is you have done, can do, and really want to do in the future. It requires taking an inventory of your education, past work experiences, and current interests, skills, and abilities. It focuses your attention around assessing major strengths and formulating a career objective that communicates accomplishments to employers.

Done right, this resume writing exercise will direct you into the civilian work world by focusing your military experience and current interests, skills, and abilities on the specific needs of civilian employers. It will help you select the proper language for communicating with civilian employers. Whatever you do in the process of making a transition to the civilian work world, make sure you start out right by compiling a dynamite resume.

You Are What You Write

At least to strangers who know little or nothing about you and your capabilities, which includes most civilian employers, you essentially are what you write about yourself. Your one- to two-page resume and accompanying cover letter succinctly say a great deal about your professionalism, competence, and personality that goes beyond just documenting your work history, experience, and education. How you present yourself and what you say through specific words, phrases, sentences, and paragraphs will make the difference between being selected or rejected for a job interview. If you have little or no civilian work experience, you must present your military experience in terms that are easily understood in the civilian world. If you want to best present your qualifications to employers, you must translate military terminology and jargon into the language of civilian employers. Above all, your new civilian resume and letter must clearly communicate to employers what it is you (1) want to do, (2) have done, (3) can do, and (4) will most likely do in the immediate future.

Your resume and cover letter must have sufficient impact to **motivate** employers to contact you, conduct a screening interview over the telephone, and hopefully invite you to a job interview that leads to a job offer and renewed career success. If you fail to properly write, produce, market, and follow up your resume, you will most likely conduct an ineffective job search.

Becoming More Effective

When did you last write a resume and job search letters? How important was the selection of language in summarizing your experience? How well did you write, produce, distribute, and follow up your resume? Who evaluated it and how? Did it immediately grab the attention of employers who called you for interviews? Would it also do well in the face of today's electronic scanning technology? How well did your resume and letter stand out from the crowd of other resumes and letters? Did they clearly communicate your qualifications and future performance to potential employers? What did your resume really say about you as both a professional and a person? Did it become your ticket to interviews or did it dash your job search expectations?

Regardless of what resulted from your previous resume and letter writing efforts, let's turn to your future success which should include dynamite resumes and letters for making that critical military-to-civilian transition.

Much Abused and Misused Communication

Resumes are some of the most abused and misused forms of job search communication. Not knowing how to best communicate their qualifications to employers, many job seekers go through the ritual of writing uninspired documents that primarily document their work history rather than provide evidence for predicting their future performance and value to employers. Lacking a clear sense of purpose, they fail to properly connect their resume writing activities to their larger job search tasks. Rather than communicate their future performance and value to employers, they choose to document their past employment history, which may or may not be relevant to employers' immediate and future needs. In this respect individuals transitioning from the military to the civilian world are no different from many other job seekers—they make similar resume mistakes.

But writing a resume really isn't that difficult if done properly. Many individuals make it more difficult than it need be because they lack a basic understanding of how the resume should relate to all other job search activities. Indeed, after writing and producing it, many job seekers don't know how to best manage their resume in relation to potential employers. Most just send it in the mail or fax it to employers as if job interviews and offers are primarily a function of increased direct-mail and faxing activity. Preoccupied with the magic of writing right, few job seekers engage in effective resume **distribution and follow-up** activities—the keys for getting your resume read and responded to. Instead, they circulate a lot of pretty paper that often goes to all the wrong people and the wrong places!

You can do better than most job seekers if you produce dynamite resumes and letters. Unlike other resumes and letters, these are designed with the larger job search in mind—they grab the attention of potential employers who, in turn, invite you to job interviews. You conduct dynamite interviews because your answers and questions are consistent with your dynamite resumes and letters. Dynamite resumes and letters:

- Consistently observe the rules of good resume and letter writing— structure, form, grammar, word selection, categories, punctuation, spelling, inclusion/exclusion, length, and graphic design.

- Clearly communicate a sense of purpose, value, professionalism, competence, honesty, enthusiasm, and likeability.

- Specifically link your interests, skills, abilities, and experience to the employer's present and future needs.

- Are produced in a professional manner, from paper stock to ink, to further communicate your professional image.

- Include the right combination of "keywords" used by search and retrieval software for scanning resumes electronically.

- Get distributed through the proper channels and delivered into the hands of the right people—those who make the hiring decision.

- Regularly get followed up with telephone calls and letters.

- Stand out from the crowd by clearly speaking to employers—*"Let's interview this candidate who appears to have the experience and qualifications we want."*

Unlike many other resume and letter writing books, which are primarily preoccupied with presenting proper form and content on paper, or presenting numerous examples of resumes and letters, this book focuses on the whole communication process, from producing outstanding written documents (form, content, and production elements) to distributing and following up your resume and letters with maximum impact. We focus on creating resumes and letters that generate concrete **outcomes**—job interviews which then result in job offers.

In 30 Seconds You're Either In or Out

Resume writing is first and foremost a 30-second image management activity. After all, it takes employers no more than 30 seconds to read and respond to your resume. If it is scanned and processed electronically, it takes only seconds for the computer software to match keywords on your resume to determine whether or not your resume should be selected for human consideration. Therefore, you must quickly **motivate** the reader to take action. Your resume and cover letter must communicate your best professional image in writing **before** you can expect to be invited to a job interview. How and what you write, as well as which methods you choose to disseminate and follow up your message, will largely determine how effective you are in moving the employer to take action on your application.

Keep in mind that most employers are busy people who must make quick judgments about you based upon your written message. Within only 30 seconds, your written communication must motivate the reader to either take you in or take you out of consideration for a job interview. Neglect the importance of a 30-second dynamite resume and you will surely neglect one of the most important elements in a successful job search. Your resume and accompanying cover letter will join the graveyard of so many other ineffective resumes and letters.

Resumes Really Do Count

Finding employment in today's job market poses numerous challenges for individuals who seek quality jobs that lead to good salaries, career advancement, and job security. The whole job finding process is chaotic, confusing, and frustrating. It requires a certain level of organization and communication skills aimed at identifying, contacting, and communicating your qualifications to potential employers. If you want to make this process best work for you, you must do more than just mail resumes and letters in response to classified ads and vacancy announcements.

To be most successful in finding employment, you should develop a plan of action that involves these seven distinct yet interrelated job search steps:

1. Assess your skills
2. Develop a job/career objective
3. Conduct research on employers and organizations
4. Write resumes and letters
5. Network for information, advice, and referrals
6. Interview for jobs
7. Negotiate salary and terms of employment

As illustrated on page 8, each of these steps represents important **communication skills** involving you in contact with others. Assessing your skills (Step 1), for example, requires conducting a systematic assessment of what you do well and enjoy doing—your strengths or motivated abilities and skills (MAS) that become translated into your "qualifications" for employers. Conducting research on individuals, organizations, communities, and jobs (Step 4) requires the use of investigative skills commonly associated with library research. Networking and interviewing (Steps 5-6) primarily involve the use of conversational skills—small talk and structured question/answer dialogues—by telephone and in face-to-face encounters.

In the job search, paper is the great equalizer. Most employers want to see you on paper before meeting you in person.

But it is the critical resume and letter writing step (3) that becomes the major communication challenge for most job seekers. Without strong writing and presentation skills, your job search is likely to flounder. Indeed, your

Job Search Steps and Stages

Identify motivated skills and abilities	1	
Specify a job/career objective	2	INVESTIGATIVE STAGE
Research individuals, organizations, communities, and jobs	3	
Produce resumes and job search letters	4	WRITING STAGE
Conduct informational/ networking interviews	5	
Manage job interviews	6	EMPLOYER CONTACT STAGE
Negotiate salary and terms of employment	7	

ability to write dynamite resumes and job search letters largely determines how quickly you will transform your job search from the investigative stage (research) to employer contact stages (networking, interviewing, salary negotiations). Your writing skills become the key element in moving your job search from the investigative stage to the final job offer stage. Put simply, your writing is a initial indicator of your possible competence.

In the job search, paper is the great equalizer. Most employers want to first see you on paper before meeting you in person. You, along with many others, must pass the written test **before** you can be considered for the face-to-face oral test—the critical job interview. Whether you like it or not, you must put your professionalism, competence, and personality in writing before you can be taken seriously for a job interview. Thus, your writing activities may well become the most critical **transformation step** in your job search. Your writing skills become your ticket to job interviews that lead to job offers and employment.

For some reason job search writing skills usually receive little attention beyond the perfunctory *"you must write a resume and cover letter"* advisory. They also get dismissed as unimportant in a society that supposedly places its greatest value on telecommunicating and interpersonal skills. Indeed, during the past two decades many career advisors have emphasized networking as the key to getting a job; they see resume and letter writing as relatively unimportant job search activities. Some even advise job seekers to eliminate the resume altogether and, instead, rely on cold-calling telephone techniques and "showing up" networking strategies.

But such advice is misplaced and misses one of the most important points in the job search. Resumes are an **accepted** means of communicating qualifications to employers; they are becoming essential requirements for today's new electronic recruitment operations. Employers expect to receive well-crafted resumes that represent the best professional efforts of candidates. The problem is that hiring managers receive so many poorly written and distributed resumes. Indeed, many candidates might be better off not writing a resume given the weaknesses they demonstrate by producing poorly constructed resumes. Failure to develop a well-crafted resume will disqualify you for many jobs.

Resumes do not substitute for other equally important communication activities, but they do play a critical transformational role in your job search. They must be carefully linked to other key job search activities, especially networking and informational interviews, which function as important **methods for disseminating resumes**.

You simply must write a resume if you are to be taken seriously in today's job market. And you will be taken most seriously if you write a dynamite resume.

While some individuals do get interviews without writing resumes, you can do much better if you take the time and effort to develop a well-crafted resume and disseminate it properly. It should be designed for both electronic and human consumption. Your resume should focus on the employer's needs. It should demonstrate your professionalism, competence, and personality. Without an effective resume, your job search will have limited impact.

Improve Your Effectiveness

Just how effective are you in opening the doors of potential employers? Let's begin by identifying your level of job search information, skills, and strategies as well as those you need to develop and improve. You can do this by completing the following "job search competencies" exercise:

INSTRUCTIONS: Respond to each statement by circling the number on the right that best represents your situation.

SCALE:

1 = strongly agree	4 = disagree
2 = agree	5 = strongly disagree
3 = maybe, not certain	

1. I know what motivates me to excel at work.   1 2 3 4 5

2. I can identify my strongest abilities and skills.   1 2 3 4 5

3. I can identify at least seven major achievements that clarify a pattern of interests and abilities that are relevant to my job and career.   1 2 3 4 5

4. I know what I both like and dislike in work.   1 2 3 4 5

5. I know what I want to do during the next 10 years.   1 2 3 4 5

6. I have a well-defined career objective that focuses my job search on particular organizations and employers.   1 2 3 4 5

7. I know what skills I can offer employers in different occupations.   1 2 3 4 5

8. I know what skills employers most want.   1   2   3   4   5

9. I can clearly explain to employers what I do
    well and enjoy doing.   1   2   3   4   5

10. I can specify why employers should hire me.   1   2   3   4   5

11. I can gain support of family and friends for
    making a job or career change.   1   2   3   4   5

12. I can find 10 to 20 hours a week to conduct a
    part-time job search.   1   2   3   4   5

13. I have the financial ability to sustain a three-
    month job search.   1   2   3   4   5

14. I can conduct library and interview research on
    different occupations, employers, organizations,
    and communities.   1   2   3   4   5

15. I can write different types of effective resumes
    and job search/thank-you letters.   1   2   3   4   5

16. I can produce and distribute resumes and letters
    to the right people.   1   2   3   4   5

17. I can list my accomplishments in action terms.   1   2   3   4   5

18. I can identify and target employers with whom
    I want to interview.   1   2   3   4   5

19. I can develop a job referral network.   1   2   3   4   5

20. I can persuade others to join in forming a job
    search support group.   1   2   3   4   5

21. I can prospect for job leads.   1   2   3   4   5

22. I can use the telephone to develop prospects
    and get referrals and interviews.   1   2   3   4   5

23. I can plan and implement an effective
    direct-mail job search campaign.   1   2   3   4   5

24. I can generate one job interview for every
    10 job search contacts I make.   1   2   3   4   5

25. I can follow-up on job interviews.   1   2   3   4   5

26. I can negotiate a salary 10-20% above what an
    employer initially offers.   1   2   3   4   5

27. I can persuade an employer to renegotiate my
    salary after six months on the job.   1   2   3   4   5

28. I can create a position for myself in a company. 1   2   3   4   5

                                    TOTAL   _____

You can calculate your overall job search effectiveness by adding the numbers you circled for a composite score. If your total is more than 75 points, you need to work on developing your job search skills. How you scored each item will indicate to what degree you need to work on improving specific job search skills. If your score is under 50 points, you are well on your way toward job search success. In either case, this book should help you better focus your job search around the critical writing skills necessary for communicating your qualifications to employers. Other books can assist you with many other important aspects of your job search.

Your Corporate Gray Connection

This book is written in conjunction with our three military to civilian career transition guides: *From Army Green to Corporate Gray*, *From Air Force Blue to Corporate Gray*, and *From Navy Blue to Corporate Gray: A Career Transition Guide For Navy, Marine Corps, and Coast Guard Personnel*. Each of these books is a comprehensive A to Z guide for making a career transition from the military to the civilian work world. They include everything from the seven-step job search process outlined on page 8 to starting your own business, relocating to a new community, and working for defense contractors. If you do not have a copy of your respective service volume, you may want to check with your base job transition office, family service center, or library. The books also are available in bookstores or can be ordered directly from Impact Publications by completing the order form at the end of this book or by ordering through their Internet bookstores: *www.impactpublications.com* and *www.winningthejob.com*. This book, along with your relevant corporate gray volume, should provide you with most of the necessary information for launching an effective job search. We also provide additional job search assistance through our Corporate Gray website: *www.greentogray.com* or *www.bluetogray.com.*

Get Taken Seriously By Employers

The whole purpose of a job search is to get taken seriously by strangers who have the power to hire. Your goal is to both discover and land a job you really want. You do this by locating potential employers and then persuading them to talk to you by telephone and in person about your qualifications.

Being a stranger to most employers, you initially communicate your interests and qualifications on paper in the form of resumes and cover letters. How well you construct these documents will largely determine whether or not you will proceed to the next stage—the job interview.

The major weakness of job seekers is their inability to keep focused on their **purpose**. Engaging in a great deal of wishful thinking, they fail to organize their job search in a purposeful manner. They waste a great deal of time and money on needless activities. They frustrate themselves by going down the same dead-end roads. Worst of all, they turn off employers by demonstrating poor communication skills, both written and oral.

The average job seeker often wanders aimlessly in the job market, as if finding a job were an ancient form of alchemy. Preoccupied with job search **techniques**, they lack an overall **purpose and strategy** that would give meaning and direction to discrete job search activities. They often engage in random and time-consuming activities that have little or no payoff. Participating in a highly ego-involved activity, they quickly lose sight of what's really important to conducting a successful job search—responding to the needs of employers. Not surprisingly, they aren't taken seriously by employers because they don't take themselves and employers seriously enough to organize their activities around key qualifications that persuade employers to invite them to job interviews. You don't want this to happen to you.

The following pages are designed to increase your power to get taken seriously by employers. Individual chapters provide a quick primer on the key principles involved in writing, producing, evaluating, distributing, and following up your own dynamite resume and letters. It also presents military-related resume and letter examples that illustrate the key principles involved in writing these important job search documents.

Since the examples in this book are presented to illustrate important resume and letter writing **principles**, they should not be copied nor edited. As you will discover in the following pages, it is extremely important that you create your own resumes and letters that express the "unique you" rather than send "canned" resumes and letters to potential employers.

In the end, our goal is to improve your **communication effectiveness** in the job search. On completing this book, you should be able to write dynamite resumes and letters that result in many more invitations to job interviews.

Do What is Expected and Produces Results

Based on experience, we assume most employers do indeed expect to receive well-crafted resumes and letters. We proceed on the assumption that resumes and letters are key elements in the job search. Moreover, they are becoming more important than ever given the increased use of resume databases and electronic scanning technology for screening candidates.

The old interview adage that *"You never have a second chance to make a good first impression"* is equally valid for resumes and job search letters. For it is usually the resume and letter rather than your telephone voice or appearance that first introduces you to a prospective employer. Your resume and letter tell who you are and why an employer should want to spend valuable time meeting you in person. They invite the reader to focus attention on your key qualifications in relation to the employer's needs. They enable you to set an agenda for further exploring your interests and qualifications with employers.

Once you discover the importance of writing dynamite resumes and letters, you will never again produce other types of resumes and letters. Your written communications will have the power to move you from stranger to interviewee to employee. It will open many more doors to job interviews and offers!

Put Power Into Your Job Search

Whatever you do, make sure you acquire, use, and taste the fruits of job search power. You should go into the job search equipped with the necessary knowledge and skills to be most effective in communicating your qualifications to employers.

As you will quickly discover, the job market is not a place to engage in wishful thinking. It's at times impersonal, frequently ego deflating, and often unforgiving of errors. It requires clear thinking, strong organizational skills, and effective strategies for making the right moves with employers. Above all, it rewards individuals who follow through in implementing each job search step with enthusiasm, dogged persistence, and the ability to handle rejections. May you soon discover this power and incorporate it in your own resumes and job search letters for the civilian work world!

Coming Up

The following chapters take you step-by-step through the process of developing resumes and letters for the civilian job market. Chapter 2, **"Resume Myths and Mistakes,"** examines some of the most important myths and mistakes that prevent job seekers from becoming effective. Chapter 3, **"Key Resume Principles That Work,"** outlines 65 major resume principles that cover everything from writing each section to producing, distributing, and following up the resume for maximum impact. Chapter 4, **"Conduct Two Resume Evaluations,"** includes the necessary forms for conducting both an internal and external evaluation of your resume based on the 65 principles outlined in Chapter 3. Chapter 5, **"Translating Military Experience Into Civilian Language,"** examines the important issue of resume language—how to best state your military experience in the language of civilian employers.

The next two chapters build upon the principles of the previous chapters by including numerous examples of resumes for transitioning military personnel. Chapter 6, **"Conventional Resumes,"** includes 61 examples of conventional resumes which are organized by different occupational fields and reflect experience in various services and at different ranks. Chapter 7, **"Electronic Resumes and Your Job Search,"** shows how to convert conventional resumes into electronic resumes that can be scanned for keywords. Chapter 8, **"Job Search Letters You Must Write,"** outlines the four most important types of letters you must write during your job search— cover, approach, thank you, and resume. Chapter 9, **"Letter Organization and Evaluation,"** identifies 16 major letter-writing mistakes job seekers make, 12 rules for writing powerful letters, 11 elements to include or exclude in a letter, and 16 criteria for evaluating the content of each letter. The final chapter, **"Creating Your Resume Database,"** includes all the forms required for organizing information that needs to go into your resume.

Taken together, these 10 chapters provide a balanced and practical mix of principles and examples to get you started in the right direction in producing your own dynamite resumes and letters for today's civilian job market. Upon completing this book, you should be well on your way to clearly communicating your qualifications in the language of civilian employers who seek people with your kind of experience, talent, and enthusiasm!

2

Resume Myths and Mistakes

IF YOU WANT YOUR JOB SEARCH TO BE MOST EFFECTIVE, YOU must follow several principles of effective resume writing, production, distribution, and follow up. Equally important, you must regularly evaluate your progress and measure your performance. The principles range from obvious elementary concerns, such as correct spelling, punctuation, and placement of elements, to more complicated questions concerning when and how to best follow up a resume sent to an employer five days ago. Evaluation involves both internal self-evaluation mechanisms and external evaluators.

Do First Things First

But before putting the principles and evaluations into practice, we need to examine the very concept of a resume within the larger job search. What exactly are we talking about? What is this thing called a resume and how does it relate to other steps in your job search? How do readers typically respond to resumes? What are some of the major mistakes one needs to avoid?

A great deal of mystery and confusion surrounds the purpose and content of resumes. Occupying a time-honored—almost ritual—place in the job finding process, resumes remain the single most important document you will write and distribute throughout your job search. Do it wrong and your job search will suffer accordingly. Do it right and your resume should open many doors that lead to job interviews and offers.

Your Resume Should Communicate Purpose

What exactly is a resume? Is it a summary of your work history? An autobiography of your major accomplishments? A statement of your key qualifications? A catalog of your interests, skills, and experience? An introduction to your professional and personal style? Your business calling card? A jumble of keywords for triggering optical scanners?

Let's be perfectly clear what we are talking about. A resume is all of these things and much much more. It is an important **product**—produced in reference to your goals, skills, and experience—that furthers two important **processes**—"job search" for you and "screening/hiring" for employers. While it is a basic requirement when applying for many jobs, your resume plays a central role in directing you and your job search into productive information gathering and employment channels. It communicates your goals and capabilities to potential employers who must solve personnel problems—hire someone to perform particular functions and jobs. At the very least, a resume represents the "unique you" to others who may or may not know much about your particular mix of goals and capabilities. It may represent the potential solution to employers' problems.

> *A resume is an advertisement for an interview. Its purpose is to get job interviews – nothing more, nothing less.*

Better still, let's define a resume in terms of its **purpose** or **outcomes** for you in relation to hiring officials: a resume is an advertisement for an interview. In other words, the purpose of writing, producing, distributing, and following up a resume is to get job interviews—nothing more, nothing less. As such, your resume should follow certain principles of good advertising—grab attention, heighten interest, sell the product, and promote action.

Your ultimate purpose in writing a resume is to **get employers to take action**—conduct a telephone interview as well as invite you to the first of several job interviews which will eventually result in job offers and employment. Thus, the purpose is a specific outcome.

If you define a resume in these terms, then the internal resume structure and specific elements included or excluded—as well as the production, distribution, and follow-up methods you choose—become self-evident. You should only include those elements that are of interest to employers.

But what do employers want to see on your resume? They simply want to see sound indicators of your **probable future performance** rather than a summary of your professional and personal history. They want to know if you have a high probability of **adding value** to their operations. Adding value can have several meanings depending on the employment situation—increase market share, improve profitability, solve specific problems, become more competitive, introduce a new system for improving efficiency.

While the logic here is very simple, it nonetheless needs repeating throughout your job search. Since employers will be hiring your future, they are more concerned with your future performance—*"What can you do for me?"*—rather than "the facts" about your past—*"Where did you go to school and what were you doing in the service during 1998?"* Therefore, you must present your past in such a manner that it clearly indicates **patterns of performance** that are good predictors of your future value and performance.

Focus on Employers' Needs and Add Value

Without this central guiding purpose in mind, your resume is likely to take on a different form, as well as move in different directions, than outlined in this book. You simply must keep your resume writing, production, distribution, and follow-up activities focused around your purpose—getting interviews. No distractions or wishful thinking should interfere with this.

Your approach, whether implicit or explicit, to resume writing says something about how you view yourself in relation to employers. It tells readers to what degree you are self-centered versus employer-centered. Are you oriented toward adding value to the employer's operations, or are you primarily concerned with acquiring more benefits for yourself? If you merely chronicle your past work history, you are likely to produce a self-centered resume that says little or nothing about your interests, skills, and abilities in relation to the employer's needs. You say nothing about adding value to the employer's operations. Resumes lacking a central focus or purpose are good candidates for mindless direct-mail approaches—broadcasting them to hundreds of employers who by chance might be interested in your history.

On the other hand, if you thoughtfully develop a job objective that is sensitive to employers' performance needs and then relate your patterns of skills and accomplishments to that objective, you should produce a resume that transcends your history as it clearly communicates your qualifications to employers and suggests that you know how to add more value to the employer's operations. This type of resume is **employer-centered**; it addresses employers' hiring needs. Such a resume is best targeted toward a select few employers who have job opportunities appropriate for your particular mix of interests, skills, and accomplishments. The type of resume you produce tells employers a great deal about you both professionally and personally.

An intensely ego-involved activity, resume writing often goes awry as writers attempt to produce a document that they "feel good" about. Thinking a resume is analogous to an obituary, many writers believe their resume should summarize what's good about them. If the central purpose is to pile on a lot of good information about the individual's past, then a resume becomes a nonfocused dumping ground for a great deal of extraneous information employers neither need nor want. Such a resume may include lots of interesting facts that must be left to the interpretation of the reader who, by definition, is a very busy person; few such readers have the luxury of spending time analyzing and relating someone's chronicle of work history to their specific employment needs. Your resume may end up like most resumes—an uninspired listing of names, dates, and duties that are supposed to enlighten employers about your qualifications. While you may feel good writing such a document, don't expect employers to get excited enough to contact you for an interview. Your resume will likely end up in their "circular files."

Every time you make a decision concerning what to include or exclude in your resume and how and when to produce, distribute, and follow up your job search communications, always keep in mind your purpose: you are advertising yourself for a job interview. Such a single-minded purpose will serve you well. It will automatically answer many questions you may have about the details of writing, producing, distributing, and following up your resume. It will tell you what is and is not important in the whole resume writing, production, distribution, and follow-up process.

Resume Myths and Realities

Numerous myths about finding employment and contacting employers lead individuals down the wrong resume-writing paths. Keep these eleven myths and corresponding realities in mind when writing your resume:

MYTH 1:   **The resume is the key to getting a job.**

REALITY: There is nothing magical about resumes. Indeed, there are
                many keys to getting a job, from being in the right place at

the right time and having good connections to conducting an excellent job interview. The resume is only one step, albeit an important one, in the job finding process. Other steps depend on well-crafted resumes and cover letters. Remember, your resume is an advertisement for a job interview. Employers do not hire individuals because of the content or quality of their resume; the resume only gets them invited to job interviews. The job interview is the real key to getting the job; it is the prerequisite step for a job offer and employment contract. But you must first communicate your qualifications to employers through the medium of a top quality resume in order to get their attention and motivate them to take desired action—invite you to the critical job interview.

MYTH 2: **The resume is not as important to getting a job as other job search activities, such as networking and informational interviews.**

REALITY: A resume still remains one of the most important written documents you will produce during your job search. If you expect to be interviewed for jobs, you simply must produce a well-crafted resume that clearly communicates your qualifications to employers. In fact, within the past five years the resume has become even more important with the rise of Internet employment sites that incorporate resume databases. For these sites, a well-crafted electronic resume becomes the key to connecting with online employers. Whether you like it or not, employers want to see you on paper **before** talking to you over the telephone or seeing you in person. And they want to see a top quality resume—an attractive, error-free document that **represents your best self**. You should pay particular attention to the details and exacting quality required in producing a first-rate resume. Errors, however minor, can quickly eliminate you from consideration. Without such an error-free resume, you seriously limit your chances of getting job interviews. And without job interviews, you won't get job offers.

MYTH 3: **A resume should primarily document your work history for employers.**

REALITY: First and foremost, your resume should communicate to employers how you will **add value** to their operations. You include work history on a resume as evidence that you have a track record of adding value to other employers' operations. The assumption for the reader is that you will add similar value to his or her operations. Be sure you always describe your work history or experience in such value-added terms.

> *A resume should communicate to employers how you will __add value__ to their operations.*

MYTH 4: **It's best to send your resume to hundreds of employers rather than to just a few. The more resumes you send, the higher the probability of getting a job.**

REALITY: Power in the job search comes from selective targeting— not through random numbers. Success comes by making a few contacts with the right people who have a specific **need** for your particular skills and qualifications. While it may be comforting to think you are making progress with your job search by sending resumes to hundreds of potential employers, in reality you create an illusion of progress that will ultimately disappoint you; few people seriously read an unsolicited resume and thus consider you for employment when they have no need. A resume broadcast or "shotgun" approach to finding a job indicates a failure to seriously focus your job search around the **needs** of specific employers. Your time, effort, and money will be better spent in marketing your resume in conjunction with other effective job search activities—networking and informational interviews. These activities force you to concentrate on specific employers who would be most interested in your interests, skills, and qualifications. These individuals have a need that will most likely coincide with both your resume and job search timing.

MYTH 5:   **It's not necessary to include an objective on your resume.**

REALITY: Without an objective your resume will lack a central focus from which to relate all other elements in your resume. An objective gives your resume organization and coherence. It tells potential employers something important about you—that you are a **purposeful individual** who has specific job and career goals in mind that are directly related to your past pattern of interests, skills, and experience as documented in the remainder of your resume. If properly stated, your objective will become the most powerful and effective statement on your resume. Without an objective, you force the employer to "interpret" your resume. He or she must analyze the discrete elements in each resume category and draw conclusions about your future capabilities which may or may not be valid. You force the person to engage in what may be a difficult analytical task, depending on his or her analytic capabilities. Therefore, it is to your advantage to control the flow and interpretation of your qualifications and capabilities by stating a clear employer-oriented objective. While you can state an objective in your cover letter, it is best to put your objective at the very beginning of your resume. After all, letters do get detached from resumes. On the other hand, many people prefer excluding an objective because it tends to lock them into a particular type of job; they want to be flexible. Such people demonstrate a cardinal job search sin—they really don't know what they want to do; they tend to communicate their lack of focus in their resume as well as in other job search activities. They are more concerned with fitting into a job (*"Where are the jobs?"*) than with finding a job fit for them (*"Is this job right for me?"*).

MYTH 6:   **The best type of resume outlines employment history by job titles, responsibilities, and employment dates.**

REALITY: This type of resume, the traditional chronological or "obituary" resume, may or may not be good for you. It's filled with historical "what" information—what work you did, in what organizations, and over what period of time. Such resumes tell employers little about what it is you can do for them in the future. You should choose a resume format that clearly communicates your major strengths—not your historical background—to employers. Those strengths should be formulated as **patterns of performance** in relation to your goals and skills as well as the employer's needs. Your choice of formats includes variations of the chronological, functional, and combination resumes—each offering different advantages and disadvantages, depending on your goals.

MYTH 7: **Employers appreciate lengthy detailed resumes because such resumes give them more complete information for screening candidates than shorter resumes.**

REALITY: Employers prefer receiving short, succinct one- or two-page resumes. Longer resumes lose their interest and attention. Such resumes usually lack a focus, are filled with extraneous information, need editing, and are oriented toward your past rather than the employer's future. If you know how to write a dynamite resume, you can put all of your capabilities into a one- to two-page format. These resumes only include enough information to persuade employers to contact you for an interview. Like good advertisements, they generate enough interest so the reader will contact you for more information (job interview) before investing in the product (job offer).

MYTH 8: **It's okay to put salary expectations and references on your resume.**

REALITY: Two of the worst things you can do is to include salary information (history or expectations) and list your references on your resume. Remember, the purpose of your resume is to get an interview—nothing more, nothing less. Only during the interview—and preferably toward the end—should you discuss salary and share information on references. And before you discuss salary, you want to demonstrate your **value** to hiring managers as well as learn about the **worth** of the position. Only **after** you make your impression and gather information on the job, can you realistically talk about—and negotiate—salary. You can not do this if you prematurely mention salary on your resume. A similar principle applies to references. Never put your references on a resume. The closest you should ever get to mentioning names, addresses, and phone numbers—other than yours—is a simple statement appearing at the end of your resume:

"References available upon request"

You want to control your references for the interview. You should take a list of references appropriate for the position you will interview for with you to the interview. If you put references on your resume, the employer might call someone who has no idea you are applying for a particular job. The conversation could be embarrassing. As a simple courtesy, you need to ask your references ahead of time whether you may use their name as a reference. At that point, you want to brief your reference on the position you seek, explaining why you feel you should be selected by focusing on your goals and strengths in relation to the position. Give this person information that will support your candidacy. Surprisingly, though, few employers actually follow through by contacting stated references! This is perhaps one reason they often make poor hiring decisions. Many employers are surprised to later discover they had hired a problem employee who had given previous employers similar difficulties.

MYTH 9: **You should not include your hobbies nor any personal statements on your resume.**

REALITY: In general this is true. However, there are exceptions which would challenge this rule as a myth. If you have a hobby or a personal statement that can strengthen your objective in relation to the employer's needs, consider including it on your resume. For example, if a job calls for someone who is outgoing, energetic, and active, you would not want to include a hobby or personal statement that indicates that you are a very private and sedentary person, such as *"enjoy reading and writing"* or *"collect stamps."* But *"enjoy organizing community fund drives"* and *"compete in the Boston Marathon"* might be very appropriate statements for your resume. Such statements further emphasize the "unique you" in relation to your capabilities, the position requirements, and the employer's needs.

MYTH 10: **You should try to get as much as possible on each page of your resume.**

REALITY: Each page of your resume should be appealing to the eye. It should make an immediate favorable impression, be inviting and easy to read, and look very professional. You achieve these qualities by using a variety of layout, type style, highlighting, and emphasizing techniques. When formatting each section of your resume, be sure to make generous use of white space. Bullet, underline, or bold items for emphasis. If you try to cram a great deal on each page, your resume will look cluttered and uninviting to the reader.

> *You should follow up your resume with a phone call within seven days.*

You may make just the opposite impression you thought you were making in an ostensibly well organized resume—you're disorganized!

MYTH 11: **Once you send a resume to an employer, there's not much you can do except wait for a reply.**

REALITY: Waiting for potential employers to contact you is not a good job search strategy. Sending a resume to a potential employer is only the first step in connecting with a job. You should always **follow up** your resume with a phone call, preferably within seven days, to answer questions, conduct a telephone interview, get invited to a job interview, or acquire additional information, advice, and referrals. Without this follow-up action, your resume is likely to get lost among many other resumes competing for the reader's attention.

Taken together, these myths and realities emphasize one overriding concern when writing a resume:

> The key to effective resume writing is to give readers, within the space of one to two pages, just enough interesting information about your past performance and future capabilities so they will get sufficiently excited and motivated to contact you for a job interview. Your resume content should move them to take positive action.

It is during the interview, rather than on your resume, that you will provide detailed answers to the most important questions concerning the job. Those questions are determined by both the interviewer and you during the job interview. Don't prematurely eliminate yourself from consideration by including too much or too little information, or by being too boastful or too negative, on your resume before you get to the interview stage. In this sense, your resume becomes an important "window of opportunity" to get invited to job interviews that hopefully will translate into good job offers.

Common Writing Errors and Mistakes

A resume must first get written and written well. And it is at the initial writing stage that many deadly errors are made. The most common mistakes occur when writers fail to keep the purpose of their resume in mind.

Most errors kill a resume even before it gets fully read. At best these errors leave negative impressions that are difficult to overcome at this or any other point in the hiring process. Remember, hiring officials have two major inclusion/exclusion concerns in mind when reading your resume:

- They are looking for reasons or "negatives" to eliminate you from further consideration.

- They are looking for evidence or "positives" to consider you for a job interview—how much value you will likely add to their operations.

Every time you make an error, you provide supports for eliminating you from further consideration. You should concentrate, instead, on providing **supports** for being considered for a job interview.

Make sure your resume is not "dead upon arrival." Whether fair or not to you, employers tend to read a lot into resumes in the process of screening candidates. To ensure against being "screened out," avoid these most common errors reported by employers who review resumes:

- **Not related to the reader's interests or needs.** Not another one of these! Why was this sent to me? I don't have a job vacancy, nor do we perform work related to this person's skills. Did they purchase someone's mailing list? They need to take their job search seriously by being more informed about employers and organizations before sending out such junk mail. In the meantime, this person has just wasted my time, which is both limited and precious to me. I hope they don't plan to further waste my time by following up their resume and letter with a phone call! I only interview and hire people when I have a vacancy—not in response to unsolicited resumes.

- **Too long, short, or condensed.** Ugh! What a waste of time and effort. Doesn't this person have a better sense of self-esteem?

- **Poorly designed format and an unattractive appearance.** This person probably doesn't look any better in person than on paper. I have a bad feeling about this one. I've met this type before— really boring and lacks initiative.

- **Misspellings, bad grammar, and wordiness.** When will they learn to write a simple sentence that conveys a basic level of literacy? This person is either illiterate or careless—two problems I don't need to hire. I wonder what other communication problems this person brings to the job? These errors are insulting. I really don't need to hire this type of trouble.

- **Poor punctuation.** Ditto. I wonder how much training this person needs to get up to speed? This could be an expensive hire—and fire!

- **Lengthy phrases, sentences, and paragraphs.** The language we work in here is English. I wonder where they learned to do this? Maybe they talk the same way—on and on and on.

- **Too slick, amateurish, or "gimmicky."** I'm really impressed. I bet this person is thinks he's the hottest thing since sliced bread. Comes with lots of baggage. Just what I need—a manipulator on the payroll. I don't need gimmicks—only an enthusiastic individual who has a predictable pattern of performance related to what we do here.

- **Too boastful or dishonest.** I've seen this before and hired someone like this against my better judgment. This one's too hot to handle—I'll regret the day I contacted him for an interview.

- **Poorly typed and reproduced.** Isn't this nice. I'm really impressed with the quality of this individual. Maybe I'm not important enough to receive a better quality resume. Or perhaps this is their best effort!

- **Irrelevant information.** Do I really need to know height, weight, children, and spouse's name? I wonder what other irrelevancies this person can bring to the interview, and the job.

- **Critical categories missing.** Where's the objective? Where did she work? What did she do? Any special awards, recognitions, accomplishments? What about education? What years did this include? Don't they know what to include on a resume?

- **Hard to understand or requires too much interpretation.** I really don't have time to do a content analysis of this individual's skills and accomplishments. After reading two pages of military "bio facts," I still don't know what this person can do other than many different jobs in a military setting. How does this all relate in terms of skills and accomplishments to the job in question?

- **Unexplained time gaps.** What did he do between 1992 and 1994? School? Unemployed? Tried to "find" himself in Paris? A health, drug, or criminal problem? Dropped out of life?

- **Does not convey accomplishments or a pattern of performance from which the reader can predict future performance.** Interesting, but what can the person do for me? I want to be able to predict what she will likely do in my organization. Show me value and performance.

- **Text does not support objective.** Nicely stated objective, but there's no evidence this person has any experience or skills in line with the objective. Could this be a statement of "wishful thinking" or something that has been "boiler-plated" from someone else's resume or a resume-writing book?

- **Unclear or vague objective.** What exactly does this person want to do in my organization? Does she have specific goals for the next three to five years? Perhaps this person really doesn't know what she wants to do other than get a good paying job through me.

- **Lacks credibility and content—includes lots of fluff and "canned" resume language.** Where do they get all this dreadful stuff? Probably using the same old resume book that emphasizes action verbs and transferable skills but fails to advise them to include real content. Where's the beef? Show me real skills and accomplishments.

This listing of writing errors and possible reader responses emphasizes how important **both** form and content are when writing a purposeful resume. You must select an important form, arrange each element in an attractive manner, and provide the necessary substance to grab the attention of the reader and move him or her to action. And all these elements of good resume writing must be related to the **needs of your audience**. If not, you may quickly kill your resume by committing some of these deadly errors.

Remember, hiring officials are busy people who only devote a few seconds—usually no more than 30 seconds—to reading a resume and thus screening a candidate at this resume reading stage. They are seasoned at identifying errors that will effectively remove you from consideration. Above all, they want to see you error-free on paper so they can concentrate on what they most need to do—evaluate your qualifications.

Qualities of Effective Resumes

A well-crafted resume expresses many important professional and personal qualities employers seek in candidates:

- Your sense of **self-esteem and purpose**.

- Your **level of literacy**.

- Your **ability to conceptualize and analyze** your own interests, skills, and abilities in relation to the employer's needs.

- Your **patterns of performance and value-added behavior**.

- Your ability to clearly communicate **who you are** and **what you want to do** rather than who you have been, what you have done, and what you need.

- Your **view of the employer**—how important he or she is in relation to your interests, skills, and abilities. Are you self-centered or employer-centered?

These qualities are expressed through certain resume principles which you can learn and apply to most employment situations. Your resume should:

- Immediately impress the reader.

- Be visually appealing and easy to read.

- Indicate your career aspirations and goals.

- Focus on your value in relation to employers' needs.

- Communicate your job-related abilities and patterns of performance—not your past or present formal job duties and responsibilities.

- Stress your productivity potential to solve employers' problems.

- Communicate that you are a responsible and purposeful person who gets things done.

- Use a language that communicates skills required by the employer—a language that is also sensitive to resume scanning technology.

If you keep these general principles in mind, you should be able to produce a dynamite resume that will grab the attention of employers, who will be moved to action—invite you to a job interview. To do less is to communicate the wrong messages to employers—you lack purpose, literacy, good judgment, and a pattern of performance.

Always Focus on Your Audience and Purpose

When deciding what to include in your resume, always remember these important writing guidelines for creating a dynamite resume:

1. View your resume as your personal **advertisement**, one that should follow the principles of good advertising.

2. Focus on the purpose of your resume which is to get a **job interview**.

3. Take the offensive by developing a resume that **structures the reader's thinking** around your objective, qualifications, strengths, and projections of future performance.

4. Make your resume **generate positive thinking** rather than raise negative questions or confuse the reader.

5. Create an employer-centered resume that focuses on the **needs of your audience**.

6. Communicate clearly what it is you have done and then stress what you **want to do and can do** for the reader.

7. Always be **honest** without being stupid. Stress your positives; never volunteer nor confess your negatives.

If you keep these basic purposes and principles in mind, you should produce a dynamite resume as well as conduct a job search that is both purposeful and positive. Your resume should stand out above the crowd as you clearly communicate your qualifications to employers.

In the next two chapters we'll take an in-depth look at these and several other principles relevant to the whole spectrum of resume activities—writing, producing, distributing, following up, and evaluating.

3

Key Resume Principles That Work

EFFECTIVE RESUMES FOLLOW CERTAIN KEY WRITING, production, distribution, and follow-up principles that are specific to the resume medium and relevant to the job search process. These principles should be incorporated into every stage of the resume writing, production, distribution, and follow-up process. If you fail to incorporate these resume principles, your job search will most likely fail to reach its full potential.

Writing

Overall Strategy

1. **Focus on translating your military experience into civilian employment terminology:** Your resume and cover letter should present your qualifications in terminology that is readily understood by civilian employers. Most of your military experience can be easily translated into civilian terms (see Chapter 5 for details on this translation process). Begin by outlining each of your military positions and corresponding accomplishments. List the equivalent civilian terms for each. Use this "civilianized" language in presenting your qualifications to employers. Avoid using military terminology and jargon unless you are applying for a defense-related position

that requires previous military experience and you know the employer understands this language.

2. **Do first things first in making your resume represent the "unique you":** Avoid creatively plagiarizing others' resumes, however tempting and easy to do. A widely abused approach to resume writing, creative plagiarizing occurs when people decide to take shortcuts by writing their resume in reference to so-called "outstanding resume examples"; they basically edit the examples by substituting information on themselves for what appears in the example. The result is a resume filled with a great deal of "canned" resume language that may be unrelated to the individual's goals, skills, and experience.

    The best resumes are those based on a thorough self-assessment of your interests, skills, and abilities which, in turn, is the **foundation** for stating a powerful objective, shaping information in each category, and selecting proper resume language. What, for example, do you want to do before you die? Answering this question in detail will tell you a great deal about your values and goals in relation to your career objectives. You may want to incorporate this information into your resume. Do first things first by starting with a self-assessment that will help you build each section of your resume. Numerous exercises and instruments are available for conducting your own self-directed assessment of your interests, skills, and abilities. These are outlined in several career planning and job search guides, including our "Corporate Gray Series" books. Other recommended books are found in the "Career Resources" section at the very end of this book. Professional testing centers and career counselors also administer a variety of useful self-assessment devices. Information on such services is readily available through your base transition office (see Chapter 4 in the "Corporate Gray Series"), local community college, adult education programs, or employment services office.

> *Do first things first by starting with a self-assessment that will help you build each section of your resume.*

3. **Develop a plan of action relevant to your overall job search:**
Make sure your resume is part of your larger job search plan. In addition to incorporating self-assessment data, it should be developed with specific goals in mind, based on research, and related to networking and informational interviewing activities. Begin by asking yourself the broader *"What do I want to do with this resume?"* question about the purpose of your resume rather than narrow your focus on the traditional *"What should I include on my resume?"* question.

Structure and Organization

4. **Select an appropriate resume format that best communicates your goals, skills, experience, and probable future performance:**
Resume format determines how you organize the information categories for communicating your qualifications to employers. It **structures the reader's thinking** about your goals, strengths, and probable future performance. If, for example, your basic organization principle is chronology (dates you worked for different employers), then you want employers to think of your qualifications in historical terms and thus deduce future performance based upon an analysis of performance **patterns** evidenced in your work history. If your basic organizational principle is skills, then you want employers to think of you in achievement terms.

If you decide to write a conventional resume, you essentially have three formats from which to choose: chronological, functional, or combination. A **chronological resume**—often referred to as an "obituary resume"—is the most popular resume format, but it is by no means the most appropriate. Primarily summarizing work history, this resume lists dates and names of employers first and your duties and responsibilities second. It often includes a great deal of extraneous information. In its worst form—the traditional chronological resume—it tells employers little or nothing about what you want to do, can do, and will do for them. In its best form—the improved chronological resume—it communicates your purpose, past achievements, and probable future performance to employers. It includes an objective which relates to other elements in the resume. The work experience section includes names and addresses of former employers followed by a brief description of accomplishments, skills, and responsibilities rather than formal duties and responsibilities; inclusive employment dates appear at the end. Chronological resumes should be used by individuals who have a progressive record of work experience and who wish to advance within an occupational field. One major advantage of these resumes is that they include "the beef" employers wish to see.

Functional resumes emphasize patterns of skills and accomplishments rather than job titles, employers, and inclusive employment dates. These resumes should be used by individuals making a significant career change, first entering the work force, or re-entering the job market after a lengthy absence. Since many employers still look for names, dates, and direct work experience—the so-called "beef"—this type of resume often disappoints employers who are looking for more substantive information relating to "experience" and "qualifications." You should use a functional resume only if your past work experience does not clearly support your objective.

Combination resumes combine the best elements of chronological and functional resumes. They stress patterns of accomplishments and skills as well as include work history. Work history usually appears as a separate section immediately following the presentation of accomplishments and skills in an "Areas of Effectiveness" or "Experience" section. This is the perfect resume for individuals with work experience who wish to change to a job in a related career field. Many career experts consider this to be the best choice of any resume because it nicely showcases accomplishments and skills.

> *If you know your resume will be scanned, be sure to write a scannable resume that incorporates "keywords" describing your experience and skills.*

You also may want to write electronic and scannable resumes in response to new technology used in posting and screening resumes. Indeed, job seekers are well advised to write conventional, electronic, and scannable resumes for today's job market. Many employers routinely use scanning technology to initially review resumes. If you know your resume will be scanned, you must write a resume that follows the principles of scannable resumes. This involves using "keywords" or nouns that describe your experience and skills. Individuals with technical backgrounds should especially use such resumes because their resumes are most likely to be scanned by employers in search of individuals with specific "keyword" skills.

Examples of these different types of conventional and electronic resumes are included in Chapters 6 and 7. Please examine these examples for ideas in developing your own resume.

5. **Include all essential information categories in the proper order.** What you should or should not include in your resume depends on your particular goals as well as your situation and the needs of your audience. When deciding on what to include or exclude on your resume, always focus on the **needs** of the employer. What does he or she want or need to know about you? The most important information relates to your **future performance** which is normally determined by assessing your **past patterns of performance** ("experience" presented as "accomplishments," "outcomes," "benefits," or "performance"). At the very least, your resume should include the following five categories of information which help provide answers to five major questions:

<u>Information category</u>	<u>Relevant question</u>
Contact information	Who you are/how to contact you.
Objective	What you **want to do**.
Experience	What you **can do**—your patterns of skills and accomplishments.
Work history	What you **have done**.
Educational background	What you **have learned** and what you might be capable of learning in the future.

Taken together, these information categories and questions will generate important data that should clearly answer a sixth unanswered question:

What you **will most likely do in the future**.

Finding answers to this implicit question is the employer's ultimate goal in the hiring process. Employers must deduce the answer from examining what you said in each category of your one- to two-page resume. Employers must make an important **judgment** about your future performance **with them** by carefully considering what you want to do (your objective), what you can do (your experience), and what you have done and learned (your work history and education). A resume incorporating only these five information categories should answer most employers' questions.

Other information categories often found on resumes include the following:

- Community involvement
- Professional affiliations
- Special skills
- Interests and activities
- Personal statement

6. **Sequence the categories according to the principle** *"What's most important to both you and the employer should always appear first"*: You want your most important information and your strongest qualifications to always come first. As a transitioning member of the military, you will want to include your most recent military experience first. On the other hand, if you have recently completed a college degree and it appears more relevant to your next job than your most recent work experience, you may want to put your education first. Indeed, recent graduates with little or no relevant work experience should put education first since it's probably their most important "qualification" at this stage of their work life. Your educational experience tells employers what you may have learned and thus provides some evidence of a certain knowledge, skill, and motivational base from which you possess a **capacity** to learn and grow within the employer's organization, i.e., you are functionally trainable. Your education also may include important work experience and achievements that indicate a pattern of future performance. Education should also come first in cases where education is an important **qualifying criterion**, especially for individuals with

professional degrees and certifications: teachers, professors, doctors, nurses, lawyers, accountants, and counselors. The sequence of elements should be:

- Contact information
- Education
- Experience
- Work history

If you have a few or several years of direct work experience that supports your objective, and if education is not an important qualifying criteria, then your "Experience" section should immediately follow your objective. In this case "Education" moves toward the end of the resume:

- Contact information
- Experience
- Work history
- Education

Any other categories of information should appear either immediately after "Work history" or after "Education."

7. **Avoid including extraneous information which is unrelated to your objective or to the needs of employers:** However ego-involved you become in the resume writing process, always remember your goal and your audience. You are writing to a potential employer who by definition is a critical stranger who has specific needs and problems he hopes to solve through the hiring process. You are not writing to your mother, spouse, friends, or former teachers. The following extraneous information often appears on resumes:

- **The word "Resume" at the top:** The reader already knows this is your resume, assuming you have chosen a standard resume format. It's not necessary to label it as such.

- **Present date:** This goes on your cover letter rather than your resume.

- **Picture:** Include a picture only if it is essential for a job, such as in modeling or theater. A picture may indeed be worth "a thousand words," but 990 of those words need not distract the reader from the central focus of your resume! Regardless of what you and your family may think about your picture—even those wonderful glamour shots—it's safe to assume that 50 percent of your readers will like and another 50 percent will dislike your picture. You don't need this type of distraction. Concentrate instead on the words and information you can control.

- **Race, religion, or political affiliation:** Include this information only if these are bona fide occupational qualifications, which they probably aren't, given equal opportunity laws.

- **Salary history or requirements:** Never ever include salary history or expectations on your resume. If you are forced to submit this information at the initial screening stage, do so in your cover letter. Salary usually is negotiable. The salary question should only arise at the end of the interview or during the job offer—after you have had a chance to assess the worth of the job as well as demonstrate your value to hiring officials. When you include salary information on your resume, you prematurely give information on your value before you have a chance to demonstrate your value in job interviews.

- **References:** Always make your references "Available upon request." You want to control the selection of references as well as alert your references that you are applying for a specific position and that they may be contacted.

- **Personal information such as height, weight, age, sex, marital status, health:** Few, if any, of these characteristics strengthen or relate to your objective. Many are negatives. Some could be positives, but only if you are a model, karate instructor, or applying for a position for which these are bona fide occupational qualifications.

- **Any negative information:** Employment gaps, medical or mental problems, criminal records, divorces, terminations, conflicting interests. There is absolutely no reason for you to volunteer potential negatives on your resume. This is the quickest way to get eliminated from consideration. Always remember that your resume should represent your very "best self." If hiring officials are interested in learning about your negatives, they will ask you and you should be prepared to respond in a positive manner—but only at the interview stage.

Since most of this extraneous information is a real negative in the eyes of employers—and has little to do with supporting your objective as well as answering employers' six critical questions—avoid including this information on your resume.

Contact Information

8. **Put all essential contact information at the very top of your resume as the header:** The very first element a reader should encounter on your resume is an attractive header. This header should at least include your name, address, and phone number. If you have a fax number and e-mail address, be sure to include them:

JAMES LAWSON
8891 S. Hayward Blvd.
Buffalo, NY 14444   Tel. 707/331-9911
                                             laws@intra.com

JAMES LAWSON   laws@intra.com

8891 S. Hayward Blvd.   Buffalo, NY 14444   Tel. 707/321-9721

JAMES LAWSON

8891 S. Hayward Blvd.   Tel. 707/321-9721
Buffalo, NY 14444   Fax 707/331-9911
                                             laws@intra.com

JAMES LAWSON

8891 S. Hayward Blvd.   Buffalo, NY 14444   Tel. 707/321-9721
                                                       laws@intra.com

JAMES LAWSON   Tel. 707/321-9721
8891 S. Hayward Blvd.   Fax 707/331-9911
Buffalo, NY 14444   laws@intra.com

We prefer capitalizing the name, although using upper and lower case letters is fine. Any of these headers would be fine because they are very inviting to readers who quickly survey resumes.

9. **Include your complete contact information:** Employers want to know how to contact you immediately should they have any questions or wish to invite you to an interview. Therefore, include only information which enables the employer to make such a quick contact. Be sure to include **complete** contact information—name, address, phone number, and e-mail address. Avoid using P.O. Box numbers; they communicate the wrong message about your housing situation—unstable or transient. Also, include a daytime telephone number through which you can be reached. If you do not have a telephone, or if your only daytime number is with your present employer, enlist a telephone answering service or use the number of someone else number who will be available and willing to screen your calls. They, in turn, can contact you at work and then you can return the call. Include your first and last name, and perhaps your middle initial, depending on your professional style. The use of a middle initial is a sign of greater formality and is most frequently used by established professionals. However, using your full first, middle, and last name together is too formal: ROBERT DAVID ALLAN. If you prefer using your middle name rather than first name, do so either alone or in combination with your first initial: ROBERT ALLAN or J. ROBERT ALLAN. Do not include nicknames (ROBERT "BUDZY" ALLAN) unless you feel it will somehow help your candidacy, which it most likely will not! Include

any professional titles, such as M.D., Ph.D., J.D., immediately after your last name: ROBERT ALLAN, J.D. Never begin your name with a formal gender designation: Mr., Mrs., or Ms. Your address should be complete, including a zip code number. It's okay to abbreviate the state (NY for New York, IL for Illinois, CA for California) as well as certain common locations: N. for North, SW for Southwest, Ave. for Avenue, St. for Street, Blvd. for Boulevard, Apt. for Apartment. However, it's best to spell out Circle, Terrace, or Lane. Be sure to include your telephone number; you may want to preface it with "Tel." or "Tel:". If you have a fax number, you may want to include it immediately following your telephone number:

Tel. 819/666-2197
Fax 819/666-2222

If you have e-mail, include your e-mail address immediately after your fax number. In fact, an e-mail address isn expected by many employers. It's a sign that you are technologically competent in today's job market. If you are ap-

> **_An e-mail address is expected – it's a sign that you are technologically competent._**

plying for a position abroad, try to include both a fax number and an e-mail address. Do not clutter the header with extraneous information such as your age, marital status, sex, height, and weight. Such information is irrelevant—indeed a negative—on a resume. It communicates the wrong messages and indicates you don't know how to properly present yourself to potential employers. These are not qualifying criteria for most jobs. Such information should never be volunteered during your job search. In fact, this is illegal information for employers to elicit from candidates.

Objective

10. **Include a job or career objective relevant to your skills, employers' needs, and the remaining elements of your resume:** While some resume advisors consider an objective to be an optional

item—preferring to keep it general or place it in a cover letter—or provide little guidance on how to structure an objective and relate it to other resume elements, we strongly recommend including a powerful objective at the very beginning of your resume. Your objective should be the **central organizing element** from which all other elements in your resume flow. It should tell employers **what it is you want to do**, **can do**, and **will do** for them.

Put in its most powerful form, your objective should be employer-centered rather than self-centered. It should incorporate both a skill and an outcome in reference to your major strengths and employer's major needs. Rather than being a statement of wishful thinking ("A position in management") or opportunistic ("A research position with opportunity for career advancement"),

> *Your resume objective should tell employers what it is you want to do, can do, and will do for them.*

it should focus on your major strengths **in relation to** an employer's needs. Take, for example, the following objective statement:

> A position in data analysis where skills in mathematics, computer programming, and deductive reasoning will contribute to new systems development.

This type of objective follows a basic **job—skill—benefit** format:

I want a _____ where I will use my
                     position/job

_____ which will result in _____
skills and abilities to   outcomes and benefits.

Restated in this basic format, the above objective would appear in this form:

> A <u>data analysis job</u> where I will use my <u>skills in mathematics, computer programming, and deductive reasoning</u> which will result in <u>new systems development</u>.

An objective based on this originating statement follows a very specific form. The first part of this objective statement emphasizes a specific position in relation to your strongest skills or abilities; the second part relates your skills to the employer's needs. Such an objective becomes a statement of benefits employers can expect from you. All other elements in your resume (experience, work history, education, awards) should provide **supports** for your objective. Formulated in this manner, your objective becomes the most important element on your resume as well as in your job search; it directs all other elements appearing on your resume, determining what should or should not be included in each section. It also gives your job search direction, focusing your efforts toward particular employers, and helps you formulate pertinent answers to interview questions. While formulating such an objective may be very time consuming—your two- to three-line objective statement may take several days to develop and refine—the end result will be a well-focused resume that communicates your value and benefits to employers.

11. **An objective should be neither too general nor too specific:** Many resume writers prefer developing a very general objective so their resume can be used for many different types of jobs. However, highly generalized objectives often sound "canned" or are meaningless (*"A position working with people that leads to career advancement"*); they may indicate you don't know what you really want to do. Indeed, if your purpose is to apply for many different types of jobs, you are attempting to fit into jobs rather than find jobs fit for you. You appear to lack a clear focus on what you want to do. On the other hand, a very specific objective may be too narrow for most jobs; you may appear too specialized for many positions. Another alternative is to write a separate or targeted objective, responsive to the requirements of each position, every time you send a resume to a hiring official. This approach should result in resumes that are most responsive to the needs of individual employers. To accomplish this effectively, you should have word processing capabilities that allow you to custom-design each resume. An objective that is not too general nor too specific will serve you well for most resume occasions. It should indicate you know exactly what you want to do without being overly specific. Look at our examples in Chapters 5 and 6 for objectives that are neither too general nor too specific.

12. **Relate all other resume elements to your objective, emphasizing skills, outcomes, benefits, and probable future value to the employer:** All other elements appearing on your resume should reinforce your objective. When deciding what to include or exclude on your resume, ask yourself this question: *"Will this information strengthen my objective, which emphasizes my skills in relation to the employer's needs?"* If the answer is "yes," include it. If the answer is "no," exclude it. Remember, the most effective one- to two-page resume clearly and concisely communicates your objectives and strengths to employers. If you fail to organize your resume in this manner, you are likely to include a great deal of extraneous information that communicates the wrong message to employers—you don't know what you want to do; your interests, skills, and experience are peripheral or unrelated to the reader's needs; you lack a clear focus and thus appear disorganized. These are cardinal sins committed by many resume writers who produce self-centered resumes that fail to respond to the needs of employers. Make sure each section of your resume clearly and consistently communicates what it is you **want to do**, **can do**, and **will do** for employers.

Summary of Qualifications

13. **You may want to include a "Summary of Qualifications" section immediately following your "Objective":** Some resume writers prefer including a short one-line objective but immediately following it with a three- or four-line "Summary of Qualifications" statement. This statement attempts to crystallize the individual's major strengths that are also relevant to the objective. It is usually a synthesis of the "Experience" section. We consider this an optional item to be used by individuals with a great deal of work experience and who choose a chronological resume format. It is most effective on chronological resumes where the objective is weak and the experience sections are organized by position, organization, and inclusive employment dates. The "Summary of Qualifications" section enables you to synthesize in capsule form your most important skills and accomplishments as patterns of performance. Especially with chronological resumes, this can be a very effective section. It helps elevate your resume by stressing major accomplish-

ments and thus overcoming the inherent limitations of chronological resumes. An example of such a statement includes the following:

SUMMARY OF QUALIFICATIONS

Twelve years of progressively responsible experience in all phases of retail sales and marketing with major discount stores in culturally diverse metropolitan areas. Annually improved profitability by 15 percent and consistently rated in top 10 percent of workforce.

The remainder of this resume should provide supports for this statement in the "Experience" section.

Work Experience

14. **Elaborate your work experience in detail with particular emphasis on your skills, abilities, and achievements:** Next to your objective, your work experience section will be the most important. Here you need to provide key details on your past skills and related accomplishments. To best develop this section, complete worksheets which include the following information on each job:

   - Name of employer
   - Address
   - Inclusive employment dates
   - Type of organization
   - Size of organization/number of employees
   - Approximate annual budget
   - Position held
   - Earnings per month/year
   - Responsibilities/duties
   - Achievements or significant contributions
   - Demonstrated skills and abilities
   - Reason(s) for leaving

   We include several worksheets for generating this information in Chapter 10. It's best to complete these worksheets **before** starting to write your resume.

15. **Keep each "Experience" section short and to the point:** Information for each job should be condensed into descriptions of five to eight lines. The language should be crisp, succinct, expressive, and direct. Keep editing—eliminate unnecessary words and phrases—until you have short, succinct, and powerful statements that grab the attention of the reader. Lengthy statements tend to lose the reader's attention and distract from your major points. The guiding principle here is to edit, edit, edit, and edit until you get it right!

16. **Work experience should be presented in the language of skills and accomplishments rather than as a listing of formal duties and responsibilities:** Employers are not interested in learning about duties and responsibilities assigned to your previous jobs which are essentially a rehash of your formal job descriptions. These come with the position regardless of who occupies the position. Instead, potential employers want to know how well you performed your assigned duties and responsibilities as well as any additional initiative you took that produced positive results. Since they are looking for indicators of your performance, it's to your advantage to describe your previous jobs in performance terms—what skills you used, what resulted from your work, and how your employer benefitted. These are usually termed your "accomplishments" or "achievements." An accomplishment or achievement is anything you did well that resulted in a positive outcome. Accomplishments are what define your "patterns of performance." Don't just restate your formal duties and responsibilities like this:

> Responsibilities included conducting research projects assigned to office and coordinating projects with three research and development offices. Duties also involved evaluating new employees and chairing monthly review meetings.

Restate this "work experience" in terms of your actual accomplishments or achievements:

> Conducted research on transportation of hazardous wastes on interstate highways which provided the basis for new restrictive legislation (PL4921). Developed three proposals for studying the effects of toxic waste dumps on rural water supplies which received $1.75 million in funds. Chaired interdepartmental meetings that eliminated unnecessary

redundancy and improved communications between technical professionals. Recommendations resulted in reorganizing R&D functions that saved the company $450,000 in annual overhead costs.

Accomplishment statements set you apart from so many other resumes that primarily restate formal duties and responsibilities assigned to positions as "Experience." Keep focused on employers' needs by stressing your accomplishments in each of your experience statements and descriptions.

17. **When writing a conventional resume, incorporate action verbs and use the active voice when describing your experience:** Some of the most powerful language you can use in a resume incorporates action or transitive verbs. It emphasizes taking action or initiative that goes beyond just formal assigned duties and responsibilities. If your grammar rules are a bit rusty, here are some examples of action or transitive verbs:

administered	conducted
analyzed	coordinated
assisted	created
communicated	designed
developed	planned
directed	proposed
established	recommended
evaluated	recruited
expanded	reduced
generated	reorganized
implemented	revised
increased	selected
initiated	streamlined
investigated	supervised
managed	trained
negotiated	trimmed
organized	wrote

When applied to the active voice, action or transitive verbs follow a particular grammatical pattern:

Subject	Transitive Verb	Direct Objective
I	increased	profits
I	initiated	studies
I	expanded	production

If written in the passive voice, these examples would appear in the "Experience" section of a resume in the following form—which you should avoid:

"Profits were increased by 32 percent."

"The studies resulted in new legislation."

"Production was expanded by 24 percent."

The passive voice implies the object was subjected to some type of action but the source of the action is unknown. If written in the active voice, these same examples would read as follows:

"Increased profits by 32 percent."

"Initiated studies that resulted in new legislation."

"Expanded production by 24 percent."

When using action verbs and the active voice, the action verb indicates that you, the subject, performed the action. The active voice helps elevate you to a personal performance level that gets de-emphasized, if not lost, when using the passive voice.

18. **Uses "keywords" appropriate for optical scanners:** Since more and more employers use resume scanning software and automated applicant tracking systems to initially sort resumes based on key-words, it would be wise to incorporate as many keywords in your

resume as possible. Unlike the language of action or transitive verbs (Principle #17), keywords reflect the jargon of particular industries and employers—desired skills, interpersonal traits, duties, responsibilities, positions held, education attained, or equipment used. While many keywords are technical in nature, others can be more generic: "curriculum development," "customer service," "employee relations," "market research," "negotiations," "public speaking," "team building." An employer may select a list of 30 keywords which will be used for sorting resumes. If your resume includes many of the words identified in the employer's keyword profile, the higher the probability your resume will be selected for visual examination. Of course, the more research you perform on the company, the better your chances of using the right keywords. For an excellent collection of keywords, along with resume examples, see Wendy Enelow's *1500+ KeyWords For $100,000+ Jobs* (Impact Publications).

19. **Avoid using the personal pronoun "I":** When using the active voice, the assumption is that you are the one performing the action. As indicated in Principle #17, there is no need to insert "I" when referring to your accomplishments. The use of "I" is awkward and inappropriate on a resume. It makes your resume too self-centered when you should be making it more employer-centered.

20. **Use numbers and percentages whenever possible to demonstrate your performance on previous jobs:** It's always best to state action and performance in some numerical fashion. Numbers command attention and communicate accomplishments. For example, take this "experience" statement:

    "Increased sales each year for five straight years."

The same statement can be stated in more powerful numerical terms that are equally truthful:

    "Increased sales annually by 23% ($147,000) during the past
    five years."

Which of these statements makes a more powerful impression on employers who are looking for evidence of performance patterns that might be transferred to their organization? To state you "increased" sales without stating by "how much" leaves a great deal to the imagination. Was it 1 percent or 100 percent? $5 or $500,000? If performance differences appear impressive, state them in numerical terms.

21. **Include quotes relevant to your performance:** Avoid including personal testimonials that are self-serving or are assumed to be solicited; they may appear dishonest to readers. But do include any special professional praise you have received from a company award or from a performance evaluation. Statements such as "Received the Employee of the Year Award for outstanding performance" or "Praised by employer for *exceptional performance* and consistently ranked in the upper 10 percent of the workforce" can be powerful additions to your resume.

22. **Eliminate any negative references, including reasons for leaving:** Keep your language focused on describing your accomplishments in positive terms. Never refer to your previous employers in negative terms and never volunteer information on why you left an employer, regardless of the reason. If you were terminated, volunteer this information only if asked to do so. This will usually occur during the job interview—not at the initial resume and letter writing stage. If an employer wants this information, he or she will ask for it during a telephone or face-to-face interview.

> *Never refer to your previous employers in negative terms and never volunteer information on why you left an employer.*

23. **Do not include names of supervisors:** Your experience and work history sections should only include job titles, organizations, inclusive employment dates, responsibilities, and accomplishments. Names of individuals other than yourself should be subjects you address in face-to-face interviews rather than volunteer on resumes.

24. **If you choose a chronological resume, begin with your most recent job and work backwards in reverse chronological order:** In a chronological resume, your present or last job should always be

described first and in greater detail than your other jobs. The next job should be the one before that one and so on. However, it is not necessary to include or provide detailed information on all jobs you ever held—only the most recent ones. Keep in mind that hiring managers are looking for "patterns of performance." The best evidence of such patterns is found by examining your most recent employment—not what you did 10, 20, or 30 years ago. Include your most recent employment during the past 10 years. If you held several part-time or short-term jobs or your employment record goes back for many years, you can summarize these jobs under a single heading. For example:

> **Part-time employment, 1989-1993.**
> Held several part-time positions—waitress, word processor, lab assistant—while attending college full-time.

> **Leader development positions, 1983-1990.**
> Served in progressively important leadership development roles during the early stages of my military career.

25. **Be consistent in how you handle each description or summary:** The rule here is parallel construction. Each description or summary should have a similar structure and size. Use the same type of language, verb tense, grammatical structure, and punctuation in each section.

26. **For each job or skill, put the most important information first:** Since most hiring officials want to know what you can do for them, put that information first. If you choose a chronological resume, begin with your job title and unit and then stress your accomplishments. Your inclusive dates of employment should appear last, at the end of the description, rather than at the very beginning where it will tend to be the center of attention. If you choose a functional or combination resume format, put your most important accomplishments first in relation to your objective.

27. **Be sure to account for major time gaps:** If you use a chronological resume in which inclusive employment dates are prominent, check to see that you do not have major time gaps between jobs. You need to account for obvious time gaps. Were you in school or

some type of training? If you were unemployed for a short time, you can easily handle this time gap by using years rather than exact months of a year when including dates of employment. For example, rather than state your last three jobs began and ended on these dates,

> June 1995 to present
> July 1992 to April 1995
> December 1990 to February 1992

State they began and ended on these dates:

> 1995 to present
> 1992 to 1995
> 1990 to 1992

If you specify exact months you began and left jobs, you encourage the reader to look for obvious time gaps and thus raise negative questions about your employment history. If you only use years, you can cover most short-term time gaps.

28. **If you are an obvious "job-hopper," you may want to choose a functional or combination resume rather than a chronological resume:** The job descriptions associated with a chronological resume format will accentuate employment dates and make it easy for the reader to determine a pattern of career progression from one job to another. If you do not have a clear chronological pattern, you are well advised to choose another resume format that accentuates your patterns of skills.

Other Experience

29. **Include "Other Experience" only if it further strengthens your objective in reference to the employer's needs or it helps account for employment time gaps:** Standard categories include:

   - **Prior civilian work:** Describe any work experiences you may have had prior to joining the military. Make it concise and easily understood by prospective hiring managers. Describe this experience as you would your military jobs—emphasize your skills and accomplishments. Relate this experience to your job objective, if possible.

- **Civic/Community/Volunteer:** You may have volunteer experience that demonstrates skills and accomplishments supporting your objective. For example, you may be involved in organizing community groups, raising funds, or operating a special youth program. These volunteer experiences demonstrate organization, leadership, and communication skills.

In each case, be sure to emphasize your accomplishments as they relate to both your objective and employers' needs.

Education and Training

30. **State complete information on your formal education, including any highlights that emphasize your special skills, abilities, and motivation:** Begin with your most recent education and provide the following details:

- Degree or diploma
- Graduation date
- Institution
- Special highlights, recognition, or achievements (optional)

The completed section might look like this:

B.A. in Sociology, 1995:
   Ohio State University, Columbus, OH
   Highlights:
       Graduated Magna Cum Laude
       Member, Phi Beta Kappa Honor Society

B.S. in Criminal Justice, 1993.
Ithaca College, Ithaca, NY
- Major: Law Enforcement Administration
- Minor: Management Information Systems
   G.P.A. in concentration 3.6/4.0

If your grade point and other achievements are not exceptional, do not highlight them here. Your educational achievements may appear mediocre to the reader and thus your education will become a negative.

31. **Recent graduates with little relevant work experience should emphasize their educational background more than their work experience:** Follow the principle that one's most important qualifications should be presented first. For recent graduates with little relevant work experience, education tends to be their most important qualification for entering the world of work. In such cases the "Education" category should immediately follow the "Objective." Include any part-time jobs, work-study programs, internships, extracurricular activities, or volunteer work under "Experience" to demonstrate your motivation, initiative, and leadership in lieu of progressive work experience.

32. **It's not necessary to include all education degrees or diplomas on your resume:** If high school is your highest level of education, include only high school. If you have a degree from both a community college and four-year college, include both under education, but eliminate reference to high school. Individuals with graduate degrees should only include undergraduate and graduate degrees.

33. **Include special training relevant to your objective and skills:** This may include specialized training courses or programs that led to certification or enhanced your knowledge, skills, and abilities. For example,

> **Additional training, 1996 to present**
> Completed several three-day workshops on written and oral communication skills: Making Formal Presentations, Briefing Techniques, Writing Memos, Audio-Visual Techniques.

When including additional education and training, include enough descriptive information so the reader will know what skills you acquired. Don't be surprised if your special training is viewed as more important to an employer than your educational degrees.

Professional Affiliations

34. **Include professional affiliations relevant to your objective and skills:** While you may belong to many groups, it is not necessary to include all of them on your resume. Select only those that appear to support your objective and skills and would be of interest to an employer. Include the name, inclusive dates of membership, offices held, projects, certifications, or licenses. Normally the name of the group would be sufficient. However, should your involvement go beyond a normal passive dues-paying membership role, briefly elaborate on your contributions. For example,

   > **American Society for Training and Development:** Served as President of Tidewater Virginia Chapter, 1993-1995. Developed first corporate training resource directory for Southeast Virginia.

Special Skills

35. **It's okay to include any special skills not covered in other sections of your resume:** These special skills might include an ability to communicate in foreign languages, handle specific computer software programs, operate special equipment, or demonstrate artistic talent. Again, if you have special skills relevant to your job objective and which should appeal to employers, include them in a separate section labeled "Special Skills" or "Other Relevant Skills."

Awards and Special Recognition

36. **Include any awards or special recognition that demonstrate your skills and abilities:** Receiving recognition for special knowledge, skills, or activities communicates positive images to employers: you are respected by your peers; you are a leader; you make contributions above and beyond what is expected as "normal." However, be selective in what you include here by relating awards or special recognition received to your objective and skills. If you are seeking a computer programming position, including an award for "First Prize in Howard County's Annual Chili Cook Off" would distract from the main thrust of your resume! But receiving the "Employee of the Year" award in your last job or "Community Achievement

Award" would be impressive; both awards would get the attention of employers who would be curious to learn more about the basis for receiving such awards—a good interview question.

Interests and Activities

37. **You may want to include a personal statement on your resume:** Normally we would not recommend including personal information on a resume. However, there is one exception and you should include such information sparingly. In addition to keeping your resume focused on your objective and skills as well as the employer's needs, you want to make you and your resume appear unique in comparison to other candidates. You may be able to achieve this in a "Personal Statement" or "Special Interests" section. This section might include hobbies or avocations. For example, if you are seeking a position you know requires a high energy level and the employer looks favorably on stable, married, family-oriented employees, you might include some personal information as well as interests and activities that address these considerations. For example, your personal data could include the following:

> *It's okay to include personal information, but only if it enhances your job objective.*

PERSONAL: 35 . . . excellent health . . . married . . . children . . . enjoy challenges . . . focused on results

Alternatively, you could write a personal statement about yourself so that the reader might remember you in particular. For example,

SPECIAL INTERESTS: Love the challenge of solving problems, taking initiative, and achieving results . . . be it in developing new marketing strategies, programming a computer, climbing a mountain, white water rafting, or modifying a motorcycle.

Such statements can give hobbies and special talents and interests new meaning in reference to your objective. But again, be very careful about including such statements. More often than not, they can be a negative, distracting the reader from the most important information included on your resume. By all means avoid trite statements that may distract from the main thrust of your resume.

Salary History or Expectations

38. **Never include salary information on your resume:** While hiring officials are interested in your salary history and expectations, there is no good reason for including this information on your resume or even in your cover letter. Salary is something that needs to be negotiated, but only after you have had a chance to learn about the value of the position as well as communicate your value to the employer. This occurs at the end of the job interview and should be the very last thing you talk about or after receiving an offer of a position. If you include salary information on your resume or in your cover letter, you are likely to prematurely eliminate yourself from consideration—your expectations are either too high or too low.

References

39. **Never include names, addresses, and phone numbers of references on your resume:** You may want to include a final category on your resume:

    REFERENCES: Available upon request

    However, this is an empty category that does nothing to enhance your resume. Our recommendation is to eliminate it altogether or use it as filler to round out a short resume that could use more text for aesthetics. Remember, you want to control your references by providing the information upon request which usually occurs during the interview stage. If you volunteer your references on the resume, your references may be unprepared to talk about you to employers. It's best to list the names, addresses, and phone numbers of your professional references on a separate sheet of paper, but take that list with you to the job interview rather than volunteer the information on your resume. Ask your references for permission to use their names and brief them on your interests in relation to the position. Make sure they have a copy of your resume for reference.

Other Information

40. **You may want to include a few other categories of information on your resume, depending on your experience and the relevance of such information to employers:** You may want to include the following categories of information:

   - Certificates
   - Accreditations
   - Licenses
   - Publications
   - Patents
   - Foreign languages
   - Government clearances

   However, include them only if they strengthen your qualifications in reference to the needs of hiring officials. For example, if foreign languages are important to employers, include them on your resume. If you are in a professional field that requires certificates and licenses, include the appropriate information on your resume.

Language, Style, and Tone

41. **Use an appropriate language to express your productivity and your understanding of the employer's needs:** In addition to using action verbs and the active voice, try to use the language of the employer when describing your skills and experience. Use the "jargon" of the industry in demonstrating your understanding of the employer. As we note in Principle #18 (pages 50-51) and again in Principle #43 (page 61), this type of language will serve you well if your resume is electronically scanned using resume scanning software and automated applicant tracking systems. Always stress your value in relation to the employer's needs—you will **add value** to the employer's operations!

42. **Use crisp, succinct, expressive, and direct language:** Avoid poetic, bureaucratic, vernacular, and academic terms that often tend to turn off readers. For example, instead of stating your objective as:

I would like to work with a consulting firm where I can develop new programs and utilize my decision-making and system-engineering experience. I hope to improve your organization's business profits.

Re-word the objective so it reads like this:

An increasingly responsible research and development position, where proven decision-making and system engineering abilities will be used for improving productivity.

Use the first person, but do not refer to yourself as *"I"* or *"the author."* The first person *"I"* is understood but not stated. The use of action verbs and the active voice implies you are the subject. Always use active verbs and parallel sentence structure. Avoid introductory and wind-up phrases like *"My duties included..."* or *"Position description reads as follows..."* Use jargon only if appropriate to the situation or enhances keywords.

43. **Select an appropriate resume language that is particularly sensitive to today's resume scanning technology:** You should pay particular attention to the specific language you select for your resume. Indeed, the language component of resumes is now more important than ever in the history of resume writing. Given recent changes in employer resume screening techniques, there's a high probability your resume will be electronically scanned sometime during your job search. The key to getting your resume "read" in electronic screening systems is the specific language you incorporate in your resume. When scanning resumes electronically, employers select certain **keywords** which should appear on your resume. If you want to increase your probability of being "electronically acceptable" to employers, you must incorporate such keywords in your resume writing. For more information on the language requirements for electronically scanned resumes, see Peter D. Weddle, *Internet Resumes* (Impact Publications).

Appearance and Visual Techniques

44. **Use appropriate highlighting and emphasizing techniques:** The most important information on a one- or two-page resume needs to be highlighted since many readers will only spend a few seconds

skimming your resume. The most widely used highlighting and emphasizing techniques involve CAPITALIZING, underlining, *italicizing*, and **bolding** headings, words, and phrases or using bullets (●), boxes (■), hyphens (–), or asterisks (*). However, use these techniques sparingly. Overuse of highlighting and emphasizing techniques can distract from your message. A major exception to this general rule relates to electronic resumes: avoid using italics, script, and underlining if your resume is likely to be electronically scanned.

45. **Follow the "less is more" rule when deciding on format and type style:** The fear of not getting all information onto one page leads some resume writers to create crowded and cramped resumes. Be sure to leave ample margins—at least 1" top to bottom and left to right—and white space. Use a standard type style (Times Roman but not Helvetica) and size (10-11 point). Remember, the first thing a reader sees is layout, white space, and type style and size. Your resume should first be pleasing to the eye.

46. **Do not include special borders, graphics, or photos unless you are applying for a job in graphic arts or desktop publishing:** Keep the design very basic and conservative. Special graphics effects are likely to distract from your central message. However, if you are in the graphics art or related art field, you may want to dress up your resume with graphics that demonstrate your creativity and style. Your photo does not belong on a resume. The rule of thumb for photos is this: Regardless of how great you or your mother may think you look, at least 50 percent of resume recipients will probably dislike your photo—and you. The photo gives them something to pick apart—your hairstyle, smile, eyes, or dress—and thus distracts from your bona fide qualifications. Why set yourself up by including a photo that will probably work against you? Your ego is best served with an invitation to an interview based solely on the content of your resume. Focus on your language rather than your photo.

Resume Length

47. **Keep sentences and sections short and succinct:** Keep in mind your readers will spend little time reading your resume. The shorter

and more succinct you can write each section and sentence, the more powerful will be your message. Try to limit the length of each job description paragraph to five to eight lines—no more than ten.

48. **Limit your resume to one or two pages:** We agree with most resume advisors that the one- to two-page resume is the most appropriate, although one-page is preferable. We prefer it because it focuses the busy reader's attention on a single field of vision. It's especially reader-friendly if designed with the use of highlighting and emphasizing techniques. The one-page resume is a definite asset considering the fact that many hiring officials must review hundreds of resumes each week. Research clearly demonstrates that retention rates decrease as one's eyes move down the page and nearly vanish on a second or third page! At first the thought of writing a one- or two-page resume may pose

> *The shorter and more succinct you can write each section and sentence, the more powerful will be your message.*

problems for you, especially if you think your resume should be a presentation of your life history. However, many executives with 25 years of experience, who make in excess of $100,000 a year, manage to get all their major qualifications onto a one-page resume. If they can do it, so can you. When condensing information on yourself into a one-page format, keep in mind that your resume is an advertisement for a job interview. You only want to include enough information to grab the attention of the reader who hopefully will contact you for a job interview. If you must present your qualifications in two pages rather than one, consider making the second page a "continuation page" that provides additional details on the qualifications outlined on the first page.

Production

Employers also want to see your best professional effort at the production stage of resume writing. This involves making the right choices on paper color, weight, and texture as well as production methods. Above all, the resume they receive must be error free or they are likely to discard it as an example of incompetence.

49. **Carefully proofread and produce two or three drafts of your resume before producing the final copies:** Be sure to carefully proofread the resume for grammatical, spelling, and punctuation errors before producing the final copy. Any such errors will quickly disqualify you with employers. Read and reread the draft several times to see if you can improve various elements to make it more readable and eye appealing. Read for both form and content. Have someone else also review your resume and give you feedback on its form and content. Use the evaluation forms in Chapter 4 to conduct both internal and external evaluations.

50. **Choose white, off-white, ivory, or light grey 20 to 50 lb. bond paper with 100% cotton fiber ("rag content"):** Your choice of paper—color, weight, and texture—do make a difference to resume readers. These things say something about your professional style. Choose a poor quality paper and inappropriate color and you communicate the wrong messages to employers. There is nothing magical about ivory or off-white paper. As more and more people use these colors, off-white and ivory colors have probably lost their effectiveness. To be different, try a light grey or basic white. Indeed, white paper gives a nice bright look to what has become essentially a dull colored process. Stay with black ink or use a dark navy ink for the light grey paper, if you have your resume professionally printed. If you are applying for a creative position, you may decide to use more daring colors to better express your creative style and personality. However, stay away from dark colored papers. Resumes should have a light bright look to them. The paper should also match your cover letter and envelope.

51. **Produce your resume on 8½" x 11" paper:** This is the standard business size that you should follow. Other sizes are too unconventional and thus communicate the wrong message to readers.

52. **Print only on one side of the paper:** Do not produce a two-sided resume. If your resume runs two pages, print it on two separate pages.

53. **Use a good quality machine and an appropriate typeface:** It's best to produce your camera-ready copy (for reproduction) on a letter quality printer, preferably a laser printer. If you choose to have it typeset, you will loose flexibility to change elements on your resume and the process can be costly. Avoid manual typewriters that produce uneven type and look very amateurish. Never produce your resume on a dot matrix printer. Most such printers produce poor quality type that communicates a "mass production" quality. If you use a desktop publishing program, choose serif typefaces (Times Roman, Palatino, New Century). Avoid sans serif typefaces (Gothic, Helvetica, Avant Garde), which are difficult to read. Be sure you print dark crisp type.

Most individuals reproduce their resume on a copy machine. Indeed, given the high quality reproduction achieved on many copy machines available at local print shops, it's not necessary to go to the expense of having your resume professionally printed. However, if you need 2,000 or more copies—which is most unlikely unless you resort to a broadcast or "shot-gun" marketing approach—it may be more cost effective to have them printed. Just take your camera-ready copy, along with your choice of paper, to a local printer and have them make as many copies as you need. The cost per copy will run anywhere from 3¢ to 15¢, depending on the number of copies run. The larger the run, the cheaper will be your per unit cost. However, we prefer composing a resume using a standard word processing (Word or WordPerfect) or desktop publishing program (PageMaker or Ventura) that enables you to customize each resume for particular employers and then printing it on a laser printer with a dpi of 600. This approach gives you flexibility and top quality at very low cost.

Marketing and Distribution

Your resume is only as good as your marketing and distribution efforts. What, for example, will you do with your resume once you've completed it? How can you best get it into the hands of individuals who can make a difference in your job search? Are you planning to send it in response to vacancy announcements and want ads? Maybe you plan to broadcast it to hundreds of employers in the hope someone will call you for an interview? Should you become a member of an electronic resume bank? Perhaps you only want to send it to a few people who can help you with your job search? Or maybe you really don't have a plan beyond getting it produced in a "correct" form.

54. **It's best to target your resume on specific employers rather than broadcast it to hundreds of names and addresses:** Broadcasting or "shot-gunning" your resume to hundreds of potential employers will give you a false sense of making progress with your job search since you think you are actually making contact with numerous employers. However, you will be disappointed with the results. For every 100 resumes you mail, you will be lucky to get one positive response that leads to a job interview. Indeed, many individuals report no responses after mass mailing hundreds of resumes. It's always best to **target** your resume on specific employers through one or two methods:

> *Broadcasting your resume to hundreds of potential employers will give you a false sense of making progress with your job search.*

- **Respond to vacancy announcements or want ads:** Resumes sent in response to job listings also will give you a sense of making progress with your job search. Since competition is likely to be high for advertised positions, your chances of getting a job interview may not be good, although much better than if you broadcasted your resume to hundreds of employers who may not have openings.

- **Target employers with information on your qualifications:** The most effective way of getting job interviews is to network for information, advice, and referrals. You do this by contacting friends, professional associates, acquaintances, and others who might have information on jobs related to your interests and skills. You, in effect, attempt to uncover job vacancies before they become publicized or meet an employment need not yet recognized by employers who may create a position for you in line with your qualifications. The resume plays an important role in this networking process. In some cases, you will be referred to someone who is interested in seeing your resume; when that happens, send it along with a cover letter, and follow up your mailing with a telephone call. In other cases, you will conduct informational interviews with individuals who can give you advice and referrals relevant to your career interests. You should take your resume to the informational interview and, at the very end of your meeting, ask your informant to critique your resume. In the process of examining your resume, your network contact is likely to give you good feedback for further revising your resume as well as refer you and your resume to others. If you regularly repeat this networking and informational interviewing process, within a few weeks you should begin landing job interviews directly related to the qualifications you outlined in your dynamite resume!

55. The best way to broadcast your resume is to join an electronic database or use computer bulletin boards: We view the new electronic job banks as high-tech resume broadcasting methods. Resume database companies use sophisticated search and retrieval software to match job seekers with employers who use their services for locating qualified candidates. If you have the right combination of skills and experience and know how to write a dynamite resume with language sensitive to the search and retrieval software, you should be able to connect with employers through such electronic mediums.

56. Your resume should always be accompanied by a cover letter: A resume unaccompanied by a cover letter is a naked resume—like going to a job interview barefoot. The cover letter is very important in relation to the resume. After all, if sent through the mail, the letter is the first thing a hiring official reads before getting to the resume. If the letter is interesting enough, the person proceeds to read the resume. A well-crafted cover letter should complement rather than repeat the content of your resume. It should grab the reader's attention, communicate your purpose, and convince the reader to take action. If you neglect the cover letter, you may effectively kill your resume! In many cases, your cover letter may be more important than your resume in landing an interview and getting the job. Your cover letter should command as much attention as your resume.

57. **Never enclose letters of recommendation, transcripts, or other information with your resume unless requested to do so:** Unsolicited letters of recommendation are negatives. Readers know they have been specially produced to impress them and thus they may question your integrity. Like personal photos, unsolicited transcripts may communicate negative messages, unless you have perfect grades. Such information merely distracts from your resume and cover letter. It does not contribute to getting a job interview. It indicates you do not know what you are doing by including such information with your resume and letter. On the other hand, once invited to a job interview, you are well advised to put together a portfolio that includes samples of your work and other materials providing evidence of your resume claims of performance. For an excellent examination of how to compile, as well as communicate, a performance portfolio, see Rick Nelles's *Proof of Performance* (Impact Publications).

58. **Your resume should be addressed to a specific person:** Always try to get the correct name and position of the person who should receive your resume. Unless you are specifically instructed to do so, addressing your correspondence to "Dear Sir," "Director of Personnel," or "To Whom It May Concern" is likely to result in lost correspondence; the mail room may treat it as junk mail. If you later follow up your correspondence with a phone call, you have no one to communicate with. A couple of phone calls should quickly result in the proper name. Just call the switchboard or a receptionist and ask the following:

> "I need to send some correspondence to the person in charge of
> _____. Whom might that be? And what is the correct address?"

Keep in mind that the people who have the power to hire are usually not in the Personnel Office; they tend to be the heads of operating units. So target your resume accordingly!

59. **Enclose your resume and letter in a matching No. 10 business envelope or in a 9" x 12" envelope:** We prefer the 9" x 12" envelope because it keeps your correspondence flat and makes a better presentation than the No. 10 business envelope. Keep all your stationery matching, including the 9" x 12" envelope. If, however, it's difficult to find a matching 9" x 12" envelope, go with a white or buff-colored envelope or use a U.S. Postal Service "Priority Mail" envelope.

60. **Type the envelope or mailing label rather than handwrite the address:** Handwritten addresses look too personal and amateurish and give off mixed messages. This is a dumb thing to do after having enclosed a professional looking resume. Contrary to what others may tell you, in a job search handwritten addresses—and even handwritten letters or notes—do not gain more attention or generate more positive responses; they may actually have the opposite effect—label you as being unprofessional or someone who is trying to manipulate the employer with the old handwritten technique.

> *Avoid handwritten messages in your job search. You're not selling real estate or insurance. This is business correspondence requiring your best professional effort.*

Typed addresses look more professional; they are consistent with the enclosed resume. After all, this is business correspondence —not a social invitation to invite yourself to an interview. Don't confuse communicating your qualifications to employers with selling real estate or insurance—fields that tell salespeople to routinely handwrite addresses and notes to customers. Such a sales analogy is inappropriate for your job search.

61. **Send your correspondence by first-class or priority mail or special next-day services, and use stamps:** If you want to get the recipient's immediate attention, send your correspondence in one of those colorful next-day air service envelopes provided by the U.S. Postal Service, Federal Express, UPS, or other carriers or couriers. However, first-class or priority mail will usually get your correspondence delivered within two to three days. It's best to affix a nice

commemorative stamp rather than use a postage meter. A stamp helps personalize your mailing piece.

62. **Never fax or e-mail your resume unless asked to do so by your recipient:** It is presumptuous for anyone to fax or e-mail his or her resume to an employer without express permission to do so. Such faxes or e-mails are treated as junk mail and are thus viewed as unwarranted invasions of privacy. If asked to fax or e-mail your correspondence, be sure to follow up by mailing a copy of the original and indicating you sent materials by fax or e-mail on a specific date as requested. A mailed resume and letter will always look better (assuming you've followed our production advice) than faxed or e-mailed correspondence. When you e-mail your resume, do so as part of the body of your e-mail message (cover letter) and as a Word attachment. Many employers prefer receiving resumes as part of the e-mail rather than as an attachment that could include a virus.

Follow-Up

Follow-up remains the least understood but most important step in any job search. Whatever you do, make sure you follow up **all** of your job search activities. If you fail to follow up, you are likely to get little or no response to your job search initiatives. Follow-up means taking action that gets results.

63. **Follow up your resume within seven days of mailing it:** Do not let too much time lapse between when you mailed your resume and when you contact the resume recipient. Seven days should give the recipient sufficient time to examine your communication and decide on your future status. If not, your follow-up will assist in making a decision.

64. **The best follow-up for a mailed resume is a telephone call:** Don't expect your resume recipient to take the initiative in calling you for an interview. State in your cover letter that you will call the recipient at a particular time to discuss your resume:

> I will call your office on the morning of March 17 to see if a meeting can be scheduled at a convenient time.

And be sure you indeed follow up with a phone call at the designated time. If you have difficulty contacting the individual, try three times to get through. After the third try, leave a message as well as write a letter as an alternative to the telephone follow-up. In this letter, inquire about the status of your resume and thank the individual for his or her consideration.

65. **Follow up your follow-up with a thank-you letter:** Regardless of the outcome of your follow-up phone call, send a nice thank-you letter based upon your conversation. You thank the letter recipient for taking the time to speak with you and reiterate your interest in the position. While some career counselors recommend sending a handwritten thank-you note to personalize communication between you and the employer, as we noted in Principle #60, we caution against doing so. Remember, you are engaged in a business transaction rather than in social communications. We feel a handwritten letter is inappropriate for such situations. Such a letter should be produced in a typed form and follow the principles of good business correspondence. You can be warm and friendly in what you say. The business letter format keeps you on stage—you are putting your best business foot forward.

The military-to-civilian resume examples found in the remainder of this book are based upon many of these resume writing and production principles. Examine those examples for ideas on how to develop each resume section. But be sure **you write your own resume** based upon the above principles rather than on the subsequent examples.

4

Conduct Two Resume Evaluations

O NCE YOU COMPLETE YOUR RESUME, BE SURE TO EVAL-
uate it according to the principles outlined in Chapter 3. You
should do this by conducting two evaluations: internal and
external. With an **internal evaluation**, you assess your resume in
reference to specific self-evaluation criteria. An **external evaluation** involves
having someone else critique your resume for its overall effectiveness.

Internal Evaluation

The first evaluation should take place immediately upon completing the first
draft of your resume. Examine your resume in reference to the following
evaluation criteria. Respond to each statement by circling the appropriate
number at the right that most accurately describes your new resume:

1 = Strongly Agree	4 = Disagree
2 = Agree	5 = Strongly Disagree
3 = So-So	

The numbers at the end of each statement correspond to each principle
previously outlined in Chapter 3. Refer to these principles for further clarifica-
tion.

Writing

1. Translated my military experience and
    skills into civilian employment terms
    that should be readily understood by
    employers with little or no military
    experience (#1).   1   2   3   4   5

2. Wrote the resume myself—no creative
    plagiarizing from others' resume
    examples. (#2)   1   2   3   4   5

3. Conducted a thorough self-assessment
    which became the basis for writing each
    resume section. (#2)   1   2   3   4   5

4. Have a plan of action that relates my
    resume to other job search activities. (#3)   1   2   3   4   5

5. Selected an appropriate resume format
    that best presents my interests, skills,
    and experience. (#4)   1   2   3   4   5

6. Included all essential information
    categories in the proper order. (#5-6)   1   2   3   4   5

7. Eliminated all extraneous information
    unrelated to my objective and employers'
    needs (date, picture, race, religion, age,
    political affiliation, sex, height, weight,
    marital status, health, hobbies) or better
    saved for discussion in the interview—
    salary history and references. (#7)   1   2   3   4   5

8. Put the most important information
    first. (#6)   1   2   3   4   5

9. Resume is oriented to the future rather
    than to the past. (#5)   1   2   3   4   5

10. Contact information is complete—name,
    address, and phone number. No P.O.
    Box numbers or nicknames. (#8-9)   1   2   3   4   5

11. Limited abbreviations to a few accepted
    words. (#9)   1   2   3   4   5

12. Contact information attractively
    formatted to introduce the resume. (#9)   1   2   3   4   5

13. Included a thoughtful employer-oriented
    objective that incorporates both skills
    and benefits. (#10)   1   2   3   4   5

14. Objective clearly communicates to
    employers what I want to do, can do,
    and will do for them. (#10)   1   2   3   4   5

15. Objective is neither too general nor
    too specific. (#11)   1   2   3   4   5

16. Objective serves as the central organizing
    element for all other sections of the
    resume. (#12)   1   2   3   4   5

17. Considered including a "Summary of
    Qualifications" section. (#13)   1   2   3   4   5

18. Elaborated work experience in detail,
    emphasizing my skills, abilities,
    and achievements. (#14, 16)   1   2   3   4   5

19. Each "Experience" section is short
    and to the point. (#15)   1   2   3   4   5

20. Consistently used action verbs and the
    active voice. (#16-17)   1   2   3   4   5

21. Incorporated language appropriate
    for the keywords of electronic resume
    scanners. (#18)   1   2   3   4   5

22. Did not refer to myself as "I." (#19)   1   2   3   4   5

23. Used specifics—numbers and percents—
    to highlight my performance. (#20)   1   2   3   4   5

24. Included positive quotations about my
    performance from previous employers. (#21)   1   2   3   4   5

25. Eliminated any negative references,
    including reasons for leaving. (#22)   1   2   3   4   5

26. Does not include names of supervisors. (#23)   1   2   3   4   5

27. Summarized my most recent job and
    then included other jobs in reverse
    chronological order. (#24)   1   2   3   4   5

28. Descriptions of "Experience" are
    consistent. (#25)   1   2   3   4   5

29. Put the most important information on
    my skills first when summarizing my
    "Experience." (#26)   1   2   3   4   5

30. No time gaps nor "job hopping" apparent
    to reader. (#27-28)   1   2   3   4   5

31. Documented "other experience" that
    might strengthen my objective and
    decided to either include or exclude
    it on the resume. (#29)   1   2   3   4   5

32. Included complete information on my
    educational background, including
    important highlights. (#30)   1   2   3   4   5

33. If a recent graduate with little relevant
    work experience, emphasized educa-
    tional background more than work
    experience. (#31)   1   2   3   4   5

34. Put education in reverse chronological
    order and eliminated high school if a
    college graduate. (#32)   1   2   3   4   5

35. Included special education and training
    relevant to my major interests and
    skills. (#33)   1   2   3   4   5

36. Included professional affiliations and membership relevant to my objective and skills; highlighted any major contributions. (#34)   1   2   3   4   5

37. Documented any special skills not included elsewhere on resume and included those that appear relevant to employers' needs. (#35)   1   2   3   4   5

38. Included awards or special recognitions that further document my skills and achievements. (#36)   1   2   3   4   5

39. Weighed the pros and cons of including a personal statement on my resume. (#37)   1   2   3   4   5

40. Did not mention salary history or expectations. (#38)   1   2   3   4   5

41. Did not include names, addresses, and phone number of references. (#39)   1   2   3   4   5

42. Included additional information to enhance the interest of employers. (#40)   1   2   3   4   5

43. Used a language appropriate for the employer, including terms that associate me with the industry. (#18, 41)   1   2   3   4   5

44. My language is crisp, succinct, expressive, and direct. (#42)   1   2   3   4   5

45. Used highlighting and emphasizing techniques to make the resume most readable to the individual (a conventional resume); avoided such elements when writing an electronic or scannable resume. (#43)   1   2   3   4   5

46. Selected language that is appropriate for being "read" by today's resume scanning technology. (#44)   1   2   3   4   5

47. Resume has an inviting, uncluttered look incorporating sufficient white space and using a standard type style and size. (#45)   1   2   3   4   5

48. Kept the design very basic and conservative. (#46)   1   2   3   4   5

49. Kept sentences and sections short and succinct. (#47)   1   2   3   4   5

50. Resume runs one or two pages. (#48)   1   2   3   4   5

Production

51. Carefully proofread and produced two or three drafts which were subjected to both internal and external evaluations before producing the final copies. (#49)   1   2   3   4   5

52. Chose a standard color and quality of paper. (#50)   1   2   3   4   5

53. Used 8½" x 11" paper. (#51)   1   2   3   4   5

54. Printed resume on only one side of paper. (#52)   1   2   3   4   5

55. Used a good quality printer and an easy-to-read typeface. (#53)   1   2   3   4   5

Marketing and Distribution

56. Targeted resume toward specific employers. (#54)   1   2   3   4   5

57. Used resume properly for networking and informational interviewing activities. (#55)   1   2   3   4   5

58. Considered entering resume into online resume databases and responding to job listings found on several Internet employment sites. (#54)   1   2   3   4   5

59. Resume accompanied by a dynamite cover letter. (#55)   1   2   3   4   5

60. Only enclosed a cover letter with my resume—nothing else. (#56)   1   2   3   4   5

61. Addressed to a specific name and position. (#57)   1   2   3   4   5

62. Mailed resume and cover letter in a matching No. 10 business envelope or in a 9" x 12" envelope. (#58)   1   2   3   4   5

63. Typed address on envelope. (#59)   1   2   3   4   5

64. Sent correspondence by first-class or priority mail or special next-day services; affixed attractive commemorative stamps. (#60)   1   2   3   4   5

Follow-Up

65. Followed up the mailed resume within 7 days. (#62)   1   2   3   4   5

66. Used the telephone for following up. (#63)   1   2   3   4   5

67. Followed up the follow-up with a nice thank-you letter. (#64)   1   2   3   4   5

TOTAL _____

Add the numbers you circled to the right of each statement to get a cumulative score. If your score is higher than 90, you need to work on improving various aspects of your resume. Go back and institute the necessary changes to create a truly dynamite resume.

External Evaluation

In many respects the external resume evaluation plays the most crucial role in your overall job search. It helps you get remembered, which, in turn, leads to referrals and job leads.

The best way to conduct an external evaluation is to circulate your resume to two or more individuals. Choose people whose opinions you value for being objective, frank, and thoughtful. Do not select friends and relatives who might flatter you with positive comments. Professional acquaintances or people you don't know personally but whom you admire may be good candidates for this type of evaluation.

An ideal evaluator has experience in hiring people in your area of expertise. In addition to sharing their experience with you, they may refer you to other individuals who would be interested in your qualifications. You will encounter many of these individuals in the process of networking and conducting informational interviews. You, in effect, conduct an external evaluation of your resume with this individual during the informational interview. At the very end of the informational interview you should ask the person to examine your resume; you want to elicit comments on how you can better strengthen the resume. Ask the following questions:

> *"If you don't mind, would you look over my resume? Perhaps you could comment on its clarity or make suggestions for improving it?"*

> *"How would you react to this resume if you received it from a candidate? Does it grab your attention and interest you enough to talk with me?"*

> *"If you were writing this resume, what changes would you make? Any additions, deletions, or modifications?"*

Answers to these questions should give you invaluable feedback for improving both the form and content of your resume. You will be eliciting advice from people whose opinions count. However, it is not necessary to incorporate all such advice. Some evaluators, while well-meaning, will not provide you with sound advice. Instead, they may reinforce many of the pitfalls found in weak resumes.

Another way to conduct an external evaluation is to develop a checklist of evaluation criteria and give it, along with your resume, to individuals whose opinions and expertise you value. Unlike the self evaluation criteria used for the internal evaluation, the evaluation criteria for the external evaluation should be more general. Examine your resume in relation to these criteria:

INSTRUCTIONS: Circle the number that best characterizes various aspects of my resume as well as include any recommendations on how to best improve the resume:

1 = Excellent	2 = Okay	3 = Weak

Recommendations
for improvement

1.	Overall appearance	1 2 3	_____
2.	Layout	1 2 3	_____
3.	Clarity	1 2 3	_____
4.	Consistency	1 2 3	_____
5.	Readability	1 2 3	_____
6.	Language	1 2 3	_____
7.	Organization	1 2 3	_____
8.	Content/completeness	1 2 3	_____
9.	Length	1 2 3	_____
10.	Contact info/header	1 2 3	_____
11.	Objective	1 2 3	_____
12.	Experience	1 2 3	_____
13.	Skills	1 2 3	_____
14.	Achievements	1 2 3	_____

15. Education   1   2   3   _____

16. Other information   1   2   3   _____

17. Paper color   1   2   3   _____

18. Paper size and stock   1   2   3   _____

19. Overall production quality   1   2   3   _____

20. Potential effectiveness   1   2   3   _____

SUMMARY EVALUATION: _____

_____

_____

_____

_____

After completing these external evaluations and incorporating useful suggestions for further improving the quality of your resume, it's a good idea to send a copy of your revised resume to those individuals who were helpful in giving you advice. Thank them for their time and thoughtful comments. Ask them to keep you in mind should they hear of anyone who might be interested in your experience and skills. In so doing, you will be demonstrating your appreciation and thoughtfulness as well as reminding them to remember you for further information, advice, and referrals.

In the end, **being remembered in reference to your resume** is one of the most important goals you want to repeatedly achieve during your job search. As you will quickly discover, your most effective job search strategy involves networking with your resume. You want to share information, by way of the informational interview, about your interests and qualifications with those who can give advice, know about job vacancies, or can refer you to individuals who have the power to hire. Your resume, and especially this external evaluation, plays a critical role in furthering this process.

5

Translating Military Experience Into Civilian Language

ONE OF THE FIRST HURDLES YOU'LL ENCOUNTER EN route to developing a conventional or electronic resume is how to translate your military experience into civilian language. Regardless of the duties you performed in the military, it is your responsibility to convey your qualifications in terms that prospective employers will easily and quickly understand.

Check Your Language

Depending on the nature of the jobs you held, this translation process will be an easy task for some and a more challenging task for others. For example, if you were a pilot in the Air Force, a nurse in the Navy, or a military policeman in the Army and your desire is to be a pilot, nurse, or policeman, respectively, in your civilian work life, the translation should be a relatively straightforward process. If, on the other hand, your jobs were unique to military service, the task is more challenging; it requires closer identification of transferable skills, such as leadership, rather than content-specific skills like computer programming.

Before beginning the translation process, it's important that you have a complete understanding of the work you did in the military. Can you thoroughly describe the different activities you performed? How did you accomplish the associated tasks? What were the skills or knowledge you used along the way? What did you produce or accomplish?

Let's start by filling out the form on page 84. This form is intended to organize your thoughts in regard to the nature of jobs held and to trigger your thoughts with regard to analogous employment in the private sector. You may find it useful to have your resume as a reference. However, note that this exercise is not intended to duplicate your documented work history. Instead, it should help you crystallize your thoughts regarding past employment and motivate you to seek information on those civilian jobs that may allow you to build on the expertise you developed while in the military. It may be the case that you can't fill in the equivalent civilian jobs just yet. That's fine and certainly not unexpected. In the next step, however, you will research those jobs that appear to match your interests so that you will have the knowledge required.

Researching the Marketplace

To become well versed in the language of your target industry, you must thoroughly research the civilian marketplace. Where should you begin? There are numerous sources of job information. Let us suggest a few. First, you should visit your local ACAP (Army), Family Service Center (Navy), or Family Support Center (Air Force) office and read the job openings in those occupations for which you have an interest. Career counselors at these sites will be glad to help you access the Operation Transition website *(www.dmdc. osd.mil/ot)* and the DoD Job Search on America's Job Bank (*http://dod. jobsearch.org*). You can also call the Operation Transition Help Desk at 800-477-8227. When reviewing the job openings on the DoD Job Search website, pay special attention to the requirements for each job listed. As you read through these listings, think about the jobs you've held in the military and the potential connection in terms of skills employed, activities performed, work accomplished, etc. For those readers leaving the Army, there is a new, interactive, computer-based training program called **ACAP XXI**. Make sure you see your local career counselor to take full advantage of its extensive capabilities.

A second source of job information can be found in the reference section of your local base/fort/post or public library. Make sure you look at reference books like the Department of Labor's ***Occupational Outlook Handbook***. This book will give you useful information about many different types of jobs. While the information is fairly generic, it will provide you with excellent

MILITARY JOB # ____

Job Title:

_____

Education / Training Required:

_____

_____

Skills Used:

_____

_____

_____

Activities Performed:

_____

_____

_____

Certification Achieved:

_____

_____

Similar Civilian Jobs:

_____

_____

_____

Required Experience / Training:

_____

_____

_____

_____

insight into the educational, training, or work experience required for thousands of civilian jobs. You can access the handbook online through this URL: *http://stats.bls.gov/ocohome.htm*. You also can order the handbook directly from Impact Publications by completing the order form at the end of this book.

A third source of job information is right at your finger tips—the Employment section of your local Sunday newspaper. Read the employment ads for the types of jobs that interest you. Look specifically at the skills or experience required. You might also consider calling the company or employment agency to see if they could provide you with additional detail concerning the requirements for the job.

A fourth method of obtaining information on the requirements for current job openings is to engage in informational interviews. As discussed more fully in Chapter 10, "Network Your Way to Career Success," of your "Corporate Gray Series" book, the purpose of the informational interview is to solicit information in a non-threatening way, i.e., you want to let the person with whom you will be conducting the informational interview know that you will not be asking him or her for a job. Call or write those friends, colleagues, acquaintances, etc. who are currently employed in a civilian occupation in which you are interested. See if they will spend some time talking with you about the nature of their responsibilities. Remember, your interest should be on learning what it takes to be successful at the type of job they hold. You will find that most people, especially those with former military experience, will be helpful and offer you a wealth of information. During these networking sessions, we recommend following the 2/3, 1/3 rule. Approximately two-thirds of the time you should be in "listen mode," soaking up as much information as possible as the other person talks about his or her job, company, or industry. In the remaining one-third you should ask insightful, intelligent questions that trigger a more in-depth response in those areas of greatest interest to you. Naturally, the more research you do prior to any given networking session, the more likely you will be in a position to ask intelligent questions and, more importantly, have useful information revealed to you.

Fifth, you can go on-line and traverse cyberspace where a wealth of career opportunities can be found. We recommend accessing the Internet's World Wide Web and visiting the sites of organizations like Monster.com, FlipDog.com, CareerBuilder.com, CareerWeb.com, Dice.com, Headhunter.net, and HotJobs.com, which daily post thousands of job opportunities for hundreds of companies across the U.S. (and even overseas!). In addition to the numerous online job databases, you can also access other Internet services such as America Online, CompuServe, and Microsoft Internet Explorer; you can visit "chat rooms" and forums focused on your civilian career interests. In addition, we recommend "surfing the Web" prior to any networking opportunity. By using a search engine like Google (*www.google.com*), iWon (*www.iwon.com*), AltaVista (*www.altavista.com*), Yahoo (*www.yahoo.com*), and Excite (*www.excite.com*), you should find considerable information about the various companies that are in your target industry. Your goal in sifting through the volumes of information available through the World Wide Web is to build a strong repository of knowledge that you can tap whenever and wherever needed. The broader and deeper your basis of knowledge, the more impressive you will be when engaged in networking or interviews.

For additional information on these and other on-line services, see Chapter 19, "Join the Electronic Revolution," in your "Corporate Gray Series" book (*From Army Green... / From Navy Blue ... / From Air Force Blue to Corporate Gray*).

Finally, we suggest visiting and/or joining an association in your desired field of employment. Often these associations will have newsletters or web sites that contain job listings. Again, we recommend contacting these companies to better understand the skills and experience they are seeking for their respective positions. As you may be aware, there are several associations that often bridge the gap between military and civilian employment in a particular career field. An example of such an association is the Society of Logistics Engineers, or SOLE. If your work in the military involved logistics and you are interested in pursuing a logistics career in the civilian work world, then you should consider contacting SOLE and becoming a member. One of the most important benefits of joining an association like SOLE is the opportunity to talk with other career professionals, many of whom have worked in that particular career field in both the public and private sectors. Other examples of this type of association include the Society of Military Engineers, the Society of Military Comptrollers, and the American Society of Industrial Security. In addition to these industry-specific associations, we also recommend contacting more general associations such as The Retired Officers Association (TROA), the Non Commissioned Officers Association (NCOA), the Naval Enlisted Association (NEA), the Air Force Association (AFA), and the Veterans of Foreign Wars (VFW), among others. Many of these associations sponsor events or have programs that help you network with other members.

Associations can also take a more purely civilian flavor as well. There are literally thousands of civilian associations. For more information, we refer you to the *Encyclopedia of Associations*, which you can find in many base or public libraries. Using this comprehensive source of associations, you will readily find one or more associations in your desired civilian career field. Give those that appeal to you a call. Ask about their membership requirements and annual dues. You might also ask if you could attend a local meeting. Most of these associations are relatively inexpensive, charging anywhere from $20 to $100 per year for membership. We recommend joining the one or two that appear to be right for you. By participating in selected association events, we're confident you'll quickly make new acquaintances who will likely be willing to spend time talking with you about their job or industry. Remember your goal in these sessions is to practice the **5Rs** of informational interviews. You want them to 1) **read** your resume, 2) **revise** your resume, 3) **reveal** useful information to you, 4) **refer** you to others, and 5) **remember** you for future job opportunities. At the same time, you should be making a mental note of the phrases and expressions they use to describe their job, company, and industry.

We stress the importance of networking because it's central to your job search, both in terms of "learning the lingo" and learning about various civilian employment opportunities. Never forget that it is your responsibility to effectively communicate your qualifications in language that civilian hiring managers will understand and appreciate.

Military Assistance

Whether you are transitioning from the Army, Navy, Air Force, Marine Corps, or Coast Guard, your military service understands the challenge you face in translating your military work experience into civilian terms and offers tangible assistance to facilitate your efforts. Here we discuss some of the most important.

First, every separating service member is provided with DD Form 2586, "Verification of Military Experience and Training," at least 120 days prior to separation. If you did not receive the DD Form 2586, we recommend contacting your local ACAP, TAMP, or TAP office and asking for assistance in obtaining this form.

We recommend using this document as a starting point for considering how your military experience and training translate into equivalent civilian occupations. From this list identify those items that relate to the types of civilian work you are interested in pursuing. Then document your experience —both within and outside the military—that relate to this item. If you feel you need some assistance, contact your local ACAP, TAMP, or TAP office and ask to meet with a career counselor. He or she will be pleased to critique your document and provide helpful suggestions.

There are also various government-sponsored publications that you should find helpful. One of these is entitled ***Military Careers***. Developed under the auspices of the Department of Defense, this book serves as an excellent guide to understanding the almost 200 military occupations within the Army, Navy, Air Force, Marine Corps, and Coast Guard and their relevance to the civilian work world. Each occupation is described according to a template consisting of the following sections: Work Environment, Physical Demands, Helpful Attributes, Training Provided, Opportunities, and **Civilian Counterparts**. The Civilian Counterparts section should be especially helpful in that it describes those civilian occupations that require similar duties and training for the military occupation under consideration. In addition, you will learn about the types of civilian companies and organizations associated with each occupation. At the end of *Military Careers* you will find "A Dictionary of Occupational Titles (DOT) Code Index." Use this index to identify the corresponding civilian occupations specific to your background. Where can you find *Military Careers*? Since it is primarily a book for describing military career opportunities to prospective new recruits, we recommend visiting a local military recruiting office. If you want to purchase the book, call the Government Printing Office directly at 202-512-1800. To contact the organization that developed *Military Careers*, write to HQ USMEPCOM/MEPCP-E, 2564 Green Bay Road, North Chicago, IL 60064.

Six-Step Translation Process

Now it's time to take your general knowledge of the translation process and apply it to your particular situation. To assist you in this process, follow this 6-step approach:

Step 1:   On a clean sheet of paper, write down your military assignments in reverse chronological order as if you were doing a chronological resume. Under each of those assignments, describe *what* you did in detail. Across from each skill, describe how you applied the skill to accomplish a given task or project. Where possible, accentuate the content-specific (as opposed to transferrable) skills or knowledge you applied in the performance of your military duties. Don't worry at this point about using military specific terms or acronyms. We'll take care of them in a later step.

Step 2:   Based on the job-seeking research you have performed to date, make a list of the required skills or experience in which prospective employers in your chosen civilian career field have interest. Here is where your informational interviewing and other networking activities pay dividends. Because you have thoroughly researched those civilian occupations, you will know the types of skills, knowledge, and experience that hiring managers seek. If such is not the case, you might consider doing some additional research, perhaps by contacting an association in the desired industry, to better understand the language and skills relevant to individuals working in your chosen career field.

Step 3:   On another page, list your military skills in the left column and the needed civilian skills in the right. Now compare the items on these two lists. Can you connect any of the items on the first list to those on the second? If not, is it a problem of semantics (different words but similar meanings) or is it the case that you simply do not currently have the skills required? If the latter, you might consider obtaining additional training or schooling either on a part or full time basis. (Don't forget to explore your military service connected education benefits!)

Step 4:   Once you have matched items in the left and right columns, return to the detailed experience chronology you created in Step 1. For those military skills that relate to the civilian occupations in which you are interested, carefully revise your documented skills and experience by incorporating appropriate civilian expressions that relate to what you did in the military. Your objective is to accurately and honestly restate your military experience using language that civilian hiring managers will understand. Wherever you used military acronyms or unique expressions in Step 1, consider how you can restate the information in a more industry-relevant way without losing the meaning or impact of your experience.

Step 5:   Show this revised write-up to civilian friends and colleagues who are currently working in your employment field(s) of interest. Ask them to objectively critique your write-up and evaluate whether it conveys your qualifications in terms relevant to their industry. When they are done, don't forget to send them a thank-you note expressing your appreciation for the time and effort expended on your behalf. Such thoughtfulness will keep you remembered in a positive way.

Step 6:   Continually refine this document by incorporating the comments received in the previous step. The finished document should clearly and accurately portray your qualifications in terms appropriate to the industry in which you desire employment. Keep this document—it is the WORK HISTORY section of your resume.

If you follow these six steps, we're confident that you will have succeeded in translating your military experience into civilian terms. Remember that perseverance is key. You must discipline yourself to seek better ways of expressing your qualifications in words that match the needs of civilian employers.

Job Titles

As you go through this six-step process, another issue you are bound to wrestle with is the translation of your military job titles into equivalent civilian titles. Because of the large number of military job titles, we can provide only limited translation guidance. In general, we suggest using your enhanced knowledge of the civilian marketplace to help you convey the title in terms that a civilian hiring manager in your desired line of work would understand. For example, if you were an Air Force Technical Sergeant who managed electrical maintenance activities for a particular type of aircraft, we suggest using a functional title that has civilian relevance, such as Electronics Supervisor rather than a more military-specific title. Similarly, if you were a Navy officer responsible for managing the distribution of supplies and materiel across a class of ships, we suggest highlighting your functional title, Logistics Manager, rather than a military title.

For each job you held in the military, you should carefully think through the level of responsibility you had in the military and, based on the your research of the civilian marketplace, choose words that correspond to your level of responsibility in the civilian workplace. Honesty and common sense will serve you well. If you have doubts, ask a professional career counselor on base for an opinion.

At times, you may want to use your military title in lieu of a functional job title. The following table should prove to be a useful starting point.

Equivalent Titles

Military Title	Civilian Title
General Officer / Admiral (O-7 to O-10)	Senior Director Managing Director
Field Grade Officer (O-4 to O-6)	Program Director Program Manager
Company Grade Officer (O-1 to O-3)	Manager Project Officer
Warrant Officer (WO1 to CWO)	Technical Manager Technical Specialist
Senior NCO / Senior Chief (E-7 to E-9)	Operations Manager Senior Advisor
Platoon Sergeant (E6-E7)	Supervisor Foreman
Squad Leader (E5-E6)	First Line Supervisor
Asst. Squad Leader (E-3 to E-4)	Section Leader Task Leader
Crew Member (E-1 to E-2)	Team Member

Military Schools

Another important resume issue is the translation of military schools and training into civilian terms. Whether the training in question is "boot camp" or an advanced officer leadership school, your attendance and completion demonstrate to potential employers your perseverance and ability to learn. And assuming that this training was in an area roughly analogous to a private sector position, you can be assured that the civilian organization in which you are interested will value the investment the government has made in you. The reason is simple. Mainly, the company will not have to make nearly the same investment in training you as they would someone walking in off the street. Hence, they save time and money—two commodities that private sector firms cherish. You should not construe, however, that this would preclude you from receiving additional training in your new place of employment. More likely, it will enhance your chances for receiving more advanced training depending upon the nature of your responsibilities and the needs of the company.

As we know, many military schools focus on developing management and leadership skills and instilling basic military values. Other schools are more specific in focus and teach skills applicable to a given skill area. Regardless of the training you received, your task is to relate it to your job objective and target employment opportunities.

The table below offers some suggested translations. Some schools are peculiar to a given military service. For those schools/colleges whose duration exceeds three months, we also recommend listing the course length on the resume.

School Translations

Military School	Civilian Translation
War College	Executive Military Leadership School
Command and Staff College	Senior Military Leadership School
Combined Arms Staff College	Officer Leadership School
Officer Advanced Course	Advanced Officer Leadership School
Basic Officers Course	Entry Level Officer Leadership Course
Advanced Non Commissioned Officers Course (ANOC)	Advanced Leadership and Management Development Course
Basic Non Commissioned Officers Course (BNOC)	Leadership and Management Development Course
Primary Leadership Development Course (PLDC)	Introductory Leader Development Course
Advanced Individual Training (AIT)	Advanced Skill Training
Basic Training	Introductory Military Training

When you complete this process, you have the necessary information to complete the Education and Training section of your resume. In this regard, we recommend starting with any college degrees you may have (in reverse chronological order, i.e., put a Masters Degree before a Bachelors Degree), and then enter the training courses, also in reverse chronological order. You should not include all training you have ever received. Instead, including only those training programs that relate to your job objective. If you have not yet completed a college degree, we recommend that you include your high school diploma. If you are taking courses toward a college degree, it is appropriate to state that you are in the process of completing a degree.

Implementation

As in other aspects of the career transition process, success depends on implementation. Successful translation of your military experience is hard work and takes time if done right. As you go through the six-step translation process, remember what we said. This is NOT a one-time exercise. You must repeatedly refine this translation as you go through the job search process. As you learn more about the civilian workplace, you must re-examine your resume with the benefit of this enhanced knowledge and carefully consider how you can better state a given skill or accomplishment so that it better relates to those employment opportunities of interest to you. Remember that we live and work in a skills-based society. Prospective employers want to know if you are qualified for the job and whether you'll fit in with the rest of their workforce. By telling them about similar work you've done (whether in or outside your military service) in terms they will understand, you will have reassured them that you have what it takes to do the job well.

In the next chapter, we will use the knowledge gained in translating your military experience to develop a resume that gets results!

6

Conventional Resumes

WE ASSUME THAT PRIOR TO READING THIS CHAPTER, you have conducted a thorough self-assessment of your skills, abilities, and interests and have a clear understanding of what you do well, what you enjoy doing, and what you want to do in the future. In addition, we assume that you have researched the civilian marketplace in your field(s) of interest and have a solid understanding of the language used. Based on this knowledge, you must now develop a resume that effectively conveys your qualifications to prospective employers. Of course, if you are like many job seekers, you will have more than one job or career interest. Therefore, you should develop a resume for each.

Examples

To facilitate your resume writing endeavors, we have assembled a wide array of examples. The 61 resume examples presented in this chapter represent a broad cross-section of the types of jobs that most transitioning military service members would likely seek. To assist you in better understanding how effective resumes are developed, we preface each resume with a description of the job opportunity and an appropriate cover letter tailored to the specific job opening. You might start by locating those resume scenarios that most closely match your job or career interest and analyzing how the cover letter and resume relate to the job opening. Can you see how the writers tailored the correspondence to highlight the skills and accomplishments most relevant to the job requirements? If you were the prospective employer, would you be motivated to learn more about this individual and invite him or her for an interview? Remember, each person and his/her resume is unique. Your goal in writing this resume is to accurately present your qualifications in the best possible light so that the hiring managers will want to call you in for a face-to-face interview. That is the true test of an effective resume!

Whether you served in the Army, Navy, Air Force, Marine Corps, or Coast Guard, you offer prospective employers a unique set of experiences, skills, and knowledge. It's your job to convey those qualifications in terms civilian hiring managers will understand. In the final analysis, you are attempting to match your skills and knowledge with the requirements of an open position. The more insight you have into the position's requirements, the better you'll be able to map your skills and qualifications to the job.

In some cases, your background may not be a good fit for the job in which you're interested. Don't despair—there are several options. One is to seek additional training or education, either on a full- or part-time basis. Another option is to seek temporary employment in a related field for which you do qualify. For example, let's assume that you want to become a licensed electrician. If you're not quite ready to make this job leap, you might work initially as an electrician's helper to obtain some "hands on" experience and take electrical courses in the evening to develop a solid underpinning for the theory side, i.e., understanding how electricity works. By steadily enhancing your skills, work experience, and job knowledge, you will soon be a strong candidate for the position you desire.

For the time being, however, we will assume that you already have the requisite background for the types of jobs that you seek. Now it's time to get down to business. The resumes that follow are categorized by the types of positions you will find in the civilian workforce. We have followed the civilian title with a military title only to show you how these people translated their experience into relevant job-related terms.

Account Executive

Available: September 20XX

ANTHONY BROWN
123 Americana Lane
Aiken, SC 12345
H: (222) 111-8888 / W: (222) 123-4567
BrownA@aol.com

OBJECTIVE:

An account executive position where sales ability and knowledge of the aviation industry will result in increased revenue for a firm specializing in aviation-related equipment.

QUALIFICATIONS SUMMARY:

Extensive experience in purchasing and managing aviation materiel for large and diverse organizations. Excellent phone and sales presentation skills. Results-driven, detail-oriented professional who understands the importance of fulfilling customer demands in a timely manner. Know how to "close the deal."

EXPERIENCE:

Aviation Logistics Operations Director, Oceana Naval Air Station, Virginia Beach, VA, 1998-present.
- Managed a 145-person aviation supply depot with $105 million in assets. Saved $360,000 annually by streamlining maintenance procedures.
- Surpassed aircraft readiness goals by 15% in the management of over 34,000 line items, from aircraft engines to flight clothing.

Repairable Materiel Acquisition and Control Manager, Pearl Harbor, HI, 1994-1997
- Led 30-person team in aviation logistics operations. Exceeded supply effectiveness goals by 7%.
- Managed all facets of a $20 million repairable aviation materiel account with 1,700 line items. Improved purchasing, storage, and issuance procedures. Streamlined maintenance repair activities.

Squadron Supply Officer, Twentynine Palms, CA, 1990-1993
- Supervised 9-person team in squadron supply activities. Exceeded inventory accuracy goals for a $225,000 inventory by 18%.
- Surpassed timeliness standards for requisition processing in support of all equipment in air traffic control squadron.

Human Resources Manager, Camp Lejune, NC, 1987-1989
- Developed integrated training, retention, and promotion plans for 165,000 people in 330 occupational specialties.
- Used computer planning models to identify and eliminate logistics acquisition inefficiencies, resulting in a savings of $12 million.

EDUCATION:

MBA, University of Hawaii, Honolulu, HI, 1993
B.S., **Business Administration**, University of South Carolina, 1987

Administrative Assistant

Available: January 20XX

SEAN T. JEROME
1821 Pine Street
Los Angeles, CA
(213) 123-4567 (W) / (213) 345-6789 (H)
JeromeS@erols.com

OBJECTIVE:

Administrative assistant position for a professional services company seeking to benefit from proven administrative skills and experience.

SUMMARY OF QUALIFICATIONS:

- Highly organized; accomplish assigned tasks in an efficient manner.
- Goal oriented professional with excellent interpersonal and communication skills.
- Self-starter; able to work well with minimal directions.
- Computer literate with expertise in Microsoft Office.
- Five years of administrative experience.

WORK EXPERIENCE:

Administrative Assistant, Office of the Deputy Chief of Staff for Personnel, 1998-Present
Organize and direct a team of four support personnel who provide administrative services to senior military officials. Keep the calendars of these senior executives, ensuring 100% attendance at planned meetings. Process administrative actions in a timely and efficient manner. Handle confidential material with tact and discretion. Received Army Commendation medal in recognition of outstanding work.

Administrative Clerk, 82nd Airborne Division, Fort Bragg, NC, 1995-1997
Process range of administrative actions in support of a 500-person battalion. Type correspondence, answer telephone calls, and maintain extensive filing system on a daily basis. Achieved rating of outstanding in both announced and unannounced audits of administrative operations.

EDUCATION AND TRAINING:

MacArthur High School, Jacksonville, FL, 1994
Advanced Individual Training, Inventory and Supply, 1995

COMPUTER SKILLS:

Microsoft Windows 98, Microsoft Access, Internet Explorer

Aircraft Maintenance

Available: May 20XX

DANA TIMMONS
6431 Saint Thomas Lane
Alamogordo, NM 88531
W: 505-321-0189 / H: 505-432-4138
TimmonsD@Earthlink.net

OBJECTIVE Position in aircraft maintenance for a commercial airline where technical know-how and supervisory skills will improve readiness and safety rates.

QUALIFICATIONS SUMMARY

MANAGEMENT
- Supervised, managed, and trained personnel on the maintenance of assorted military aircraft, including the F-15, F-16, F-117A, and T-38A.
- Effectively supervised the inspection and maintenance activities of 20 Air Force and contractor personnel involved in the overhaul of jet aircraft.
- Managed 15-person team supporting the daily operation and maintenance of 22 F-16 aircraft. Supervised troubleshooting activities affecting major aircraft subsystems, including the hydraulics, fuel, and electrical systems.

AIRCRAFT MAINTENANCE
- Over 20 years experience in all aspects of aircraft operation/maintenance.
- Supervised maintenance inspections of the F-117A aircraft. Ensured repair and rigging of major airframe components were done correctly, reducing error rates by 14% within one year.
- As an aircraft maintenance specialist, performed troubleshooting of flight controls, hydraulics, engine components, and fueling subsystems.
- FAA-certified Airframe and Powerplant mechanic.

QUALITY CONTROL
- Hand-picked by senior management to ensure contracted repair work was performed in accordance with manufacturer-directed requirements.
- Coordinated inspection maintenance plans with scheduling managers, production superintendents, and 1st level managers. Inspection team was rated in the top 5%.
- As a Project Control specialist, proposed several operational improvements that enhanced the safety of the F-15, F-117A, and T-38A aircraft. Adoption of ejection seat redesign resulted in 40% decrease in probability of injury.

EMPLOYMENT HISTORY

Maintenance Supervisor, Holloman Air Force Base, NM, 1998-Present
Aircraft Inspector, Langley Air Force Base, VA, 1994-1997
Quality Assurance Manager, McGuire Air Force Base, NJ, 1991-1993
Line Supervisor, Randolph Air Force Base, TX, 1987-1990
Aircraft Maintenance Specialist, Lackland Air Force Base, TX, 1982-1986

EDUCATION & TRAINING

A.A. Aircraft Technology, College of the Air Force, 1997
Eisenhower High School, Dallas, TX, 1981

Airline Pilot

Available: April 20XX

CHARLES SCHUSTER
9851 Kennedy Lane, Apt. #123
Travis Air Force Base, CA 32542
W: 904-232-1832 / H: 904-763-1321
SchusterC@aol.com

OBJECTIVE

Position as a pilot for a well-established commercial airline where extensive flight experience will positively impact the carrier's safety and on-time performance record.

SUMMARY OF QUALIFICATIONS

Air Force pilot with 20 years of single- and multi-engine aircraft experience in domestic and international environments. Technically proficient leader with over 6,000 flight hours in a variety of high-performance jet aircraft, including the C-130 and B-1. Polished communicator who inspires and motivates subordinates to excel in all assigned tasks. Consistently accomplished difficult missions while minimizing the associated risks to assigned crews. Caring leader who sets and enforces high standards of personal and professional conduct. Active DoD Secret clearance.

PROFESSIONAL EXPERIENCE

Squadron Commander, Eglin Air Force Base, FL, 1998-Present
> Responsible for successful performance of a B-2 squadron supporting operations in Haiti. Plan, organize, and lead the activities of 25 pilots. Maintain combat readiness through efficient execution of training sorties. As the senior safety officer, ensure pilots and their crews adhere to flight procedures and policies. Strictly enforce rules of engagement for assigned aircraft. Effectively guide and advise pilots in all aspects of flight operations.

Operations Officer, Eglin Air Force Base, FL, 1995-1997
> As second in command of a B-1 bomber squadron, ensured the combat readiness of all pilots assigned to the squadron. Performed numerous flight evaluations of B-1 pilots to verify their flying skills. Performed safety checks of squadron pilots, assessing crew's knowledge of safety procedures, and ensured combat readiness of aircraft. High quality program resulted in perfect safety record.

Staff Officer, Operations and Plans, Office of the Air Force Deputy Chief of Staff, Operations, Pentagon, Washington DC, 1991-1994
> Served as a principal advisor to the Deputy Chief of Staff for Operations and Plans. Developed plans and policies affecting the worldwide operation of Air Force aircraft. Wrote decision papers and prepared briefings for senior management. Interfaced effectively with members of the House and Senate Armed Services Committees on national security issues.

Instructor Pilot, C-130, Kelly Air Force Base, TX, 1987-1990
> Instructed over 60 student pilots through C-130 jet training in all phases of flight, including aerobatics, formation, instrument, and navigation. Enhanced the existing training program by integrating new, innovative training techniques that reduced the training period by a week, thereby saving the government $50,000 per student. Maximized the use of simulator training. Trained new instructors on the use of simulators. Voted top instructor by 3 consecutive classes.

Aircraft Commander, Travis Air Force Base, CA, 1985-1989

Supervised 4-member crew in all phases of C-130 flight operations. As the lead pilot, flew 2200 hours both domestically and internationally under all weather conditions. Managed, supervised, and evaluated the performance of aircrew personnel. Instructed crew members on all aspects of flight operations, aircraft maintenance, and safety procedures. Developed a strong team atmosphere to accomplish assigned missions.

Pilot, U.S. Air Force, 1980-1983

Gained extensive flying experience in both day and night environments, both domestically and internationally. Overseas flight experience in South and Central America, Europe, Canada, Southeast Asia, and the Pacific Rim. Consistently rated as one of the best pilots in the squadron.

EDUCATION

M.S. Aeronautical Engineering, Air Force Institute of Technology, 1984
B.S. Aeronautical Engineering, U.S. Air Force Academy, 1980

TRAINING

Air Command and Staff College, 1995
Pilot Instructor Training, Air Training Command (Distinguished Graduate), 1990
Instrument Flight Course, Strategic Air Command, 1983
Squadron Officer School, 1980

Attorney

Available: August 20XX

STEVEN MARSH

2001 West James Ct.
Seattle, WA 98322

Home: 501/789-4321
Work: 501/789-5539

OBJECTIVE

A position in aviation law where proven management, organization, and supervisory skills and an exceptional record of success in investigating, adjudicating, settling, defending, and prosecuting cases will be used in settling cases to the benefit of employer and clients.

EXPERIENCE

Chief Circuit Defense Counsel, Davis Air Force Base, Ogden, UT, 1999-Present
Personally defended all Flying Evaluation Boards, winning every one. Successfully defended felony trials covering offenses of drug use, distribution, assault, DUI, and perjury. Supervised, trained, and directed 22 attorneys and 17 paralegals responsible for total defense services across 16 Air Force installations located in 12 states. Included oversight of over 500 trials with every offense up to and including premeditated murder.

Chief, Aviation Settlement Branch, U.S. Air Force, Washington, DC, 1997-1998
Directed the investigation, adjudication, and either settlement or litigation of all aviation, environmental, medical malpractice, and other tort claims filed against the Air Force. In 1993, this topped a $40 billion dollar exposure with the percentage of payout to claimed amount the lowest in over a decade. Supervised staff of 13 attorneys and 5 paralegals. Re-formulated U.S. Air Force policy on tort claim and litigation matters in conjunction with the Department of Justice, leading to a better concept and application of paying the losers and spending time and resources to win the winners.

Chief, Tort Section, U.S. Air Force, Washington, DC, 1994-1996
Supervised the investigation and recommended adjudication or litigation of all aviation tort claims against the Air Force, including the last of the Agent Orange cases and the KAL 007 Korean airliner shoot-down by the Soviet Union. Supervised staff of 3 attorneys and 1 paralegal. Recommended U.S. Air Force policy change on aviation tort claims that directly resulted in greater Agency latitude for meritorious claims independent of the previously required GAO Office requirements.

Staff Judge Advocate, Stevens Air Force Base, Miami, FL, 1992-1993
Advised top management of all legal issues to include the convening of Aircraft Accident Boards and Flying Evaluation Boards. Directed tort, labor, environmental, procurement, and criminal law procedures. During this period, defended two state environmental Notice of Violations successfully, and over 40 criminal cases were prosecuted without a single acquittal. Served as management's Chief Labor Resolution Negotiator securing settlements at 60 percent of the previously approved maximums. Supervised staff of 4 attorneys and 5 paralegals.

Assistant Staff Judge Advocate, Lowry Air Force Base, CO, 1987-1990
Served as government prosecutor for over 35 trials with no acquittals. Served as government representative in over 20 administrative hearings with no losses. Counseled clients on rights/duties under state and federal law.

Area Defense Counsel, Marshall Air Force Base, Austin, TX, 1983-1986
Defended over 300 clients in criminal trials, administrative hearings, or minor disciplinary concerns.

Assistant Staff Judge Advocate, Myrtle Beach Air Force Base, SC, 1980-1981
Investigated and adjudicated all claims arising from a major B-52 bomber aircraft accident, supervising team of paralegals. Government prosecutor for 12 trials and boards, with zero losses.

EDUCATION

J.D., Boston University College of Law, Boston, MA, 1980
B.A. (Political Science), University of North Carolina, Chapel Hill, NC, 1977

TRAINING

Air War College, USAF, Seminar Program, 1998
Armed Forces Staff College, Joint Service Program, Residence, 1995
Air Command and Staff College, USAF, Seminar Program, 1994

AWARDS

Stuart Reichart Award, Senior Attorney, HQ USAF, 1997
Ramirez Award, Outstanding Attorney Tactical Air Command, 1993
Outstanding Attorney, U.S. Air Forces Colorado, 1990

OTHER EXPERIENCE

U.S. Parole Board Hearing Member, USAF, 1995
Joint Services Consolidation Committee, 1993-1994

BAR MEMBERSHIPS

U.S. Supreme Court, 1997
U.S. Court of Appeals, 4th Circuit, 1993
U.S. Court of Military Appeals, 1990
Supreme Court of Massachusetts, 1986

Aviation Maintenance Supervisor

Available: August 20XX

SAMUEL ADAMS
2913 West Broad St.
Fairfax, VA 22313
(703) 888-3333
AdamsS@erols.com

OBJECTIVE   Supervisory position where aviation maintenance experience can be used to improve the effectiveness and quality of an airline's maintenance operations.

QUALIFICATIONS SUMMARY

MAINTENANCE
- Extensive maintenance experience in a variety of jet aircraft, including the B-1, and C-117, and C-130.
- Innovative problem solver who developed efficient methods for ensuring aircraft were maintained at peak levels. Recommended cost-cutting measures that saved the Air Force $1.5 million over a 3-year period.
- Developed maintenance checklists and enforced compliance, resulting in a perfect safety record for all assigned aircraft.

MANAGEMENT
- Evaluated performance of 15 maintenance technicians on a daily basis.
- Developed customized maintenance training program, which resulted in a 98% pass rate for staff under my supervision.
- Executed action-oriented plans, ensuring assigned missions were accomplished on time and within budget.

COMMUNICATION
- Effectively communicated aircraft maintenance tasks to fellow teammates.
- Briefed senior leaders on the readiness status of aircraft. Developed innovative plans for repairing defective components.
- Taught aviation maintenance courses to newly assigned staff.

EMPLOYMENT HISTORY

Assistant Director, Maintenance, 79th Tactical Air Wing, Hanscom AFB, 1997-Present
Manager, Aircraft Maintenance, 339th Fighter Squadron, Nellis AFB, NV, 1994-1996
Staff Non Commissioned Officer, Andrews AFB, MD, 1990-1993
Aviation-related leader development positions, 1981-1990

EDUCATION & TRAINING

A.S. Aircraft Maintenance, Community College of the Air Force, 1996
Aircraft Maintenance Training, Nellis AFB, NV, 1994
Basic Training, Randolph AFB, TX, 1981

Commercial Helicopter Pilot

Available: July 20XX

DAVID P. JONES
322 Gregor Street
Fort Rucker, AL 22311
W: (999) 222-3333 / H: (999) 222-4444

OBJECTIVE

Position as a helicopter pilot where military aviation experience and skills can be used by a commercial firm located in a major metropolitan area.

SUMMARY OF QUALIFICATIONS

Exceptionally skilled aviator with over 20 years experience flying various types of Army helicopters. Logged over 18,000 hours of flight time under all weather conditions. Hand-picked for several critical missions affecting U.S. national security. Experienced flight trainer with an unblemished safety record. Recognized by senior Defense Department officials as one of the best Army aviators.

PROFESSIONAL EXPERIENCE

Safety Evaluator, Fort Rucker, AL, 1998-Present
　　Inspect U.S. Army aviation sites to ensure 100% compliance with the Defense Department's aviation safety policies. Evaluate Army aviators' knowledge of safety procedures and practices in all phases of flight operations. Inspect aviation accident sites worldwide to identify common shortfalls in training or procedures. Recommended changes in pre-flight inspections that reduced the number of accidents annually by 27%.

Instructor Pilot, Fort Rucker, AL, 1995-1997
　　Instructed Army aviators on all phases of flight operations involving the Blackhawk helicopter. Incorporated state-of-the-art flight simulator equipment into all aspects of training, shortening course by 1 week for a savings of $75,000 per student aviator. Evaluated students' flight performance. Rated 1st out of 9 instructors.

Pilot, 101st Airmobile Division, Saudi Arabia, 1993-1994
　　Logged 55 air combat missions during Operations Desert Shield/Desert Storm while flying the Army's Blackhawk helicopter. Supported troop and logistics transport to Army combat units. Flew day and night missions under severe environmental conditions. Received Bronze Star.

Pilot, 1st Infantry Division, Fort Riley, KS, 1990-1992
　　Logged over 2000 hours of flying time in the Blackhawk helicopter. Flew numerous missions under all weather conditions. Trained and evaluated supporting flight crew, raising readiness level by 18%.

Pilot, 1981-1989
　　Piloted the Huey helicopter in assignments spanning North America, Europe, and Southeast Asia. Excelled in all phases of flight operations. Received many awards for outstanding performance.

EDUCATION & TRAINING

B.S., Aeronautics, University of Alabama, 1980
Black Hawk Training, Fort Rucker, AL, 1990
Flight Training, Fort Rucker, AL, 1981

Construction Supervisor

Available: June 20XX

Michael Ramirez
313 Bradley Drive
Bremerton, WA 90972
W: (206) 222-3333 / H: (206) 888-3321
RamirezM@aol.com

OBJECTIVE   A foreman position where skills and experience as a construction supervisor will benefit a firm seeking to expand its scope of construction operations.

QUALIFICATIONS SUMMARY

MANAGEMENT
- Supervised construction crew of 25 personnel involved in building new homes and offices.
- Trained numerous junior operators on the proper use and maintenance of construction equipment.
- Attained a 100% safety record through strict adherence to standard operating procedures.

CONSTRUCTION OPERATIONS
- Operated bulldozers, roadgraders, and other heavy equipment in building over 25 miles of runway in record time, under combat conditions.
- Used scrapers and other heavy machinery to remove ice and snow from runways.
- Operated winches, cranes, and hoists in constructing over 200 new homes.

INTERNATIONAL
- Fluent in Spanish.

WORK HISTORY

Construction Supervisor, 23rd Engineer Battalion, McChord AFB, WA 1998-Present
Construction Equipment Operator, 110th Construction Battalion, Keesler AFB, MO, 1994-1997

EDUCATION & TRAINING

A.A., Construction, Washington Community College, Seattle, WA, 2000
Air Force certified apprenticeship program in Heavy Construction, 1996
Diploma, Homer High School, Homer, NY, 1996

Contracts Manager

Available: September 20XX

DANA T. EDWARDS
1187 MacArthur Blvd.
Springfield, VA 22121
H: (703) 888-3333 / W: (703) 111-2345
EdwardsD@aol.com

OBJECTIVE

Senior contracts manager for a management consulting firm interested in reducing costs and improving acquisition efficiencies.

QUALIFICATIONS SUMMARY

CONTRACT
MANAGEMENT

- Initiated and administered invitations for bid and requests for proposals. Awarded over 250 contracts valued in excess of $900,000.
- Negotiated/contracted for commodities, facilities, maintenance, and services.
- Prepared formal contracts and ensured all Government terms, specifications, legal requirements, and restrictions were incorporated and satisfied.
- Expert knowledge of federal acquisition guidance (FAR, DFARS, & FIRMR).

PROJECT
MANAGEMENT

- Directed 37 system engineers responsible for acquiring the equipment necessary to support 5 Government research & development laboratories.
- Led the Tactical Exploitation of National Capabilities Program, directing the acquisition activities of 89 staff. Responsible for administering $8 million annual budget.
- Effectively managed two major weapon system projects valued in excess of $250 million. Increased accuracy of system deliveries ten-fold through stringent enforcement of technical specifications.

CERTIFICATIONS

- Warranted U.S. Government contracting officer
- Certified GSA Trail Boss

EMPLOYMENT HISTORY

Chief, Advanced TENCAP Plans & Programs, Space Applications Project Office, 1998-Present
Deputy Director, Key Technologies, Air Force Ballistic Missile Defense Program, 1995-97
Reconnaissance Liaison Officer, Combined Field Army, Air Liaison Office, Seoul, Korea, 1993-94
Chief, Reconnaissance/Intelligence Plans & Programs, HQ Air Force Systems Command, 1988-92
Flight Instructor, Academic Instructor, Flight Test RF-4C, 1980-1987

EDUCATION & TRAINING

M.S., Systems Management, U.S.C., 1996
B.S., Contract Administration, University of Maryland, 1980
Air Command and Staff College, Maxwell AFB, Alabama, 1992

ASSOCIATIONS

Treasurer, National Contract Management Association
Vice President, National Association of Purchasing Managers

Corporate Communications

Available: May 20XX

KAREN BENTON
200 West Brookfield Place
Palm Springs, CA 92200
(619) 321-0987
BentonK@aol.com

OBJECTIVE

Corporate Communications position for a large, international defense firm where proven communication skills will enhance internal coordination and strengthen the firm's public image.

PROFESSIONAL SKILLS PROFILE

Training & Development. Strong qualifications in the design, development and instruction of field and classroom training programs for professional, management and support personnel. Created training manuals and handbooks. Trained other trainers.

Administrative Operations. Detail-oriented with strong organizational and project management skills. Evaluated existing operations, standardized operating procedures to streamline core operating functions, and introduced quality, efficiency and productivity initiatives. Excellent qualifications in office management, policy/procedure development, employee performance measurement and cross-functional team leadership.

General Management. Cross-functional experience in business development, sales, personnel recruitment training, customer relationship management, accounting, financial reporting and administration. Strong decision-making, problem solving and crisis management skills.

Graphic Arts & Communications. Creative and artistic with the ability to translate concepts and images into strong visual presentations. Designed business marketing and promotional materials.

PC Skills. Proficient in Microsoft Word, Excel, and PowerPoint.

PROFESSIONAL EXPERIENCE

U.S. AIR FORCE   1980-2000

Fast-track promotion through a series of increasingly responsible technical and supervisory positions. Held multi-functional responsibility for the receipt, processing and control of sensitive electronic information, developed operating plans and procedures, and coordinated the deployment of assigned personnel and equipment during crisis situations. Top security clearance. Career highlights include:

Command & Control Supervisor, Utah & Germany
Command & Control Technician, California & Germany
Avionics Communications Specialist, Arizona

Had management oversight for a team of six responsible for technical assessment, maintenance and troubleshooting of high-tech information systems. Maintained computer systems and automated data processing equipment for worldwide military command. Assumed additional management role for monitoring all aircraft traveling throughout Europe, Africa and the Middle East to facilitate rapid deployment in the event of a crisis.

Wrote complete training instruction procedures for command computer systems. Led training, development and certification programs for new personnel. Evaluated and documented performance of systems team. Led monthly readiness training sessions to enhance the unit's response capability. Conducted on-site inspections of numerous command centers to audit reporting procedures, identify deficiencies in quality control, and ensure compliance with all military and federal regulations. Presented findings to headquarters for evaluation.

Communications Technician

One-year position between tours of duty with the U.S. Air Force. Directed building control, alarm and security systems for the university's Plant Services Division. Designed and implemented procedures to dispatch law enforcement, medical and rescue personnel in response to emergency and crisis situations including power loss, fire, vandalism and burglary.

EDUCATION & TRAINING

Eisenhower High School, Biloxi, MI, 1980

Completed numerous programs sponsored by the Air Force and regional community colleges. Course highlights included:

- Staff Development Training
- Computer Data Handling
- Human Resource Management
- Management Communications

Electronic Maintenance Supervisor

Available: June 20XX

THOMAS JONES
2121 Main Street
Norfolk, VA 22211
H: (757) 333-4444 / W: (757) 112-2345
E-mail: ThomasJ@aol.com

OBJECTIVE

Electronics Maintenance Supervisor position where electronics expertise and management know-how can be used by an aerospace firm to significantly improve its maintenance operations.

SUMMARY OF QUALIFICATIONS

- Results-oriented professional with significant management and hands-on electronic and mechanical maintenance experience.
- Skilled technician with expertise in an array of electro-mechanical disciplines.
- Articulate communicator who conveys technical concepts in clear terms.
- Adept problem solver who easily transfers knowledge to teammates.

PROFESSIONAL EXPERIENCE

MANAGEMENT

- Supervised over 45 electronics technicians in 5 shops performing a wide range of electrical and mechanical repair on over 20 aircraft.
- Coordinated and implemented technical training and reassignment of technicians in a manner that mitigated the impact of manpower shortages.
- Maintained 100% accountability of over 2,000 component parts, electronic test equipment, and materials with inventory values in excess of $3 million.
- Ensured strict adherence to quality control in repair cycle by conducting receiving, in-process, and final inspections of electronic systems and associated components.

ELECTRONIC REPAIR

- Repaired electrical and electronic aircraft systems and components using industry-standard equipment, such as oscilloscopes, signal generators, voltmeters, ammeters, and time domain reflectometers.
- Employed standard troubleshooting methods using technical manuals, wiring schematics, block diagrams, and drawings to rapidly isolate malfunctions in system wiring, sub assemblies, and other components.
- Skilled at wire, cable bundle, coaxial, and connector repair.

TRAINING & EDUCATION

Total Quality Management Training, 1998
Advanced Electrical/Electronic Technical Training, 1996
Miniature Electronics Repair QA/Supervisor Course, 1994
Diploma, Martin Luther King High School, Biloxi, MI, 1993

Electronics Technician

Available: February 20XX

DALE PARKER
200 Main St, #2
Middlesex, NJ 08820
(908) 543-2111
ParkerD@aol.com

OBJECTIVE: Electronics technician for an international Defense firm where experience, leadership, and communication skills will strengthen a small-to-medium sized staff.

HIGHLIGHT OF QUALIFICATIONS

- Eight years experience as a RF Telecommunications specialist.
- Two years experience as a supervisor/manager.
- Implemented successful inventory control management system to include a database.
- Trained in basic AC/DC principles, solid state and digital devices, control systems and communication theory.
- Experienced in development and implementation of training requirements.
- Held Top Secret security clearance. Recent Special Background Investigation.

PROFESSIONAL EXPERIENCE

UNITED STATES NAVY, Electronics Technician, 1990-Present

Technical Knowledge:

- System diagnosis and quality assurance of Submarine Communications Equipment to component level using schematics, blueprints and technical manuals.
- Operate and coordinate Communication Systems including automated networks, satellite data links, and a full spectrum of voice, teletype and data circuits.
- Identified a difficult Antenna problem resulting in a cost savings repair to the Navy of over $28,000.
- Repaired or replaced electrical/electronic cables and cable connectors.
- Knowledge of basic test equipment.
- Operation of signal converters, modems, associated peripheral communication equipment.
- Trained in Hydraulic and Pneumatic systems and compliance with a variety of extensive procedures.

Administration:

- Extensive office skills to include filing, copying, maintaining multiple files and logs, typing messages and reports and administrative control over various collateral duties.
- Organized and corrected Hazardous Material/Waste System; familiar with E.P.A. requirements.
- Two years experience managing the security access of a U.S.Navy submarine.

EDUCATION/TRAINING

Basic Enlisted Submarine School
Submarine Electronic Technical Training School
Submarine Radioman A (Basic) School
Submarine Radioman C (Advanced) Receivers Combined Maintenance School
Submarine Radioman C (Advanced) Special Communications School
Submarine Radioman C (Advanced) Tactical Communications School

Electronics Repair

Available: December 20XX

DONALD J. BUOY
834 Market Lane
Groton, CT 98031
W: (206) 918-7623/ H: (206) 231-8710
BuoyD@aol.com

OBJECTIVE

Electronics System Repair position where technical training and skills can benefit a large aerospace firm that also manufactures major weapon systems.

QUALIFICATIONS SUMMARY

- Electronic weapon systems repairer with over 10 years hands-on and supervisory experience.
- Recognized expert in the maintenance of multiple weapon systems electronics. Troubleshoot and solve difficult electrical faults.
- Extensive experience adjusting weapon systems' firing guidance and launch sub-systems using electronic test equipment, calibrators, and other fine precision instruments.
- Knowledgeable in the repair and maintenance of missile mounts, platforms, and launch mechanisms.
- Demonstrated ability to use schematics and underlying knowledge of electronic principles and techniques to diagnose electrical system failures.
- Certified electronic weapons system repairer.

WORK HISTORY

Shop Supervisor, San Diego Coast Guard Station, San Diego CA, 1998-Present
Responsible for ensuring all electrical repairs are done on time and to standards. Schedule work and training assignments for 25 personnel. Provide technical guidance and advice to shop personnel on a daily basis. Inspect and approve all electronic weapons system repair work performed in the shop.

Senior Electronic Weapon System Repairer, Coast Guard Station, Melbourne, FL, 1994-1997
Set up and ran electronic test equipment used to repair Coast Guard weapon systems. Installed and calibrated guidance, telemetry, and electronic fire control subsystems to ensure accurate firing of weapons systems. Used wiring system knowledge and troubleshooting techniques to detect faulty electronic parts and identify causes for system breakdowns. Provided on-the-job training to new technicians; assisted them with difficult electrical repairs.

Electronic Weapon System Repairer, Coast Guard Station, San Diego, CA, 1992-1993
Troubleshot electronic components of various weapon systems by analyzing associated mainte-nance and wiring diagrams. Repaired or replaced faulty electrical components. Used electronic equipment and test probes to check missile fire control guidance systems.

EDUCATION & TRAINING

Diploma, Miami Central High School, Miami, FL, 1991
Advanced Supply School, 7th District, FL, 1993
Coast Guard Basic Training, 1992

Electronics Technician

Available: June 20XX

SANDY FISHER
101 Arlington Blvd.
San Diego, CA 92100
(619) 512-3456
FisherS@aol.com

Objective

Position as an Electronics Technician for a West Coast firm seeking to strengthen its engineering staff with a dedicated, experienced, and highly motivated professional.

Qualifications Summary

- Expert in testing, troubleshooting and repairing complex navigation, fire control, and display systems.
- Proficient in the operation, calibration, and maintenance of multimeters, oscilloscopes, signal analyzers, and numerous types of test equipment.
- Utilized total quality management to develop valuable time/stress management skills.
- Exceptional interpersonal, client service, and liaison skills.
- U.S. Navy Electronics Instructor
- Expertise in WordPerfect, MS Windows 2000, and the Internet.
- Quality Assurance inspector.

Work History

- *Electronics Technician*, U.S. Navy - USS Coronado (AGF-11), 1998-Present
- *Electronics Instructor*, U.S. Navy - Service School Command, Naval Training Center, San Diego, CA, 1993-1997

Education and Training

- Associate of Science Degree
- Total Quality Management Training
- Instructor Training School
- Various U.S. Navy Electronics Schools

Emergency Medical Technician

Available: October 20XX

KATHLEEN SMITH
8841 Greensboro Drive
Boston, MA 01755
W: 617-632-1343 / H: 617-232-3212

OBJECTIVE

Position as an Emergency Medical Technician where my military-refined health care skills and experience will benefit a private health care facility seeking to improve the quality of its patient care.

SUMMARY OF QUALIFICATIONS

- Over 10 years experience in the health care profession as a Navy corpsman.
- Trained to provide emergency medical care in response to accidents, fire, natural disasters, etc.
- Proficient in a variety of first-line tasks, including: recording of vital signs, reading and updating of patients' medical records, and taking of blood for laboratory analysis.
- Communicated effectively with patients and administrators.
- Demonstrated ability to work well under stressful conditions.

WORK HISTORY

Emergency Medical Technician, **U.S.S. Mercy, 1998-Present**

Provide first-line emergency medical care to sailors and Marines onboard ship. Take patients' vital signs, including temperature, pulse, and blood pressure. Prepare patients for follow-up treatment by registered nurses or medical doctors. Update patients' medical records.

Medical Service Technician, **Bethesda Naval Hospital, MD, 1994-1997**

Responsible for ensuring 500 patients' records were properly filed. Responded to record requests by nurses and doctors. Performed quality assurance checks of medical records. Identified missing documents and persevered until records were properly completed. Recommended an innovative color-coding scheme that reduced confusion and saved health care professionals' time.

Medical Service Technician, **Tripler Army Hospital, Honolulu, HI, 1991-1993**

Drew patients' blood for analysis by laboratory technicians. Resuscitated those patients who fainted during the procedure. Explained the importance of wellness programs that emphasize proper diet and exercise.

EDUCATION AND TRAINING

Emergency Medical Training, Bethesda Naval Hospital, MD, 1989
St. Elizabeth Seton High School, Rockville, MD, 1988

Engineering Manager

Available: May 20XX

LEE CHAPPEL
50 Winding Road
Darien, CT 06000
(203) 444-7890
Chappel@aol.com

OBJECTIVE

Position as an Engineering Manager for a Fortune 500 manufacturing firm where extensive experience, broad technical knowledge, and proven management skills will further strengthen a quality organization.

EDUCATION

M.S., Mechanical Engineering, Rensselaer Polytechnic Institute, 1999
B.S., Mechanical Engineering, University of New Haven, 1996, Summa Cum Laude, 3.97/4.0 GPA

PROFILE

- Proven performer in development and implementation of quick turnaround solutions to interdisciplinary engineering problems in a fast-paced environment.
- Team player with extensive engineering background developed over 25 years of experience in Naval Engineering and Naval Nuclear Propulsion.
- Extensive knowledge of industry standards, military standards, and military specifications.
- Trained and proficient in Total Quality Management (TQM) methods.

PROFESSIONAL EXPERIENCE

PLANNING OFFICER, Naval Submarine Support Facility New London, 1998-Present

- Coordinated efforts of 40 planner/estimators in preparation of detailed, step-by-step, user-friendly technical work procedures in support of 1,000-man production work force.
- Organized interdisciplinary teams eliminating craft barriers. Resulted in 20% reduction in planning lead time; elimination of revisions and associated work stoppage caused by inaccurate job scope of inadequate procedures.
- Trained craftsman in skills required of effective planners: ship checks; technical research; technical writing; quality assurance; make/buy decisions; long lead-time material identification/resolution; identification of problem causes vs. symptoms; assessment of shop capabilities; development of critical path timelines.
- Specified, procured, installed, and trained personnel in use of a Local Area Network (LAN). Streamlined procedure preparation, improved accuracy, enabled repetitive use procedures.
- Essential member of department Quality Management Board and command Automatic Data Processing/Management Information Systems Steering Committee.

ASSISTANT ENGINEER, Commander, Submarine Squadron Two, 1995-97

- Actively managed efforts of multiple industrial activities in execution of extensive shipyard maintenance periods. (Average of 120,000 man-days/$50 million per year.)
- Provided liaison between shipyard, squadron, customer, and Naval Sea Systems Command management to resolve schedule conflicts, arrange shipchecks, review work packages, and train ship's company. Ensured best product, least cost, shortest time.

- Evaluated Propulsion Plant watchstanding/administration. Resulted in significant improvements in the proficiency and performance of new construction crews in meeting crew certification milestones, and in the performance of operating crews on Operations Reactor Safeguards Exams.
- Monitored Radiological Controls, Nuclear Work Practices, and Quality Assurance Procedures. Assisted in identification and correction of deficient work practices, material deficiencies, and documentation problems before they impacted production.
- Coordinated the efforts of four major industrial activities in intensive maintenance period including first dry-docked battery replacement and major repairs/replacement of unique propulsion shafting. *Commended for direct role in early completion.*

NUCLEAR REPAIR OFFICER, USS Fulton (AS-11), 1992-94

- Directed all phases of Nuclear Repairs to submarine Nuclear Propulsion Plants including planning, qualification, and continuing training, production, production management, and quality assurance.
- Project Officer for major inspection of steam generating equipment: selected, trained, and qualified personnel; researched, ordered, staged material and special equipment; developed computerized logistic support database; implemented stringent cost controls resulting in savings of $350,000; directly supervised procedure preparation; actively managed production and testing phases. *Personally commended for cost savings, incident free inspection, and early completion.*
- Supervised restoration of Ship Service and Main Propulsion Generators and Main Propulsion Motors following major fire in FULTON's aft engine room: arranged outside technical support; organized assets; trained technicians. Restored to full capability, in place, in one-half time, saving $500,000.

PROJECT OFFICER, Supervisor of Shipbuilding, Conversion & Repair, San Francisco, 1989-91

- Led project team of 50 contract administrators/surveyors, engineers, contract specialists in management of multiple intensive Nuclear Aircraft Carrier industrial maintenance periods (1000 man-days/day). Average total contract value of $100 million/period. Funds administrator.
- Worked directly with structural engineers, loftsmen, and production to design, loft, fabricate, and install stabilizing fin to reduce shaft vibration and propeller cavitation. Completed in half the time at one-third of the estimated cost due to innovative pre-fabrication of major subassemblies.

ADDITIONAL EXPERIENCE

- Nuclear Propulsion Plant Engineering Watch Supervisor/Mechanical Division Superintendent.
- Mechanical Systems Instructor, Naval Nuclear Power Training Unit, Idaho Falls, Idaho.
- Highest security clearance held: Top Secret.

AFFILIATIONS

American Society of Mechanical Engineers, Vice President of local chapter.
American Nuclear Society, active member.

Executive Assistant

Available: July 20XX

PATRICK SMITH
20 Elm Street
Norwich, CT 06300
(860) 890-1234
SmithP@erols.com

OBJECTIVE: Executive Assistant for a Defense contractor where experience, motivation, and knowledge of the military will increase the number of contracts awarded annually.

SUMMARY OF QUALIFICATIONS

- 20 years experience as an administrative assistant and supervisor. Processed correspondence, transmitted messages, and operated sophisticated communications equipment.
- Computer proficient—expertise in MS Word, Excel, Access, and Powerpoint.
- Polished communicator with excellent interpersonal skills.
- Supervised 25 staff members.
- Hold a Top Secret clearance with current SBI.

PROFESSIONAL EXPERIENCE

United States Navy. Senior Communications Specialist. 1980-Present

OFFICE AND ADMINISTRATIVE MANAGEMENT

- Responsible for the operations of a 20-person staff, comprised of culturally diverse members who implemented beautification program for a submarine base.
- Possess strong clerical skills; able to type 50 wpm. Experience with Xerox, fax machines, and multi-line telephones.
- Safeguard classified material as the Confidential Material Control Clerk. Collect, distribute, file all documents and computer disks. Maintain accurate log of all material transferred.

SUPERVISION/TRAINING

- Taught Recruit Training to over 400 students maintaining the highest class average for a female group in Orlando, FL. Instructed a company of 80 on all facets of Basic training
- Supervised up to 10 staff members training on routing Naval messages, use of Message Distribution Terminal system, and Digital Encryption equipment.
- Trained and supervised 25 staff members to prepare facilities for top level civilian and military executives at the annual national Security Industrial Association (NSIA) Conference. *"...successfully planned and flawlessly executed countless details which went into making every facet of the seminar a resounding success."* (CAPT A.B. Jones, 1998)

EDUCATION & TRAINING

Bachelor of Science Degree (Candidate, 2001), Eastern Connecticut State, CT
Associates Degree, St. Petersburg Junior College, FL, 1995
Relevant training:
    Navy Leadership and Development Program for Supervisors
    Instructor Basic Course/Fundamentals of TQL
    Basic and Advanced Communications

Financial Management

Available: June 20XX

JEFFREY SIMMONS
2913 West Broad St.
Fairfax, VA 22313
(703) 888-3333
SimmonsJ@erols.com

OBJECTIVE   Financial management position where extensive finance and accounting background can be used to improve a startup company's financial operations.

QUALIFICATIONS SUMMARY

ACCOUNTING
AND FINANCE
- Experience in general ledger, financial analysis, budgets, projections, cash management, and supervision of accounting staff.
- Project manager for conversion to new computerized accounting system, which saved $1 million annually through reductions in personnel expenses.
- Senior accountant for a $10 million organization involved in national defense.

PLANNING
- Accurately forecasted organizations' expenditures over a 5 year period.
- Projected shortfalls and modified plans to mitigate the impact.
- Developed financial plans for organizations ranging in size from 300 to 10,000.

MANAGEMENT
- Supervised groups of 5-37 personnel involved in all facets of finance and accounting operations.
- Trained and mentored staff in both individual and team-based settings.
- Evaluated employee performance and provided suggestions for improvement.

EMPLOYMENT HISTORY

Senior Finance Director, Defense Information Systems Agency, Arlington, VA, 1998-Present
Finance Manager, Fort Hood, TX, 1995-1997
Staff Finance Officer, Fort Carson, CO, 1992-1994

EDUCATION & TRAINING

M.B.A., Finance, American University, 1999
B.S., Accounting, University of Colorado, 1992
Planning, Programming, and Budgeting Course, Fort Harrison, IN, 1994

Financial Services

Available: August 20XX

MARK BRANSCOM
2913 West Broad St.
Philadelphia, PA 19199
555-222-2121 (H) / 555-222-1212 (W)
MBranscom@aol.com

OBJECTIVE:	A financial services position for a brokerage house where strong communication and leadership skills will result in increased sales.

ACCOMPLISHMENTS:

Financial Management	Assisted in developing a $12 million annual budget for a department of 180 employees. Introduced new cost-cutting measures that resulted in saving $500,000 per year.
Leadership	Excelled in progressively responsible leadership positions as an officer in the U.S. Army. Natural leader who received numerous awards for excellence. Motivated and inspired organizations ranging in size from 30 to 300 personnel. Set and enforced high standards of personal and professional conduct.
Communication	Designed and developed an innovative aviation training program for the Third Armored Division. Incorporated state-of-the-art flight simulators, saving over $45,000 per month in fuel costs. Aviation training was rated the best in Europe.
Training	Raised training ratings from the worst to the best for six helicopter attack companies on two evaluations. Received a Zero Aircraft Accident Safety Award, and raised aircraft readiness rate to 85%—15% above the standard.
WORK HISTORY:	**Assistant Athletic Director, Administration**, U.S. Military Academy, 1997-Present
	Division Aviation Staff Officer, Third Armored Division, GE, 1994-96
	Aviation Company Commander, 11th Helicopter Company, Fort Rucker, AL, 1992-93
	Infantry Officer, U.S. Army, 1981-1991
EDUCATION:	**University of Michigan, Ann Arbor, MI** M.S. in Business Administration, Fuqua School, Duke University, 1988
	United States Military Academy, West Point, NY B.S. in General Engineering, 1981

Food Service

Available: June 20XX

William Lane
301 Westmoreland Street
Philadelphia, PA 19199
555-222-2121 (H) / 555-222-1212 (W)
MBranscom@aol.com

OBJECTIVE: Restaurant Manager for a national food service chain.

EDUCATION/TRAINING:

Associate Degree, Food Management, Central Texas College, 1997
Certified Food Manager, International Food Service Executive Association, 1999
Food Service Specialist Advanced Individual Training - 8 weeks, 1992
Basic Food Service Course - 16 weeks, 1990

EMPLOYMENT HISTORY: United States Army, 1990-Present

2nd Infantry Division, Camp Casey, Korea, 1999-Present
Senior Food Operations Manager
Supervise and assist three Food Operations Managers in the feeding of over 3,200 soldiers daily. Key accomplishments include:
- Established effective food service training programs.
- Worked with Food Operations Managers in the planning and delivery of food service.
- Conducted periodic unannounced inspections to ensure quality of food service remained consistently high.

82nd Airborne Division, Fort Bragg, NC, 1996-1998
Senior Food Operations Manager
Responsible for daily food service operations that supported 4,500 soldiers. Key accomplishments include:
- Instituted an innovative culinary specialist competition that resulted in enhancing the overall quality of dining services.
- Provided training and professional development for 65 food service person-nel, including four dining facility managers.
- Ensured high quality food handling and sanitation standards through frequent checks and inspections.
- Received Commanding General's Award for best dining facility.

Various Army Bases 1990-1995
Soldier
Learned basic soldiering skills. Served in a variety of positions as a soldier in the U.S. Army. Developed sense of commitment, integrity, loyalty, and honesty.

Healthcare Administration

TRACY LAKELAND
2913 West Broad St.
Fairfax, VA 22313
H: (703) 888-3333
LakelandT@erols.com

OBJECTIVE   Healthcare administrator position where extensive financial management experience can be used to improve the profitability of a multi-specialty ambulatory care clinic.

QUALIFICATIONS SUMMARY

HEALTHCARE
ADMINISTRATION

- Ten years experience in Healthcare Administration in positions of increasing responsibility within the U.S. Navy.
- Managed health service activities, including plans and operations, human resources, logistics, patient administration, and finance.
- Directed the hospital accreditation program, which was successfully completed two months ahead of schedule.

FINANCIAL
MANAGEMENT

- Managed departments from 25-600 personnel, responsible for direct supervision of up to 10 second line supervisors.
- Established and administered a $15 million budget.
- Increased third party collections by 45% while reducing expenditures by $3 million through aggressive follow-up communication.
- Developed automated financial plan, which was adopted and implemented, saving the hospital approximately $39,000 annually.

CERTIFICATION

- Certified Healthcare Executive
- Member, ACHE's Regents Advisory Council for the Army Regent

EMPLOYMENT HISTORY

Director, Healthcare Services, Walter Reed Army Medical Hospital, 1998-Present
Senior Healthcare Service Administrator, Walter Reed Army Medical Hospital, 1993-1997
Healthcare Service Administrator, Eisenhower Army Medical Center, Fort Gordon, GA, 1989-1992
Developmental Medical Service Corps positions, U.S. Army, 1980-1988

EDUCATION & TRAINING

MBA, Finance, University of Maryland, 1999
B.S.N., Penn State University, 1980

Heavy Manufacturing

Available: October 20XX

THOMAS F. JONES
3212 Cravens Drive
Quantico, VA 29036
W: (703) 123-4567 / H: (703) 321-9999

OBJECTIVE

A supervisory position with a large manufacturing company seeking an experienced machine operator with demonstrated management skills to improve its operations.

HIGHLIGHT OF QUALIFICATIONS

- Dedicated professional with over 15 years experience in heavy machinery.
- Expert knowledge of the operation and maintenance of a wide variety of equipment.
- Possess both hands-on and supervisory experience in heavy machinery.
- Adept, skillful communicator who interacts well with all levels of staff and management.

AREAS OF EXPERTISE

Management

Effectively supervised a staff of 30 personnel who operated and maintained heavy armor equipment. Raised the organization's equipment maintenance status 35% by instituting an innovative quality control program that stressed attention to detail in all facets of maintenance operations. Set and enforced high standards.

Heavy Equipment Maintenance

Demonstrated expertise in troubleshooting inoperable equipment using computer-based diagnostic equipment. Applied ingenuity to quickly restore equipment to operable condition. Received recognition for successfully maintaining assigned equipment at a high state of readiness throughout Operation Desert Storm.

Training

Provided expert training to monthly classes of up to 25 personnel in the operation and care of heavy armor equipment. Made course interesting while ensuring full understanding of key concepts. Received highest possible instructor rating over a three-year period.

EMPLOYMENT HISTORY

Platoon Sergeant, 18th Marine Regiment, Quantico, VA, 1998-Present
Operations Sergeant, 2nd Marine Expeditionary Unit, Camp Lejeune, NC, 1995-1997
Tank Commander, 3rd Marine Expeditionary Unit, Twentynine Palms, CA, 1992-1994
Developmental leadership positions, 1980-1991

EDUCATION & TRAINING

Cortland High School, Cortland, NY, 1980
Material Maintenance Course, Camp Lejeune, NC, 1984

Human Resources

Available: August 20XX

JOHN C. DILLON
342 Lincoln Lane
Fayetteville, NC 91901
H: (919) 111-2222 / W: (919) 123-4567
DillonJ@aol.com

OBJECTIVE   Human Resources manager for a dynamic manufacturing firm rapidly expanding its operations and seeking to build a quality work force.

QUALIFICATIONS SUMMARY

PERSONNEL
PLANNING

- Assisted senior Army leaders in developing personnel plans and policies that improved leadership opportunities for 80,000 Army officers.
- Developed and presented briefings to senior officials on the implementation of new programs designed to reduce costs and improve quality of life.
- Recommended effective strategies for producing a smaller yet equally effective force through the use of simulation and modeling techniques.

MANAGEMENT

- As the senior officer in charge of a 500-member organization, led and executed national security-related operations.
- Effectively managed a $75 million budget.
- Instituted innovative training program that raised the overall proficiency of unit by 20%, as measured by independent Defense Department evaluators.
- Supervised and directed a staff of 30 personnel on a daily basis.

MULTICULTURAL

- Supervised 21 local national staff while stationed in Germany
- Fluent in Spanish, conversant in German

EMPLOYMENT HISTORY

Executive Officer, DCSPER, Pentagon, 1998-Present
Battalion Commander, 23rd Infantry Battalion, Germany, 1995-1997
Professor of Military Science, Bucknell University, 1991-1992
Developmental Leadership Positions, 1980-1990

EDUCATION & TRAINING

M.S., Business Administration,Wharton School, University of Pennsylvania, 1994
B.S., General Engineering, U.S. Military Academy, West Point, NY, 1980

Industrial Engineer

Available: December 20XX

TERRY HARPER
139 Georgia Avenue
Denver, CO 80808
499-217-3219 (H) / 499-217-9123 (W)
HarperT@earthlink.net

OBJECTIVE: An industrial engineering position with a broad-based manufacturing firm in the Northeast where leadership experience and technical skills will enhance operations.

EXPERIENCE: <u>**Operations Research Analyst**</u>, U.S. Total Army Personnel Command, Alexandria, VA (1998 to present)
Direct a four-person analytical team developing, evaluating, and recommending personnel reduction policies mandated by Congress.

- Applied SAS programming expertise to develop computer models that optimized employees' opportunities to advance based on performance and organizational needs.
- Created and implemented a system acceptance testing plan for a $3 million out-sourced optimization model. Resulted in four critical design enhancements and an 8.2% reporting accuracy increase.

Personnel Officer. US Army, 3rd Support Command, Germany, 1995-97
Managed human resource matters for a 750-employee organization including finance, education, legal support, performance appraisals, reassignments, and personnel strength.

- Standardized office on the Microsoft suite, reducing administrative processing time by 35%.
- Achieved marked improvements in personnel action processing time through enhanced training and motivational techniques.

<u>**General Manager**</u>. US Army, 32d Air Defense Command, Germany, 1992-94
Supervised 180 employees with 34 different specialty skills performing maintenance and supply operations. Managed a 24-hour repair and warehouse facility servicing 13 retail customers' vehicles, missile, and communications equipment valued at $2.1 million.

- Reduced annual operating expenses from $1.5 million to $1.3 million in first year of operation while increasing customer support levels by 7.2%.
- Decreased maintenance backlog by 62.4% in three months through production control policy changes.
- Relocated $20.3 million supply stockage increasing on-hand inventory accountability by 7.8%.

EDUCATION: **Louisiana State University**, Baton Rouge, LA.
B.S. in Industrial Engineering, 1992, Deans List

Industrial Painter

Available: December 20XX

TONI BLAKE
4212 Banters Lane
San Diego, CA 99812
W: 991-221-3232 / H: 991-332-4545

OBJECTIVE: Industrial Painter for a manufacturing firm in the Southeast that values high quality work and attention to detail.

SUMMARY OF QUALIFICATIONS:

- Four years experience as a Navy aircraft painter.
- Painted over 150 aircraft and associated equipment.
- Hands-on experience as a Quality Control Representative.
- Adept ability to operate and maintain hand and power tools.
- Excellent team leader and motivator, easily adapt to situations.

PROFESSIONAL EXPERIENCE

Professional painter with extensive experience in the proper use and maintenance of paint guns and other power tools. Consistent performer who ensures assigned paint tasks are thoroughly planned and executed. Expert in the repair of paint guns. Resourceful and innovative—will get the job done even under conditions of high stress. Recognized expert in the paint field.

Painting Experience
- Sandblasted and sprayed ship hulls with airless operated paint units.
- Prepared surfaces to be painted; sanded walls, ceilings and woodwork.

Troubleshooting Equipment/Tools
- Keen ability to rapidly identify potential problems and take proactive steps to avert trouble.
- Excellent troubleshooter who uses technical knowledge of paint guns and other power tools to minimize time required to fix equipment.

Quality Control
- Ensure proper use of prescribed safety equipment, such as safety glasses, helmets, goggles, respirators and protective clothing. Certified to inspect completed paint work.

TECHNICAL TRAINING

Paint Finish and Insignia School	125 hrs
Aircraft Corrosion Control School	55 hrs

ON-THE JOB TRAINING

Personnel and Equipment Safety Training	50 hrs
Quality Assurance Certification	75 hrs
Tool Control Training	30 hrs

Information Systems

Available: December 20XX

STEPHEN AKROYD
321 Memory Lane
Bethesda, MD 32112
AkroydS@aol.com
Home: 301-666-7787 / Work: 202-331-1234

CAREER OBJECTIVE

Information Systems position in a high technology firm where management and technical skills can be leveraged to the benefit of the company.

KEY SUCCESS FACTORS

Leadership: Outstanding ability to influence others to cooperate by use of common sense, personal example, persuasion and encouragement. Comfortable with authority and decision makers in crisis situations.

Management: Uses all resources to achieve goals and objectives—on time and on budget. Constantly evaluating management effectiveness, eliminating systems that are of little value.

Methodology: Reducing a problem to its basic components; determining where we are, where we want to be, and how to get there. Familiar with various philosophies including "Catalyst."

Planning: Envision "end-state"; identify requirements, research and choose alternatives, develop a blueprint for success, and develop an exit plan.

Organization: Staying logically oriented with respect to time, space, resources, information schedules and events using state of the art information and computer systems management tools.

PROFESSIONAL ACHIEVEMENTS

Information Systems   1998-Present

Considerably improved military email systems connectivity between 29 aviation sites and Washington, DC headquarters. Accomplished in both PC and Macintosh system hardware and software. Oversaw usage of a sophisticated computer tracking system for analyzing manpower flow and demographic data. Developed a web-based system capable of downloading data from several mainframe systems for demographic cost analysis and sourcing skill levels. Extensive computer network and information technology support for annual briefing requirements.

STEPHEN AKROYD

Strategic Planning Officer 1995-1997

A senior manager in procurement, strategic planning and acquisition in a fast-paced diverse environment with multilevel demands. Directed progress development and tracking of multi-million dollar major aeronautical and facility end-items. Coordinated detailed acquisition schedules and prioritized plans of actions and milestones. Personally introduced the largest free-world heavy lift helicopter into the Reserve program. This first time capability in reserves required extensive liaison with Congressional, Industry and DoD leadership.

Systems/Training Manager (Operations Officer) 1993-1994

Directed office and field personnel conducting logistical and information coordination for updates to thousands of personnel reporting to 47 separate sites. Successful in mobilizing individual reservists for Desert Storm in the first major call-up since the Korean War.

Team Director (Base Realignment Team Leader) 1990-1992

Successfully lead BRAC 95 process action teams (PAT) of diverse ethnic, gender and cultural personnel in a crisis situation with extreme time pressured deadlines. Eliminated and reduced wasteful expenditures saving $150 million dollars. BRAC teams utilized computers, equipment and subject matter experts to successfully influence the national evaluation of facilities and space. Received Meritorious Service Medal Award for these efforts. Automated and archived approximately 100K pages of BRAC process data enabling smooth and easy retrieval. Commercial/Instrument ratings with 2500 Helicopter and multi-engine aircraft hours.

Corporate Planning Director (Reserve Aviation Plans Officer) 1987-1989

Developed plans for modernization of aviation assets through the year 2005. Wrote concept papers and briefed senior level executives on budget, joint military issues and congressional plans. Established a legacy formulating the squadron designation of new revolutionary tilt-rotor aircraft. Prepared Powerpoint briefs for executive level review.

Variety of increasingly responsible Army leadership positions,1981-1986

EDUCATION

MBA in Business Administration   National University 1989
JD (Juris Doctor) in Law   Campbell University 1984
BAA in Business Administration   Campbell University 1981

Intelligence Analyst

Available: February 20XX

CHRIS SIMPSON

2312 Columbus Ave
Fort Meade, MD 99902

W: (222) 231-1232
H: (222) 231-5423

OBJECTIVE   Intelligence Analyst position where imagery interpretation and data analysis skills will benefit a Government contractor seeking to expand its intelligence support.

QUALIFICATIONS SUMMARY

IMAGERY
INTERPRETATION

- Over 10 years of specialized imagery experience with the U.S. Army.
- Keen ability to translate and interpret imagery data.
- Applied imagery interpretation skills to identify equipment location, troop movement, and other intelligence information.

SUPERVISION

- As a manager, applied technical imagery interpretation knowledge and skills to expertly guide and advise staff in all facets of imagery interpretation.
- Briefed senior management on imagery interpretation findings.
- Maintained detailed files on imagery interpretation data and findings.

PROJECT
MANAGEMENT

- As the project leader for a new imagery system, provided technical guidance and direction that ensured the system met all requirements.
- Participated in all phases of system development. Evaluated operational effectiveness of imagery interpretation equipment. Suggested cost reduction measures that, when implemented, resulted in savings of $1.5 million.

TRAINING

- Trained classes of 35 students on imagery activities, including imagery interpretation methods, computer renditions, and pattern recognition.
- Developed innovative curriculum that blended classroom training with hands-on field exercises requiring demonstrated proficiency. Evaluated student understanding of imagery interpretation theory through oral and written exams.
- Ensured students mastered the use of sophisticated imagery equipment.

EMPLOYMENT HISTORY

Intelligence Project Specialist, Fort Meade, MD, 1999-Present
Intelligence Manager, 23rd Military Intelligence Detachment, Fort Drum, NY, 1995-1998
Intelligence Specialist, 22nd Military Intelligence Battalion, Baumholder Germany, 1992-1994
Intelligence Specialist, 12th Military Intelligence Battalion, Fort Polk, LA, 1989-1991

EDUCATION & TRAINING

B.S., Geology, University of Maryland, College Park, MD, 2000
Military Intelligence Warrant Officer Technical Certification Course, 1993
Army Basic and Individualized Training, 1989

PERSONAL

Top Secret security clearance with recent Special Background Investigation.

Law Enforcement

Available: February 20XX

JOSEPH A. MARTINEZ
95 Colgate Drive, Apt. 131
Kileen, TX 45886
H: (333) 222-1256 / W: (333) 111-5667

OBJECTIVE

Law enforcement position where leadership skills and military police experience will benefit a large metropolitan police force seeking dedicated, community-sensitive law enforcement professionals.

SUMMARY OF QUALIFICATIONS

- Over 10 years experience as a military policeman.
- Extensive training in traditional law enforcement operations.
- Hand-picked for clandestine counter-drug operations.
- Developed innovative and highly effective approaches to crime solving.
- Qualified expert in 9 mm hand gun.

PROFESSIONAL EXPERIENCE

Counter-Drug Specialist, 109th **Military Intelligence Company, Fort Bliss, TX, 1999-Present**

Infiltrate drug operations in an effort to curtail the import of illegal drugs. Employ specialized police training techniques to identify and eradicate illegal substances in foreign countries. Train foreign security forces in counter-drug techniques.

Operations Manager, 35th **Military Intelligence Detachment, Fort Polk, LA, 1996-1998**

Assigned tasks daily to 15 military police professionals responsible for maintaining law and order in a community of 25,000. Interacted with colleagues on a daily basis to ensure complete understanding of assigned tasks. Assisted in the training and evaluation of 9 junior military police specialists. Counseled and mentored assigned staff.

Supervisor, 12th **Military Police Company, Fort Lewis, WA, 1993-1995**

Supervised activities of 8 military personnel responsible for maintaining law and order. Trained and led personnel in all facets of daily police operations. Motivated staff to attain high levels of weapons proficiency. Ensured team members acted professionally and courteously at all times.

Military Policeman, 53rd **Military Police Company, Fort Bragg, NC, 1990-1992**

Served with distinction as a member of the 82nd Airborne Division's Military Police company. Skillfully applied military police training. Handled infractions with minimal confrontation. Received Commendation Medal for excellent police work.

EDUCATION

High School diploma, Martin Luther King High School, Atlanta, GA, 1990

Logistics Management

Available: February 20XX

MICHAEL FISHER
7829 Newbury Drive
Los Angeles, CA 92101
E-Mail: fisherm@pacbell.net

H: 619-123-5678

W: 619-222-3333

OBJECTIVE: Management level position for an aerospace firm where extensive logistics management expertise can be used to help achieve significant cost reductions and improved operating efficiencies.

QUALIFICATIONS SUMMARY:

- Over 20 years of professional experience in logistics and materials management
- Exceptional knowledge of inventory, stockage control, security, and distribution.
- Keen trouble shooter with impressive analytical, verbal, and listening skills.
- Customer-oriented professional with strong interpersonal and communication skills

PROFESSIONAL EXPERIENCE:

Chief, Management and Systems Division, McChord AFB, 1998-Present
- Analyzed trends and set procedural guidelines to correct deficiencies in a $748 million account.
- Established and enforced quality performance measurements and implemented quantifiable improvements in stockage procedures, resulting in 99% inventory accuracy.
- Initiated a study of an aging document imaging system. Revised replacement approach resulted in $35,000 savings over a contractor's estimated replacement cost.

Chief, Materiel Management Division, Homestead AFB, 1995-1997
- Achieved stockage effectiveness rate of 87% for over 100,000 line items of property in support of 120 aircraft of 32 different makes, models, designs, and series.
- Coordinated materiel management activities with over 45 organizations to ensure most critical assets were available during a period of tight budgetary constraints.
- Managed the design and installation of a $3 million automated warehouse system, resulting in a 40% increase in warehouse space and a 20% reduction in processing time.

Superintendent, Operations Support Division, Scott AFB, 1992-1994
- Developed training program for research and order placement of priority requirements. Average order time was reduced from four hours to one.
- Addressed Air Force level problems with method of transportation used to deliver parts. Recommendations resulted in 25% pipeline delivery for priority requirements.

Supply Manager, MacDill AFB, FL, 1989-1991
- Led team of 80 logistics technicians in inventorying, accounting, and securing $75 million in critical jet aircraft components in 30 days.
- Achieved established production goals in reconstituting 250 depleted part kits to 100% completion in record time.
- Eliminated duplication of services at two sites, saving 1,000 staff hours monthly, doubling warehouse capacity, and improving customer service.
- Analyzed and solved significant transportation problem affecting multiple sites. Solution resulted in reworked transportation network that resulted in documented savings of $50,000 annually.

Developmental Leadership Positions, 1980-1988
Served in progressively more responsible leader development positions in the logistics field. Consistently recognized as a superlative performer. Received numerous leadership awards.

CAREER HIGHLIGHTS:

Demonstrated leadership abilities resulted in rapid advancement to Chief Master Sergeant, the highest enlisted grade in the U.S. Air Force (top 1% of the enlisted corps). Recognized as Superintendent of the Year twice at the local level (1st out of 40 peers) and once at the Headquarters level (1st out of 200 peers).

EDUCATION:

B.S., Business Management, University of Miami, 1991
A.A., Logistics Management, Community College of the Air Force, 1989
Over 100 hours of executive Total Quality Management training.

Logistics Supervisor

Available: June 20XX

EDWARD DANIELS
2813 Lincoln Lane
Tacoma, WA 98031
W: (206) 918-7623 / H: (206) 231-8710

OBJECTIVE   Logistics Supervisor position for an international distribution company where leadership skills and supervisory ability will enhance operational effectiveness and increase profitability.

QUALIFICATIONS SUMMARY

LOGISTICS
- Assisted in directing logistics support operations of 9 Federal Aviation Administration sites and 4 Air National Guard units.
- Executed the redistribution of 2,500 items of supply from deactivating sites.
- Optimized maintenance cycles, thereby decreasing time on aircraft repairable from 72 to 12 hours and costs by 28%.
- Provided subject matter expertise to the development of the Air National Guard's Mission Critical Logistics Reporting System, which enhanced the effectiveness of air operations management.

DISTRIBUTION
- Directed the requisitioning and control of aircraft parts to support a fleet of 54 aircraft and 680 vehicles. Cited by senior leaders as a major contributor to improved efficiency of warehouse operations.
- Developed the first Air National Guard inspection checklist for warehouse operations, thereby reducing customer complaints by 55% in the first year.

SUPERVISORY
- Led and guided four inspectors in performing quality control evaluations of 24 line personnel. Achieved 23% increase in proficiency without deviating from standards.
- Coordinated technical training for approximately 300 personnel over 24 month period.
- Prevented the loss of $109,000 in equipment assets by developing and enforcing strict accounting and control procedures.

INTERNATIONAL
- Extensive experience in Europe.
- Fluent in Italian.

EMPLOYMENT HISTORY: U.S. Army, 1980-Present

Warehouse Supervisor, McChord Air Force Base, WA, 1998-Present
Distribution Manager, Travis Air Force Base, CA, 1993-1997
Quality Assurance Manager, Aviano AB, Italy, 1990-1992
Training Supervisor, Andrews Air Force Base, MD, 1987-1989
Developmental Logistics Assignments, U.S. Air Force, 1980-1986

EDUCATION & TRAINING

A.A., Business Administration, San Francisco State University, San Francisco, CA, 1991
Relevant Training: Total Quality Management Course (1985); NCO Academy (1984), Airman Leadership Course (1979)

Maintenance Supervisor

Available: February 20XX

TERRY GRAHAM
5 High Street
Groton, CT 06300
H: (860) 456-7890 / W: (860) 123-4567
GrahamT@erols.com

OBJECTIVE: Maintenance supervisor for a company in the Midwest where expertise in electro-mechanical equipment will enhance the company's maintenance operations.

PROFESSIONAL EXPERIENCE

UNITED STATES NAVY, 1989-Present

<u>Senior Electrician</u>

- Operate, repair and maintain components associated with electric and nuclear reactor plants; specifically, turbine and diesel generators.
- Expert knowledge of AC/DC motors and controllers, 60 Hz motor generators, circuit breakers, and voltage regulators.
- Lead troubleshooting efforts on complex electrical equipment minimizing critical equipment downtime
- Perform preventive and corrective maintenance and document repair procedures.
- Involved in complicated testing of steam and reactor plants during initial criticality and steaming of two different reactor/steam plants.
- Assess equipment during normal operation to anticipate problems.
- Read and interpret blueprints, schematics and technical manual associated with maintenance procedures.
- Solely responsible for daily operation of electric power generation during normal and casualty operations.

<u>Supervisor/Project Management</u>

- Engineering Watch Supervisor. Manage 6-10 team members in daily operation of engineering propulsion and power generation plant.
- Network administrator for 2 server Novell Local Area Networks.
- Inspect completed maintenance items to ensure all regulations and specifications are adhered to.
- Assess and prioritize job orders and assign appropriate personnel to promote timely completion.
- Liaison with Navy and civilian contractors for successful installation of a Novell Local Area Network.
- Evaluate performance, document progress, counsel and motivate staff to continually improve operations.

<u>Instructor</u>

- Taught formal classes and On-The-Job Training on operation, maintenance and theory of electrical equipment.
- Reviewed and updated course curriculum, lesson plans, and tests.
- Effectively counseled students with academic and personal problems.

EDUCATION/TRAINING

Electrician's "A" School (640 hours)
Reactor Principles (80 hours)
Naval Nuclear Power School (1040 hours)
Naval Nuclear Power Training Unit (1040 hours)
Equipment Control and Distribution (80 hours)
Quality Assurance Inspector (40 hours)
Digital and Microprocessor Basics (96 hours)

Basic Novell Administration (40 hours)
Basic UNIX (40 hours)
Computer hardware/Novell installation (80 hours)
Instructor Training School (40 hours)
Sexual Harassment Prevention
Equal Opportunity Employment and Affirmative
  Action
Safety Training

PERSONAL

Currently hold Secret Security Clearance

Management Consultant

Available: January 20XX

ALEX SMITH
200 Meadow Crossing Way
Sterling, VA 20100
W: (703) 910-1234

OBJECTIVE

A management consultant position where international operations experience, strategic planning, and project management expertise in the former Soviet Union will translate into additional business.

HIGHLIGHT OF QUALIFICATIONS

- Successful, performance-oriented manager/leader. Strong interpersonal skills, excellent organizer, analyst/strategist. Outstanding writing and speaking skills.
- Proven success in strategic planning, coordinating requirements, and leading teams to project completion.
- Demonstrated ability to solve complex problems.
- Extensive experience in multi-cultural environments.
- Fluent in Russian, conversational in German and Ukrainian.
- Computer literate and competent with IBM-compatible programs.
- Top Secret security clearance with Special Background Investigation/polygraph.

EDUCATION

M.A., Soviet and Eastern European Studies, University of Kansas, Lawrence, KS, 1995
B.S., General Engineering, United States Military Academy, West Point, NY, 1982

PROFESSIONAL ACHIEVEMENTS

INTERNATIONAL OPERATIONS MANAGEMENT

As Site Commander, actively managed the operations of a $30 million nuclear missile production monitoring site established under the Intermediate-Range Nuclear Forces (INF) Treaty at Votkinsk, Russia. More recently managed a similar $5 million monitoring site at Pavlograd, Ukraine and consistently exercised all U.S. treaty rights under the Strategic Arms Reduction Treaty (START). At both facilities, supervised the daily operations and inspection activities of 30 U.S. officers and technicians. Interfaced daily with Russian/Ukrainian officials to improve the harsh living conditions and morale of U.S. treaty monitors.

HIGH-LEVEL INTERNATIONAL NEGOTIATIONS

Served as the principal On-Site Inspection Agency representative to the U.S. Ambassador, advising him on current and projected arms control treaties. Interfaced daily with officials from the Ukrainian Ministries of Defense and Foreign Affairs to resolve and implement treaty issues.

PROJECT AND ANALYTICAL MANAGEMENT

Supervised 10 highly trained civilian and military imagery interpretation specialists. Consistently managed limited personnel resources and improved production of intelligence in response to critical intelligence requirements from the National Security Council, Department of State, and other national agencies.

LOGISTICS AND TRANSPORTATION MANAGEMENT

Hands-on experience in supervising the palletization, uploading, air-transport, downloading, and joint inventory with Ukrainian Customs officials of 100 tons of monitoring equipment and supplies for the establishment of the START monitoring facility at Pavlograd, Ukraine.

SECURITY AND TRAINING MANAGEMENT

Actively managed all intelligence and security matters for a 4,100-man armored cavalry regiment. Improved the Opposing Forces training and physical security of the regiment. Supervised the Special Armor Program during the unit's initial acquisition of new M1A1 Abrams tanks.

COMMUNICATIONS/TECHNICAL EQUIPMENT MAINTENANCE MANAGEMENT

Achieved outstanding ratings during NATO tactical evaluations for managing a 30-person imagery interpretation, photo reproduction, and tactical communications unit.

ADMINISTRATIVE AND PERSONNEL MANAGEMENT

Increased assignments of critical intelligence specialists and improved the personnel management of a 700-person organization dispersed in eight locations in Germany and the United Kingdom.

EMPLOYMENT CHRONOLOGY

Commander, On-Site Inspection Agency (OSIA), Washington DC	1998-Present
Principal Advisor, Arms Control Implementation Unit, OSIA, Kiev, Ukraine	1995-1997
Branch Chief, Defense Intelligence Agency, Washington, DC	1990-1993
Staff Officer, 3rd Armored Cavalry Regiment, Fort Bliss, Texas	1987-1990
Commander, 582nd Military Intelligence Detachment, Alconbury, UK	1985-1987
Personnel Officer, 2nd Military Intelligence Battalion, Pirmasens, Germany	1984-1985
Operations Officer, 2nd Military Intelligence Battalion, Zweibrucken, Germany	1982-1984

ADVANCED TRAINING

Certificate, Russian Foreign Area Officer, U.S. Army Russian Institute, Garmisch, Germany, 1996
Graduate, Army Command and Staff College, Fort Leavenworth, Kansas, 1994
Certificate, Defense Sensor Interpretation and Application Training Program, Offutt, NE, 1990

Manufacturing

Available: June 20XX

JOHN T. BARNES
3212 Hunter Lane
Fayetteville, NC 92012
(919) 322-8828
BarnesJ@earthlink.net

OBJECTIVE: Production supervisor position where applied leadership, discipline, and esprit is needed to improve the efficiency and profitability of manufacturing operations.

QUALIFICATIONS SUMMARY

MANAGEMENT
- Successfully led teams ranging in size from 10 to 150 personnel in challenging national security-related missions. Applied leadership skills and motivational techniques to ensure success.
- Demonstrated the ability to quickly decompose complex tasks into smaller components, assign responsibilities, and direct operations.
- Effectively translated guidance between different management levels. Ensured team members were well informed and focused on accomplishing assigned tasks with minimum expenditure of resources.

PLANNING & ORGANIZATION
- Planned and led various teams in physically demanding operations requiring close coordination with the other military services.
- Organized and directed the actions of 30 team members involved in various activities, ranging from scuba diving to mountain climbing.
- Devised and executed a strategy that resulted in the recovery of over $350,000 in government supplies.

COMPUTER SKILLS
- Experienced in several computer software packages, including Microsoft Word, Excel, and Access.

INTERNATIONAL
- Lived and worked in several countries.
- Fluent in Spanish, conversant in German.

EMPLOYMENT HISTORY

First Sergeant (Senior Personnel Advisor), 7th Special Forces Gp, Fort Devens, MA, 1998-Present
Operations Manager, 7th Special Forces Group, Fort Devens, MA, 1995-1997
Operations Team Leader, 10th Special Forces Unit, Fort Bragg, NC, 1991-1994
Member, Special Forces team, Fort Bragg, NC, 1990-1991
Squad Leader, Fort Benning, GA, 1989
Infantry Trainee, 1987-1988

EDUCATION & TRAINING

B.S. (Candidate, 2001), Industrial Engineering, University of Maryland
Special Forces Course (U.S. Army leadership course), 1992
Advanced NonCommissioned Officers Course, 1991
Basic NonCommissioned Officers Course, 1990
Army Basic Training, 1986

Network Specialist

Available: December 20XX

DAVID P. JONES
2311 Park Avenue
Langley AFB, VA 22312
Work: 540-123-4567 / Home: 540-123-1234
JonesD@aol.com

OBJECTIVE

Position as a Network Specialist for a small-to-medium size telecommunications firm where proven communication skills and self-motivation will help the organization obtain increased market share.

SUMMARY OF QUALIFICATIONS

Technically adept technician with over seven years experience providing telecommunications support to executives at the highest levels of the U.S. Government. Significant experience installing and maintaining cellular, VHF, UHF satellite, wireline, and line of sight voice and data systems. Articulate, motivated professional with strong desire to excel. Possess a Top Secret security clearance with SCI and Presidential Access Security Clearance.

PROFESSIONAL EXPERIENCE

Senior Radio Technician, White House Communications Agency, 1998-Present
Supervised five to eight person teams deployed worldwide to provide uninterrupted communications support for Presidential-level officials. Managed $80 million worth of communications equipment with no loss or damage. Received Army medal for outstanding communications support provided to the President and his staff.

Mobile Communication System Technician, White House Communications Agency, 1994-97
Designed and implemented a mobile communications system that provided secure/non-secure voice, data, and facsimile service via cellular, VHF, UHF satellite, and HF mediums. Ensured high level government officials had uninterrupted communications service regardless of their itinerary. Maintained 98% readiness rate on fleet of 25 mobile communication vehicles.

Radio Operator, 101st Airmobile Division, Fort Cambell, KY, 1991-93
Operated radio communication systems in support of unit operations. Set up and tuned radio equipment to pre-established frequencies. Transmitted, received, and logged radio messages according to military procedures. Maintained equipment in operational condition.

EDUCATION AND TRAINING:

A.S., Computer Technology, Northern Virginia Community College, 1997
Tactical Satellite/Microwave Communications, Fort Gordon, GA, 1991

Outside Sales

LOU MADISON
345 Ashford St.
Arlington, VA 22000
(703) 456-7890

OBJECTIVE

A position in Outside Sales for a small, entrepreneurial firm where demonstrated ability to bring in new accounts will be instrumental in building the firm's business base.

EXPERIENCE SUMMARY

Over twenty years of success in demanding positions in administrative management, with focus on special projects, program management, and customer and employee relations. Excellent interpersonal skills. Extensive success in recruiting with the uncanny ability to find new market pools. Primary strengths include a creative self-starter with excellent oral communication abilities coupled with many years of public speaking. High degree of personal and professional dedication to loyalty and integrity. Computer literate with knowledge of several software applications (Microsoft Suite, Lotus Notes, Windows, and Netscape). SECRET NATO clearance.

PROFESSIONAL ACHIEVEMENTS

Quality Control and Reengineering
Fort Myer, VA   **1998-1999**

Served as Project Manager on Army Performance Improvement Criteria team. Utilized the Malcolm Baldrige National Quality Award criteria to interview employees, directors, and assess historical data. Collated data and recommendations to existing processes to improve service and support for customers throughout the Washington Metro area. Received commendations from U.S. Army and Department of Defense senior leadership for producing outstanding results. Actions resulted in the reengineering of several processes.

Human Resource Management
Fort Myer, VA   **1995-1997**

Served as First Sergeant for the single largest unit in the United States Army. Serviced over 55 Federal Government agencies employing personnel in 40 states and 28 countries. Upgraded personnel qualifications systems to better ensure the maintenance of employee training, administrative and organizational requirements. Oversaw the administration and enforcement of company personnel programs and policies. Received meritorious recognition from senior executive leadership for efforts and results.

Recruiting
Denver Recruiting Region, Denver, CO   **1992-1994**

Served as a recruiter and regional recruiting office manager. Managed recruiting offices in rural and metropolitan areas consisting of up to seven recruiters. Developed new or improved existing recruiting markets extending up to 80,000 square miles of territory. Results included several awards as Top Producing Office, both regionally, and nationwide (continuously 150-220% above production requirements), and Recruiter of the Year, worldwide.

Marketing and Sales Research and Analysis
Denver Recruiting Region, Denver, CO   **1990-1991**

Developed a Market Analysis for a District Recruiting Headquarters representing a four-state region. Collected and collated statistical data from local, county, state, and federal agencies. Efforts resulted in a market analysis, which reflected growth patterns from the past ten-year period with projected figures for the next decade that allowed for the realignment of resources. Completed project in 25% less time than any other region nationwide, with fewer resources. Commended by senior leaders for superior results.

Administrative Management

U.S. Army (Various locations worldwide)   **1980-1989**

Supervised staffs over a 20-year period ranging from 3 to 25 personnel. Improved administrative management support for employees ranging from 400 to 6,000. Updated several organizational strategic and routine plans on a variety of personnel models. Managed troubleshooting of projects involving personnel and facilities. Planned, generated, executed organization-wide support for a $2 million upgrade to facilities housing over 500 personnel. Oversaw the overall property management and security of three installations housing over 1,000 soldiers and their families. Coordinated an office-automated system to improve information flow to over 55 government agencies and 2,500 personnel. Handled a myriad of daily and long-term care issues ranging from family domestic, alcohol and drug abuse cases, to assisting in major criminal investigations. Received numerous commendations from Department of Defense for improvements in administrative, morale, facilities maintenance and upkeep, and security support areas.

EDUCATION & TRAINING

B.S., Management Studies, University of Maryland, 1998

A.A. in General Studies, University of Maryland, 1994

Relevant training:

Certificate, Advanced Staff Management, Sergeant Major Academy, U.S. Army, Fort Bliss, TX

Certificate, Total Quality Management, Defense Management College, Fort Belvoir, VA

Certificate, Advanced Recruiting and Sales Management, U.S. Army, Fort Ben Harrison, IN

Certificate, Personnel Management, U.S. Army, Fort Bragg, NC

Personnel Management

Available: January 20XX

LOUISE ARMSTRONG
4221 Apple Lane Court
Fort Hood, TX 77777
(678) 123-4567
larmstrong@ix.netcom.com

OBJECTIVE:

Personnel manager for a mid-to-large sized manufacturing company where proven leadership skills and a disciplined approach to problem solving will result in improved operating efficiency and increased team morale.

SUMMARY OF QUALIFICATIONS:

- Fifteen years experience in office supervision and personnel management.
- Reliable and highly motivated self-starter with an aptitude for quickly learning new tasks.
- Improved efficiency of operations through skilled application of computer technology.
- Proficient in a variety of office automation software, including Microsoft Word, Power-Point, Excel, and Microsoft Mail.
- Fifteen years experience in office supervision and personnel management.

EMPLOYMENT EXPERIENCE:

Personnel Manager, Dyess Air Force Base, TX, 1998-Present
Provide accurate responses to over 14 inquiries daily using PC SAS and ATLAS, two commercial software packages. Provide instruction in the use of these packages to approximately 30 personnel per month. Recognized as a top instructor through both supervisor and student ratings.

Personnel Supervisor, Andrews Air Force Base, MD, 1995-1997
Managed the Air Force's largest personnel database with a staff of eight. System administrator for eight AT&T 3b2s in a network supporting over 400 users. Achieved 99% reliability rate over a two year period. Developed and met goals aligned with management's vision.

Personnel Inspector, Langley AFB, VA, 1992-1994
Inspected and evaluated various personnel management systems. Recommended changes that were adopted and resulted in a 29% increase in transaction processing efficiency. Trained staff of three personnel in inspection techniques.

Personnel Systems Technician, Travis AFB, CA, 1988-1991
Assisted users in preparing decision briefs for senior Air Force managers. Coordinated actions and followed up on assigned tasking responsibilities to ensure projects were completed successfully.

EDUCATION

B.S., Business Administration, University of Maryland, 2000.
A.S., Computer Systems, Community College Air Force, 1996.

PROFESSIONAL ACHIEVEMENTS

Navy Achievement Medal for superior performance in leadership and technical abilities.
Three Letters of Commendation for superior performance and leadership.

Project Management

Available: August 20XX

LYNN JONES
1229 East York Ave.
New Livery, CT 09558
(Home) 913-558-9877 / (Work) 913-487-8993

OBJECTIVE: A product management position in a fast growing cellular communication company where organization, leadership, and communication experience will be used for improving product quality and innovation.

EDUCATION & TRAINING:
- B.S., Electrical Engineering, Brigham Young University, Salt Lake City, UT, 1992
- Information Management Course, Fort Gordon, GA, 1997
- U.S. Army Signal Officer Advanced Course, Fort Gordon, GA, 1995
- U.S. Army Signal Officer Basic Course, Fort Gordon, GA, 1992

EXPERIENCE: 1992-Present, U.S. Army, Captain, Signal Corps

Organization Designed and coordinated communications for Pacific Command Joint Training Exercises. Organized and chaired engineering conferences. Presented decision briefings and prepared staff action papers for a variety of communication-related issues of considerable importance to the command. Served as Watch Officer during operations and exercises.

Leadership Installed, operated, and maintained satellite, switching, cable, and message communications in support of numerous U.S. Army units distributed throughout central Germany. Led 110 soldiers in performing all assigned communications missions. Total responsibility for the training, morale, welfare and discipline of all the soldiers under my command.

Communication Planned and supervised installation of telecommunication systems of V Corps exercises. Maintained and accounted for vehicle and communications equipment valued at approximately $1.5 million. Planned and conducted individual and collective training in technical skills and general military subjects. Supervised, trained, and led 23 personnel.

WORK HISTORY: *Communication Staff Officer*, 12th Signal Brigade, Fort Lewis, Washington, 1998-Present

Communications Company Commander, C Company, 430th Signal Battalion, Mainz, Germany, 1995-1997

Platoon Leader, B Company, 17th Signal Battalion, Hoechst, Germany, 1992-1994.

Project Manager

Available: March 20XX

PETER R. SMITH
2913 West Broad St.
Fairfax, VA 22313
H: (703) 888-3333 / W: (202) 132-7654
SmithP@aol.com

OBJECTIVE   Project Management position where organizational and technical skills will assist an international telecommunications firm implement systems on time and within budget.

QUALIFICATIONS SUMMARY

PLANNING &
ORGANIZATION
- Created and implemented world-wide ISDN installation plan, which was completed on schedule and 15% below budget.
- Developed and used PERT charts to manage 18-month project to upgrade a telecommunications network, reducing system downtime by 20%.
- Coordinated multi-service exercises with other military services and NATO countries. Validated interoperability of communications systems.

MANAGEMENT
- Managed a 150-person mobile communications unit that was consistently rated best in the organization (1st of 4).
- Re-engineered a personnel management process, resulting in a 20% improvement in staff efficiencies.
- Integrated innovative training techniques that reduced the program course length by one week, saving the government $500,000 per year.
- Planned, programmed, budgeted, and executed an X.400-based electronic mail program for 5,000 users, reducing dependency on proprietary systems.

TECHNICAL
- Registered Professional Engineer.
- Over 20 years experience in systems engineering, telecommunications, and management information systems.
- Led technically complex acquisition project involving the development and fielding of an all-digital, fiber optic communications network.
- Designed and developed AI-based quality control system that reduced processing errors by 50%.

EMPLOYMENT HISTORY

Communications Director, Fort Hood, TX, 1998-Present
Project Officer, Defense Information Systems Agency, Arlington, VA, 1995-1997
Communications Operations Staff Officer, Frankfurt, Germany, 1992-1994
Communications Manager, Fort Gordon, GA, 1989-1991
Systems Analyst, The Pentagon, Washington, DC, 1985-1987
Various Engineering and Junior Management Positions with the U.S. Army, 1979-1984

EDUCATION & TRAINING

M.S., Computer Science, Cornell University, Ithaca, NY, 1988
B.S., General Engineering, U.S. Military Academy, West Point, NY, 1979
Relevant training:
   Courses and seminars on Project Management, Systems Engineering, Advanced Resource Management, Total Quality Management, and Budgeting

Public Relations

Available: July 20XX

JESSE JONES
200 Goldstar Road
Riverside, CA 92508
(909) 654-3210

Objective:

Senior Public Relations official for a large defense contractor where extensive experience, dedication, and personal commitment to excellence will enhance the company's image in the U.S. and abroad.

Highlights of Qualifications:

- 20 years of proven professional public relations experience.
- Personable and persuasive in communications skills
- Excellent trainer and motivator
- Self-motivated "team player" confident in making independent decisions.
- Excellent organization and leadership skills.
- Awarded numerous recruiting, advertising, and training honors.

Management and Training Experience:

- Expertly developed and managed an account base of $4.45 million
- Directed advertising department with annual budget of $1.5 million.
- Spearheaded training program, developing lessons plans and providing sales, cold calls, and motivational training for recruiting personnel.
- Expert Regional Manager of urban inter-city recruiting stations. Provided professional guidance, career counseling, professional training and motivation for recruiting personnel.
- "Determined troubleshooter"—As recruiter-in-charge of various recruiting stations, transformed personnel into productive, contributing members of recruiting command.
- Integral part of the executive steering committee for Total Quality Management implementation.

Sales and Marketing Experience:

- Experienced in micro computer, hardware and software sales solutions. Routinely developed proposals, presented products, requested educational grants, and prepared price bid quotations.
- Possess expertise in recruiting/career counseling programs and policies.
- Dynamic public speaker—Routinely represented employer at National Broadcasting Convention, Computer Conventions, NAACP Job Fairs, Southern Baptist Leadership Convention. Also made presentations to the student body of Colleges, High Schools, and Middle Schools throughout Southern California.
- Innovatively developed and analyzed marketing statistics and strategies, increasing production 40%.

Employment History:

Senior Public Relations Officer, Office of the Vice Chief of Staff, U.S. Air Force, 1998-Present
Public Relations Officer, Office of the Chief of Plans, U.S. Air Force, 1996-1997
Communications Officer, Pope AFB, NC, 1994-1995
Progressive leadership development positions within the U.S. Air Force, 1980-1993

Education and Training:

Southern Illinois University—B.S., Workforce Education and Development, 2000
Career Counseling Course
Career Recruiting Academy
Total Quality Management Techniques
Advertising Tracking and Development Course
Hawthorne High School—Diploma, 1979

Public Relations

Available: June 20XX

THOMAS HART
3212 Eisenhower Lane
Waldorf, MD 20717

Home: (301) 111-2222   Work: (202) 765-4321   E-mail: HartT@aol.com

---

PUBLIC RELATIONS / MEDIA RELATIONS / COMMUNICATIONS / SPECIAL EVENTS

Talented public relations strategist and campaign director with 10 years professional experience. Expertise in community/public outreach, multimedia communications, publications management, and crisis management. Accomplished in managing relationships with major print and broadcasting media nationwide. Skilled in large-scale event coordination and management. Consistently effective in meeting budget and schedule requirements.

PROFESSIONAL EXPERIENCE: 1990-Present, U.S. Army, Captain

Public Relations Officer, 1995-Present
UNITED STATES NAVY—Washington, D.C. /California/Virginia/Pennsylvania

Fast track promotion through a series of increasingly responsible public relations/public affairs positions nationwide as one of only 200 designated spokespersons in the U.S. Navy. Won several distinguished commendations for outstanding performance in the management of sensitive public relations programs and initiatives.

Public Relations / Public Affairs, *1990-1994*

- Rebuilt and revitalized inactive public relations function aboard the USS Kitty Hawk.
- Developed course content and taught public relations at seminars to 12 Naval organizations.
- Publicized the Navy's assistance to victims of earthquakes and other natural disasters, winning positive media coverage and strengthening the Navy's image.
- Launched high-profile public relations campaigns to recruit community board members and to gain public access to information concerning two hazardous waste removal projects.
- Wrote public relations guidelines for Congressional visits emphasizing the management of high profile events and strategies to leverage media exposure.
- Trained and supervised teams of up to 24 PR specialists in printing, graphic arts, photography, media relations, community outreach, and administrative support.

Media / Press Relations

- Represented the U.S. Navy in front of major print and broadcast media nationwide, including network affiliates, national and local correspondents, National Public Radio, and several major newspapers, including the Washington Post, New York Times, Los Angeles Times, Wall Street Journal, Time, and Newsweek.
- Managed liaison affairs with local, national, and international press, White House Press Office, Arlington National Cemetery, and National Cathedral for national coverage of memorial services for national dignitaries.
- Spokesperson in regional and national media markets.
- Coordinated media events for the first U.S. port visit by Russian warships in 20 years. Managed affairs for 300+ media over a five-day period.

Education: B.A., English Literature, Norfolk State University, 1990

Registered Nurse

Available: January 20XX

MARY BARKELY
2913 West Broad St.
Fairfax, VA 22313
(703) 888-3333
BarkelyM@erols.com

OBJECTIVE   Full-time Nurse Practitioner in a Family Practice or Primary Care facility that seeks the services of an experienced and dedicated registered nurse.

QUALIFICATIONS SUMMARY

NURSE PRACTITIONER
- Provided direct nursing care for a variety of acutely/chronically ill adult and pediatric patients in both an in-patient and out-patient care setting.
- Experienced in Pediatrics and Neonatal Intensive Care Units.

MANAGEMENT
- Developed management policies and operating instructions that resulted in more timely and higher quality health care.
- Defined scope of patient care based on doctor prognosis.
- Implemented quality improvement initiatives that generated positive patient feedback on received healthcare.

TRAINING
- Developed and presented educational workshops for staff personnel.
- Delivered professional weekly training classes on diabetes.

NURSING ADMINISTRATION
- Oversaw daily clinical/administrative operations for a 500-bed hospital.
- Supervised, trained, and evaluated 105 nurses, paraprofessionals, and administrative support personnel.
- Planned and directed nursing care activities in Intensive Care Unit.

CERTIFICATIONS
- Certified in Medical Surgical Nursing by the American Nurses Credentialing Center.
- National Certification Corporation for the Obstetric, Gynecologic, and Neonatal Nurse Specialties.
- Advanced Cardiac Life Support Certification.
- Basic Cardiac Life Support Certification.

EMPLOYMENT HISTORY

Department Head, Eisenhower Army Medical Center, Fort Gordon, GA, 1999-Present
Nurse Practitioner, Walter Reed Army Medical Hospital, 1993-1998
Registered Nurse, Surgical Room, Tripler Army Medical Hospital, Honolulu, HI, 1987-1991
Registered Nurse, Emergency Room, Tripler Army Medical Hospital, Honolulu, HI, 1982-1986

EDUCATION & TRAINING

M.S., Nursing, Central Michigan, 1992
B.S., Nursing, University of North Dakota, 1982

Sales Trainer

Available: June 20XX

JAMES L. PARK
2829 Creekview Court
Quantico, VA 22312
W: (703) 290-1212 / H: (703) 291-9999
ParkJ@aol.com

OBJECTIVE	Sales training position for a consumer products company seeking highly motivated individual with outstanding salesmanship skills.

QUALIFICATIONS SUMMARY

RECRUITING
- Interacted with candidates and their parents on a daily basis. Highlighted the benefits of military service.
- Surpassed recruitment goals by 15% annually.
- Visited over 100 local high schools and community colleges to attract top-notch Marine candidates.

TRAINING
- Indoctrinated 150 new recruits into the traditions and practices of the Marine Corps.
- Physically and mentally challenged new recruits, preparing them for a wide range of national security related assignments.
- Trained new recruits on the use of various weapon systems. Achieved unit proficiency rating of 95%.

MANAGEMENT
- Led and directed the activities of a 10-member team; improved both their individual and team skills.
- Counseled and mentored subordinates; evaluated their performance and provided development advice.

EMPLOYMENT HISTORY

Recruiter, US Marine Corps, Atlanta, GA, 1998-Present
Drill Instructor, US Marine Corps, Parris Island, SC, 1994-1997
Squad Leader, US Marine Corps, Okinawa, Japan, 1991-1993
Squad Member, US Marine Corps, Okinawa, Japan, 1988-1990

EDUCATION & TRAINING

A.S., Business Administration, Albany Community College, GA, 1999
Marine Corps Recruiter's School, 1998
Advanced Leadership Training, 1991
Marine Corps Basic Training, 1988

Security

Available: January 20XX

FRANCIS MITCHELL
1100 Main Street
Dugway, UT 84000
Home: (801) 890-1234 / Work: (801) 123-4567
Mitchell@earthlink.net

PROFESSIONAL PROFILE

Over 15 years experience in Security and Intelligence Operations worldwide. Combines strong planning, analysis, organizational and communications skills with excellent qualifications in the development of security operations. Skilled personnel manager and budget administrator. Expertise includes:

- Scientific & Technical Intelligence
- Tactical Assessment/Planning
- Document Security/Control
- Security Training & Team Leadership

- Operations & Personnel Security
- Counter-Terrorism
- Counter-Espionage
- Reporting/Analysis

Excellent knowledge of the Freedom of Information Act and security policies of U.S. and foreign governments. Familiar with general security practices followed by major industries and corporations nationwide. Held highest level U.S. Government security clearance and positions of trust. PC proficient.

PROFESSIONAL EXPERIENCE

Intelligence & Security Officer, U.S. Army   1985 to Present
Logistics Officer, U.S. Army   1980-1984

Fast-track promotion throughout career. Advanced through a series of increasingly responsible security and intelligence positions with organizations operating worldwide. Won numerous honors and commendations for capabilities in threat analysis, intelligence collection/analysis, security operations planning and personnel training. Career highlights include:

Security Operations Planning & Management

- Authored several major documents impacting security and intelligence operations worldwide. Provided the strategy, organizational structure and processes for security operations development, management and expansion in response to changing demands of worldwide operations.

- Hosted two intelligence planning committees of multi-disciplinary intelligence and operating management personnel challenged to enhance security and operations planning worldwide.

- Provided high-level security and intelligence support to technologically advanced systems and engineering projects.

Intelligence Collection & Analysis

- Directed large-scale intelligence research, collection, analysis and dissemination operations to provide top management with critical information regarding potential threats, breeches to security and technical intelligence.

- Initiated processes to overcome shortcomings in intelligence collection and analysis vital for the success of major projects.

- Authored reports, led executive-level presentations and coordinated information flow between various public and private organizations.

Personnel Training, Supervision & Development

- Designed and led training programs in security and intelligence for operative personnel, management and executives worldwide. Created customized presentations to meet specific operating requirements of each organization.

- Trained, scheduled, supervised and evaluated work performance of up to 85 personnel.

Budgeting & Financial Management

- Participated in the long-term administration of a $7 million annual budget. Provided timely and accurate input to high-level reports and discussions addressing operations planning and budget requirements.

Achievements & Project Highlights

- Developed processes to maintain control of more than 70,000 sensitive security documents.

- Managed systems development and implementation project to computerize a large technical scientific library and integrate advanced optical data technology for long-term document retention.

- Built cooperative working relationships with government agencies worldwide to facilitate the timely exchange of information critical to intelligence and security operations.

- Extensive technical knowledge of chemical, biological, and radiological security threats, electronic surveillance technology, electronic counter-measures and munitions technologies.

EDUCATION

Bachelor of General Studies, Kent State University, 1980

Completed 350+ hours of continuing professional training in Security and Intelligence. Program included scientific and technical intelligence collection/analysis, leadership and supervisory skills, and tactical assessment.

Security Management

Available: January 20XX

WARREN THOMAS
2480 Davis Circle
Washington, DC 29036
H: (202) 111-2222 / W: (202) 222-3345
ThomasW@aol.com

OBJECTIVE: An organizational development position with a security company requiring discipline, strength, and management expertise.

SUMMARY: Motivated, charismatic leader who seeks responsibility and accomplishes tasks in a professional, timely manner. Strong interpersonal skills have been demonstrated in a range of security-related assignments. Quickly adapt to new and physically challenging environments. Strong leadership skills were refined throughout Army service.

EXPERIENCE   **Leadership**. Responsible for the well-being, discipline, morale, and readiness of a 30-member unit. Set and enforced high standards in the areas of personal appearance, physical fitness, and weapons qualifications. Demonstrated leadership, supervision, management, and team building skills.

Training. Assisted in developing weekly training and development plans. Helped establish and conduct training programs in the areas of nuclear, biological, and chemical protection, physical fitness, land navigation, weapons qualifications, and equipment maintenance.

Management. Organized and led a 10-member team through numerous missions. Planned team work schedules and training for accomplishing mission objectives. Set and enforced high standards of performance.

Supervision. First line supervisor responsible for the productivity of a four-man team. Organized training, planned daily activities, and supervised team members.

WORK HISTORY   **Platoon Sergeant**, 3rd US Infantry, Fort Myer, VA, 1998-present
Training Supervisor, 3rd US Infantry, Fort Myer, VA, 1995-1997
Infantry Squad Leader, 3rd US Infantry, Fort Myer, VA, 1992-1994
Team Leader, 197th Infantry Brigade, Fort Benning, GA, 1989-1991

EDUCATION   ▪ Infantry Advanced Noncommissioned Officers Course, 1995
▪ Infantry Basic Noncommissioned Officers Course, 1993
▪ Leadership Development Course, Noncommissioned Officers Academy, 1991
▪ Infantry Basic Training, 1989

Senior Electrician

Available: August 20XX

CHRIS BRADLEY
2813 Lincoln Lane
Las Vegas, NV 98031
W: (206) 918-7623 / H: (206) 231-8710

OBJECTIVE

Senior electrician position for a commercial aircraft manufacturer seeking to benefit from the experiences of a highly trained and motivated aircraft electrician.

QUALIFICATIONS SUMMARY

Air Force electrician with over 8 years of first-hand experience in the installation and maintenance of electrical systems on jet aircraft. Trained in effectively troubleshooting electrical systems using specialized diagnostic and test equipment. Dependable, hard-working professional who perseveres until all tasks are successfully accomplished. Recipient of numerous military awards for outstanding service as an electrician.

WORK HISTORY

Electrical Supervisor, Nellis Air Force Base, NV, 1998-Present

Oversaw the electrical maintenance activities in a large Air Force maintenance shop. Designed and implemented maintenance procedures for fellow electricians. Performed numerous quality control checks. Trained electricians on various electrical maintenance activities. Improved aircraft readiness level by 32%.

Senior Electrician, Kelly Air Force Base, 1995-1997

Responsible for maintenance of all electrical components in the C-5 aircraft. Supervised nine electricians in all facets of operations. Developed maintenance checklists to ensure major electrical components were 100% operational before release. Used computer-based diagnostic equipment to rapidly isolate deficiencies. Repaired electrical components, including generators and electric motors.

Electrician, Travis Air Force Base, CA, 1991-1994

Used wiring diagrams in the maintenance of various electrical components in the U.S. Air Force's F-16 jet fighter. Repaired or replaced various electrical instruments, including tachometers, temperature gauges, and altimeters. Used soldering equipment to solidify electrical connections. Replaced faulty wiring.

EDUCATION & TRAINING

A.A., Electrical Theory, Community College of the Air Force, 1999
Fundamentals of Electricity, 1991

Senior Operations Manager

Available: February 20XX

MARK FRANCIS
Box 900
APO AE 09120
011-49-711-678-1234
FrancisM@aol.com

OBJECTIVE

Senior operations manager for a Defense-related firm where discipline, drive, energy, and innovation will contribute to improved organizational performance.

CAREER PROFILE

Distinguished management career leading the planning, staffing, budgeting, technology and operations of organizations throughout the U.S. and abroad. Expert in cross-functional team building and leadership, multi-cultural communications, change management, organization development and quality/performance improvement. Traveled, lived and/or worked in more than 30 countries worldwide.

PROFESSIONAL EXPERIENCE

UNITED STATES MARINE CORPS   1980 to Present

Branch Chief / Commanding Officer / Executive Officer
Operations Officer / Logistics Officer / Safety Director

Fast-track career promotion through a series of increasingly responsible management positions leading large-scale operations worldwide. Currently hold the rank of Lieutenant Colonel. Received numerous commendations and awards for leadership.

Operations Management

- More than 20 years' management experience in the strategic planning, staffing, budgeting, resource allocation and leadership of administrative, field, flight, maintenance equipment, technology, training and logistics operations worldwide. Skilled policy-maker.
- Direct and decisive leadership qualifications with particular strengths in planning, performance improvement, quality improvement and productivity gain.
- Experienced in the start-up and leadership of new operations and organizations.

Human Resources Affairs & Team Leadership

- Led teams of up to 500 personnel with full responsibility for work assignments, scheduling, performance review, disciplinary action and long-term career planning/development/ promotion.
- Expert qualifications in evaluating personnel needs and developing responsive training programs.
- Early career experience managing the audit and examination of personnel records to ensure regulatory compliance.

Budgeting & Financial Management

- Administered up to $50 million in annual budgets to support operations worldwide.
- Expert in evaluating organizational funding requirements, preparing/leading formal budget presentations, allocating the distribution of funds, and managing complex financial analysis and reporting functions.

Safety Management

- Extensive qualifications in the planning, development and leadership of occupational, workplace, transportation and aviation safety programs supporting operations throughout the U.S. and abroad.
- Equally extensive qualifications in safety training program design and instruction.

Technology Management

- Spearheaded the operational test, analysis and review of advanced navigational, telecommunications and operating support systems to evaluate performance and reliability.
- PC skills in word processing, database and spreadsheet applications.

Flight Operations

- Planned, staffed, budgeted and directed flight transportation operations worldwide.
- Directed flight planning and scheduling, aircraft operations, aircraft maintenance, aviator training and flight instructor training programs.
- Designated Naval Aviator with over 6100 hours of total flight time with no incidents.
- Four-year tenure as Presidential Command Pilot.

Project Coordination & Leadership

- Planned and directed cooperative operations between the U.S., France, Germany and the United Kingdom through direct leadership of multinational teams.
- Led joint efforts on behalf of the U.S. Government, U.S. embassies, Pentagon and State Department to facilitate emergency relief, assistance and humanitarian programs.

Communications

- Strong written communication, public speaking, and senior-level presentation skills.

EDUCATION & TRAINING

M.A., International Relations, University of Southern California, 1988
B.A., History, Indiana University, 1980

Graduate of numerous management and leadership training programs.

Senior Program Administrator

Available: June 20XX

SAM MATTISON
10 Parkwood Lane
Groton, CT 06300
(860) 412-3456

OBJECTIVE

A Senior Program Administrator position where knowledge and technical expertise in facilities management will improve the efficiency of a firm's manufacturing operations.

PROFESSIONAL EXPERIENCE

UNITED STATES NAVY, 1977-Present

Project/Program Manager

- Managed a $200 million budget in an increasingly constrained and technically complex environment. *Saved $6 million in maintenance resources through skillful fixed-price negotiations.*
- Monitored General Electric operations of four Nuclear Propulsion Prototypes ensuring compliance with Naval Reactors, OSHA and EPA procedures for training and test requirements. Graded satisfactory on annual audits.
- Directed multiple industrial activities: job scoping and sequencing; quality control procedures; and personnel training. Ensured best product, least cost, shortest time.

  Special recognition: *"The success of the NR-1 $80 million Refueling Overhaul is due to LCDR Mattison's superior management and attention to detail."*—J. P. Smith, Vice Admiral, Navy Commendation Medal

Supervisor/Trainer

- Directed and supervised 40 technical writers in preparation of detailed, step-by-step, user friendly preventive and corrective maintenance procedures (3M) for a 1000-man production work force.
- Assessed department needs and problems, identified and recommended solution, developed realistic and achievable goals, and designed on-the-job training programs to eliminate discrepancies, increased productivity and enhanced skills of employees. (e.g., revised the Basic Nuclear Electrician's Rate curriculum. *Reduced attrition by 3% and improved GPA by 0.3 points.)*
- Evaluated personnel semiannually: focused on contributions, character and accomplishments; counseled on ways to increase skills and advance in career. *Achieved a 95% success rate for electricians' advancement to E-5. Eighteen students were selected for officer commissioning programs.*
- Administered and implemented preventive and corrective maintenance program (3M), assigned and scheduled technicians based on skill and experience, inspected work ensuring compliance with regulations and technical specifications, and verified accurate documentation into records.

Technical

- Researched, compiled and evaluated data and statistics to write reports and make formal presentations, with decision points to department heads and Chief Executive Officers. *Saved $2 million by identifying and eliminating an outdated time phased hydraulic control valve maintenance program.*

- Planned, scheduled and directed attack submarine employment, resulting in on-time departure and electronic suite certification.
- As quality assurance office continuously inspected Naval equipment to ensure operational readiness in a safe manner.

Quality Control

- Implemented radiological controls, nuclear work practices, radiographic operations and quality control procedures. Identified and developed solutions to resolve work practices discrepancies, before they impact production.
- Sent weekly letters to the Director, Naval Nuclear Propulsion Program, on mechanical and fluid systems compliance, with recommended solutions. *One recommendation to a nuclear valve was incorporated locally and fleet-wide, saving an estimated $1 million in corrective maintenance.*

EDUCATION & TRAINING

B.S., Nuclear Engineering Technology, Thomas Edison State College, Trenton, NJ, 1999
Associate of Science Degree, University of New York, 1993

3,000+ hours of Navy training in nuclear power, engineering, leadership, supervision, and project management.

PROFESSIONAL AFFILIATIONS

American Nuclear Society
American Society of Mechanical Engineers
Advanced Training Institute of America

HONORS/AWARDS

Numerous awards and citations for leadership, supervision, technical coordination, and project management.

"Singled out by Squadron Four Commanding Officers and the Force Commander for timely and expert preparation of four SSN's for deployment."—A. W. Adams, Commodore, Navy Commendation Medal

"Conceived and implemented a harbor tug overhaul plan with a cost savings of $750,000. The success of this project was due to his thorough planning and resourceful initiatives by obtaining a harbor tug from Naval Station Rota, Spain."—M. D. Frank, Commodore, Navy Achievement Medal

Senior Program Manager

KEVIN LINCHBAUGH
123 North Main Street
Fairfax, VA 22322
(703) 888-9999

OBJECTIVE

Senior level program management position with an aerospace firm where mature leadership and extensive aviation experience will be used for developing new aircraft systems.

SUMMARY

Over 20 years of program management experience. Demonstrated success as an Aircraft Systems Manager; Air Station Operations Officer, Executive Officer, and Commanding Officer. Fixed and rotary wing pilot. Instill loyalty and a commitment to excellence.

Skills include:

- TEAM BUILDING
- MARKETING
- CHANGE MANAGEMENT

- COMMUNICATIONS
- SCHEDULING
- ADMINISTRATION

PROFESSIONAL ACCOMPLISHMENTS

Team Building

As Commanding Officer, operated with 1/3 fewer aircraft, a 40% lower budget, and 10% fewer employees than any other Coast Guard Air Station, yet exceeded readiness standard by 7.1%. Also, achieved an aircraft availability rate of 78%, exceeding fleet-wide average by 13 points.

As Operations Officer and Commanding Officer, delivered over 10,000 accident-free flight hours by setting high standards, motivating crews, and achieving high levels of training.

Change Management

As Commanding Officer, safely transitioned unit from the HH-52A helicopter to the HH-65A helicopter, flew all scheduled program hours, met operational commitments during height of Search and Rescue (SAR) season with one-third of employees away for training. Completed advanced training for pilots, aircrew, and maintenance employees at unit.

As Operations Officer, coordinated unit's downsizing and extremely successful HH-3F transition at height of SAR season; completed 2 weeks ahead of schedule; managed all pilot and airmen training; met all operational contingents.

Scheduling

Managed program introduction of 41 business jets (HLJ-25A) into Coast Guard service, including pilot and aircrew training. Rescheduled aircraft and employees to maintain schedule and operational capabilities when faced with availability rates 50% below projections.

Managed the Coast Guard's HU-16E and HC-131A fleets. Kept these aging aircraft in service until HU-25A deliveries began. Overcame problems with fuel supply, corrosion, etc. to maintain operational capabilities.

Marketing   As Commanding Officer, increased productivity and reduced training overhead by aggressively marketing our services to local public safety agencies.

As Operations Officer, marketed services to government agencies in 5 states, increased operational productivity 70%. Reduced training overhead 28%.

EDUCATION

B.S., Aeronautical Engineering, Ohio State University, 1980

Senior Welder

Available: January 20XX

DANA WILLIAMS
100 Berry Drive
Groton, CT 05500
(860) 432-1066

OBJECTIVE: Senior welder position for a large shipbuilding company where demonstrated expertise can be used to expand the range of client services.

SUMMARY OF QUALIFICATIONS

- 8 years of military service as a welder, pipefitter, shipfitter, instructor, leader, and supervisor.
- Experienced working from complex plans, blueprints, and sketches in conjunction with fabricating or repairing existing or new equipment of steel structures.
- Excellent interpersonal communication skills.
- Work well independently and as a team member.

WORK EXPERIENCE

United States Navy, 1991-Present

- Identify metals using a variety of methods from continuous identification system to spark configuration.
- Strictly adhere to all safety procedures and regulations associated with cutting welding, and with all shop equipment.
- Administer and perform formal preventive and corrective maintenance program which decreased maintenance cost and equipment failures by 50%.
- Hands-on supervisor and senior technician directly responsible for all aspects of safety, repair, maintenance of 17 different types of steel structures and piping.
- Assess job order and assign personnel according to capabilities, ensuring all work is completed in a timely and professional manner.

EDUCATION AND TRAINING

Bachelors Degree (Candidate, 2001), Liberal Arts, Boston University
Welder, Journeyman License, 1995

Relevant training:

— General Maintenance Welding
— Prevention of Sexual Harassment
— Non-Nuclear Power Plant Component Welding

— Sewage and Sanitation Systems
— Supervision and Management
— Metallurgical Theory

Senior Welder

CHRIS THOMAS
2813 Lincoln Lane
San Diego, CA 98031
W: (206) 918-7623 / H: (206) 231-8710
ThomasC@aol.com

OBJECTIVE

Welding position for a company seeking experienced, dedicated welders to improve their business through on-time delivery and a commitment to excellence.

QUALIFICATIONS SUMMARY

Over 5 years of first-hand experience as a welder for the U.S. Navy. Trained and proficient in the use and care of various types of welding equipment, including torch tips and fill rods. Accomplished ship welder who enjoys physical work in both team and individual settings. Persevere until jobs are done right.

WORK HISTORY

Senior Welder, **Naval Base Norfolk, 1995-Present**

Led a team of 7 welders responsible for welding ship hulls and other components. Provided advanced training in the safe use and maintenance of welding equipment. Performed more complex welding tasks under minimal supervision.

Welder, **Long Beach, CA, 1991-1994**

Performed basic welding functions. Continuously improved welding techniques while working under the supervision of more experienced welders. Applied training in cutting, brazing, and heat treating of metal parts. Forged and repaired over 75 line items.

EDUCATION & TRAINING

Advanced Welding, Naval Base Norfolk, VA, 1995
Introduction to Welding, Naval Base Norfolk, VA, 1991
Thomas Jefferson High School, Oklahoma City, Oklahoma, 1990

Software Engineer

Available: May 20XX

DAVID M. JACKSON
8841 Greensboro Drive
Bedford, MA 01755
W: 617-632-1343 / H: 617-232-3212

OBJECTIVE

Software engineering position for a small to mid-sized firm where information technology skills can be used in all phases of software development life-cycle.

SUMMARY OF QUALIFICATIONS

Software Engineer with over 10 years experience in the U.S. Air Force. Skilled in the design and development of large-scale, object-oriented software applications. Demonstrated expertise in C, C++, and SQL programming languages. Experience includes systems analysis and programming in hardware environments ranging from desktops to IBM mainframes. Expert software trainer with strong interpersonal and communication skills. Recognized as a skilled programmer who can rapidly adapt to a variety of challenging environments.

PROFESSIONAL EXPERIENCE

Software Engineer, Hanscom Air Force Base, MA, 1998-Present
Developed custom software applications using 3rd and 4th generation programming languages (e.g., C, C++). Hands-on experience in the use of CASE and other information engineering tools. Reduced projected software development time 25% through effective software module reuse.

Systems Analyst, Travis Air Force Base, CA, 1995-1997
Co-wrote the specifications for a large-scale software system designed to provide automated logistics support. Modular, top-down design enabled programmers to concurrently work on different subsystems. Disciplined approach was credited with saving the government over $55,000.

Senior Computer Programmer, Travis Air Force Base, CA, 1991-1994
Designed and developed complex software applications involving the transport of air passengers using the "C" programming language. Innovative software design was credited for decreasing development time by 23%. Assisted in the implementation and fielding of the software modules at over 15 Air Force bases where manifests had previously been done manually. Provided training to over 225 users at bases worldwide.

Computer Programmer, Travis Air Force Base, CA, 1988-1991
Designed and developed COBOL-2 software applications that increased the efficiency of personnel processing actions affecting the records of approximately 8,000 military personnel. Programming was done on an IBM 3090 mainframe running MVS/TSO. Received Air Force commendation medal for saving the government over $25,000 in labor costs annually.

EDUCATION AND TRAINING

A.A., Computer Programming, College of the Air Force, 1994
Special Courses and Seminars: Systems Analysis, Programming in "C++", Object Oriented Programming and Design, 1992

Staff Recruiter

Available: June 20XX

MARY TYLER
2122 Maryland Avenue
Fort Meade, MD 20311
W: (333) 222-3334 / H: (333) 555-4444
TylerM@aol.com

OBJECTIVE

In-house staff recruiter for an international consulting firm needing assistance in attracting and recruiting high quality professional staff.

SUMMARY OF QUALIFICATIONS

Resourceful military recruiting specialist with over 7 years experience. Exceptional interpersonal skills demonstrated in several successful assignments as a recruiter. Adept salesperson accustomed to meeting and exceeding demanding recruitment targets. Strong communicator with polished interpersonal skills.

PROFESSIONAL EXPERIENCE

Senior Recruiter, Baltimore, MD, 1997-Present
Exceeded target enlistment goals by 23%. Recruited high quality (Category I) candidates at the highest rate ever recorded in the state of Maryland. Recognized by the Eastern Region recruiting officer for the outstanding results attained. Received Navy Recruiter of the Year award for 1996.

Recruiting Specialist, Dallas, TX, 1995-1997
Totally revamped the Dallas recruiting program. Aggressively identified and recruited candidates from diverse ethnic backgrounds. Ensured recruitment candidates understood the responsibilities and rewards of Naval service. Raised percentage of recruits with high school degrees by 21% over 3 years.

Personnel Specialist, Naval Air Station, Oceana, VA, 1991-1994
Assisted in the coordination and distribution of Naval policies related to recruiting. Quickly learned all facets of the recruitment business. Rapidly comprehended complex personnel matters in minimal time. Recommended for early promotion and assignment as a Naval recruiter.

EDUCATION & TRAINING

A.A., Personnel Administration, Towson State University, MD, 1995
Naval Recruiters School, Norfolk, VA, 1995
Basic Training, Charleston, SC, 1992

Systems Engineer

Available: July 20XX

JEFFREY P. McCORMICK

1900 Novak Street   Office: (703) 903-2245
Carlton, Virginia 22400   Residence: (703) 432-1234

Objective:

Systems engineering position for an engineering consulting firm where technical skills and proven management expertise will further enhance the firm's reputation for excellence.

Summary of Qualifications:

Talented executive with proven skills in systems engineering, design engineering, installation team supervision, and budget management. Extensive experience working with leaders of key organizations to facilitate project implementation. Superb negotiating skills to resolve issues and ensure successful project implementation. Ability to hire and supervise large, talented, and motivated staff. Aggressive at identifying and resolving inefficient procedures.

Professional Experience:

Computer Network Systems Analyst
Pentagon, Washington, DC, November 1998-Present
Office of Secretary of Defense

> Responsible for computer network management and data traffic analysis for a computer networking system consisting of a fiber optic baseband Ethernet backbone supporting 10 subnets arranged in a star/bus topology. System provides office automation, file transfer, electronic mail, calendar, and various other functions, to over 4,000 users, through four communications protocols: Transmission Control Protocol/Internet Protocol (TCP/IP), Xerox Network System (XNS), Novell Interpacket Exchange (IPX), and Digital Network (DecNet). Directly responsible for monitoring system errors and difficulties, engineering solutions, ordering equipment, and working with commercial vendors to implement.

Deputy Commander
Osan Air Base, Korea, 1992-1994

> Directed operation and maintenance (O&M) of vital communications and computer systems supporting 15,000 people. Managed 680 people, $2.5 million budget, and equipment assets worth $200 million. Developed emergency evacuations and operational plans for imminent natural disaster—subsequent implementation proved flawless. Planned and supervised removal of Department of Defense communications assets after volcanic eruptions. Involved planning to satisfy ongoing communications requirements, developing removal schedules, making team assignments, identifying budgeting methods, and arranging equipment transportation. Directly supervised 230-person workforce consisting of civilian contractors, foreign nationals, and military personnel.

Director of Communications
New Boston Air Force Station, New Hampshire, 1993-1994

Directed operations and maintenance of communications and computer systems supporting satellite operations. Directly supervised 23 people. Managed annual budget of $1.5 million and equipment assets worth $10 million. Developed and implemented plan to merge two organizations. Reduced manpower by 10% and administrative costs by 20% by upgrading computer systems. Worked with home office to validate requirement for new telephone switching equipment. Engineered solution, identified acquisition methods, obtained funding, and resolved contracting issues.

Commander
Zweibrucken Air Base, Germany, 1989-1992

Responsible for engineering, procurement, manufacturing, and installation of command post voice and data communications throughout Europe. Controlled annual budget of $2 million and warehouse stock exceeding $2 million. Supervised 150 employees. Turned a faltering, inefficient organization around in 3 months with dedicated group of professionals. Ensured functional integration of all communications systems, including VHF, UHF, and HF radios, telephone systems, secure communications systems, and teleconferencing equipment. Developed and implemented extensive quality assurance program and created specialized manufacturing and installation teams. Results: quality product, manufacturing costs cut by 30%, travel expenses reduced by 50%.

Executive Officer/Chief of Staff
Tinker Air Force Base, Oklahoma, 1988-1989

Responsible for tasking management staff directing 29 organizations involved in engineering, manufacturing, installation, and maintenance of communications systems throughout the world. Systems included VHF/UHF radios, radio control tower consoles and communications, computer systems, weather equipment and satellite terminals. Developed and implemented procedures for installation team deployment and progress reporting. Increased on-time starts by 20% and eliminated work stoppages. Directed implementation of systems engineering approach for all large projects, eliminating engineering errors and duplication. Provided customers with high quality communications systems.

Communications Systems Engineer
Griffiss Air Force Base, New York, 1986-1987

Designed, procured, and installed complex communications systems using a systems engineering approach. Handpicked as part of elite team of system engineers tasked with upgrading Berlin radar approach control facility and communications systems; served as on-site engineer during installation efforts. Supervised on-site installation teams and developed standard engineering procedures for over 100 locations.

Education:

M.S., Aviation Science, Embry-Riddle Aeronautical University, AZ, 1993
B.S., Electrical Engineering, University of New Hampshire, NH, 1983

Telecommunications Management

JOHN PAYNE
3120 Morningside Drive
Marietta, GA 30303
(716) 888-8888
PayneJ@earthlink.net

OBJECTIVE

Management position with an aggressive, multi-national telecommunications firm where leadership skills and telecommunications experience will assist in capturing market share.

AREAS OF EXPERTISE

Leadership: Motivated and inspired staff to excel in tasks involving the installation and maintenance of mobile communication systems. Ensured effectiveness of the unit through intensive training program. Cited for exceptionally high level of readiness under very demanding conditions.

Communications: Assisted in the installation, operation, and maintenance of communication systems during numerous field training exercises. Continuously sought ways to improve the effectiveness of the training and communications knowledge of the training participants. Employed both team-based and individual instruction. Advised senior managers on alternative solutions to communication challenges.

Project Management: Coordinated the acquisition of communications equipment and spare parts. Assisted in the translation of communications manuals into German, thereby facilitating training with host country forces.

WORK EXPERIENCE

Senior Communications Manager: Camp Lejuene, NC, 1998-Present
Communications Instructor: Quantico, VA, 1995-1997
Project Manager: Quantico, VA, 1991-1994
Communications Center Operator: Camp Lejuene, NC, 1989-1991
Communications Technician: Twentynine Palms, CA, 1985-1988

EDUCATION & TRAINING

B.S., Communications (Candidate, 2000), University of Maryland
Field Radio Operators School, U.S. Marine Corps, 1989
High Frequency Communication Center School, U.S. Marine Corps, 1980

Telecommunications Specialist

CHRIS R. KELLY
112 Oleander Road
Quantico, VA 21221
W: (777) 795-1467 / H: (777) 775-1988

OBJECTIVE

A Local Area Network administrator position where LAN skills and knowledge will improve the range of services offered by a small to mid-sized telecommunications firm located in the Southeast.

HIGHLIGHT OF QUALIFICATIONS

- Telecommunications professional with over 12 years experience in the installation, operation, and maintenance of local area networks.
- Expertise in local and wide area networks, intra-networking, and network management.
- Demonstrated knowledge of telecommunication protocols, including TCP/IP and IPX. Extensive experience in Banyan Vines and Novell networks.
- Designed and installed LANs of various configurations and topologies.
- Expert troubleshooter adept at solving complex communication problems.
- **Microsoft Certified Network Engineer.**

AREAS OF EXPERTISE

Network Administration: Installed and administered Banyan Vines LANs that interconnected 100 microcomputer users in an MS Windows environment. Expertly employed network management software to optimize network performance. Upgraded communications equipment and operating system software in a manner that minimized disturbances in LAN operations. Maintained accurate list of authorized users. Controlled passwords for direct and remote access to the LAN. Hands-on experience with many communication protocols.

Communications Training: Provided classroom and 1-on-1 telecommunications training for the organization's 200+ computer users. Instructed staff on the use of various applications, including electronic mail (cc:Mail), Internet/World Wide Web, and office automation software (Microsoft Office). Developed course curriculum and taught specialized courses. Received Marine Corps Achievement medal

Computer Operations: Maintained large tape and disk library for 300-staff organization in an IBM mainframe environment. Coordinated activities and briefed senior operations managers on important issues. Interfaced with the organization's staff members to answer computer-related questions. Facilitated mainframe connection by installing Etherlink processor cards in IBM-compatible personal computers. Maintained accurate inventory of computer and peripheral equipment valued at $1.5 million.

EMPLOYMENT HISTORY

Computer Operations Supervisor, Henderson Hall, VA, 1995-Present
Network Supervisor, Cherry Point, NC, 1991-1994
Computer Network Specialist, San Diego, CA, 1986-1990

EDUCATION

B.S. (Candidate, 2001), Information Systems, George Mason University, Fairfax, VA
A.A., Computer Technology, North Carolina State University, 1995

Telecommunications Specialist

Available: June 20XX

JENNIFER R. JOEL
112 Oleander Road
Mystic, UT 85220
Home: (801) 795-1467 / Work: (801) 775-1988
JoelJ@erols.com

OBJECTIVE

Network administrator position with a startup telecommunications firm where certified expertise in LAN installation and configuration will enhance the firm's ability to deliver technically sound solutions.

HIGHLIGHTS OF QUALIFICATIONS

- **Novell Certified Network Engineer (CNE).**
- Five years of hands-on experience installing Windows NT and Novell networks.
- Expertise in numerous communication protocols, including X.25 and TCP/IP.
- Skilled in recognizing and troubleshooting network problems quickly and efficiently.

RELEVANT EXPERIENCE

Network Administrator, Fort Stewart, GA, 1998-Present

- Administered 150-terminal, 200-user Novell Network.
- Managed user mail groups in an efficient manner.
- Controlled network access through password and other authentication techniques.
- Tuned network for optimal performance; balanced network loads as appropriate.
- Solved user networking difficulties in a patient, caring manner.

Network Instructor, Fort Lee, VA, 1994-1997

- Trained users to be self-sufficient on a 100-terminal, 200-user LAN:
  — Instructed on the Windows 95 operating system
  — Instructed students on the Novell network operating system
  — Taught the Microsoft electronic mail program
- Taught advanced word processing and desktop publishing, using the latest versions of Microsoft Word and Aldus Page Maker.

EDUCATION AND TRAINING

B.S., Computer Information Systems, University of Georgia, 1999
Novell Network Installation and Administration training, 1997

Telecommunications Specialist

Available: January 20XX

CHARLES A. LINCOLN
32 Virginia Ave
Portsmouth, VA 23032
W: (803) 111-1111 / H: (803) 888-2222
LincolnC@aol.com

OBJECTIVE	A telecommunications specialist position where my sonar and radar experience will benefit a rapidly expanding firm seeking to enhance its range of professional services.

QUALIFICATIONS SUMMARY

MANAGEMENT	■ Managed a staff of 15 U.S. Navy radar specialists ■ Planned, scheduled, and evaluated radar and sonar training for new technicians. Over 95% receiving rating of acceptable or higher. ■ Assigned staff and determined work priorities; provided technical advice and assistance. ■ Prepared reports, correspondence, and technical instructions.
RADIO COMMUNICATIONS	■ Received and transmitted over 1,000 radio messages from ship-to-shore and ship-to-ship. ■ Detected and tracked position, direction, and speed of aircraft, ships, submarines, and missiles on a 24-hour basis under all weather conditions. ■ Set up and operated radar equipment. ■ Monitored early warning air defense systems. Stayed alert to interference, jamming, and masking techniques.
SONAR	■ Expert in sonar operations; logged over 7,000 hours under all weather conditions. ■ Used sonar equipment to monitor passage of friendly ships and detect presence of foreign vessels. Demonstrated constant vigilance and concentration in high stress environments. ■ Maintained 100% accurate log of events at sea.

EMPLOYMENT HISTORY

Operations Superintendent, Norfolk, VA, 1998-Present
Radar Supervisor, Norfolk, VA, 1995-1997
Radar Operator, San Diego, CA, 1992-1994
Sonar Operator, Rota, Spain, 1989-1991
Apprentice Sonar Operator, Norfolk, VA, 1986-1988

EDUCATION & TRAINING

A.A. Naval Oceaneering, Virginia State University, 1996

Trainer

Available: July 20XX

KELLY RODRIGUEZ
100 Packard Dr.
Groton, CT 06300
(860) 213-4657

OBJECTIVE

A training position where a strong blend of technical expertise and propensity to train will enable a firm to rapidly enhance the technical depth of its staff.

SUMMARY OF QUALIFICATIONS

- Over 8 years training and experience operating and maintaining Naval nuclear propulsion plants and electrical generation/distribution systems.
- Experience in adult education, technical training, and program management/development.
- Outstanding technical background in power plant operations and maintenance supervision.
- Strong interpersonal skills, meticulous administrator, and an enthusiastic instructor.
- Excel in either individual or team-based setting.
- Fluent in Spanish

WORK EXPERIENCE

United States Navy, 1991-Present

Instructor

- Train junior and senior staff in electrical theory, operating procedures, maintenance techniques, and safety precautions.
- Compile a comprehensive exam bank, write and administer exams, report results to department head.

Program Manager/Developer

- Assess division's training needs, identify weaknesses, develop and implement short-range and long-range training plans.
- Administer qualification program, assign goals, track progress, and verify individuals' compliance with qualification requirements.
- Confer with chain of command and administrators of local community college, arrange for college level English course to be taught to crew members, expanding crew's educational opportunities.

"His meticulous administration and outstanding effort as Electrical Division Training Petty Officer ensured the highest quality training."—Rear Admiral A. C. Hogan

EDUCATION

B.S., Education, Southern Illinois University, 1991

Transportation

Available: June 20XX

JOHN BECKETT
123rd Street
Las Vegas, NV 12345
(333) 123-4567
BeckettJ@aol.com

OBJECTIVE

Facilities Director for a large manufacturing plant where the application of experience-proven management expertise will result in improved operating efficiency and profit margins.

SUMMARY OF QUALIFICATIONS

Twenty-year Naval career with expertise in personnel management within large organizations. Experience in executive leadership positions managing organizations up to 300 people with total budgets in excess of $3 million annually. Extensive hands-on experience in facilities maintenance, organizational development, training, and time management. Strong communication and interpersonal skills.

ACHIEVEMENTS

Chief, Sealift Transportation, U.S. Atlantic Command, 1999-Present
- Planned and executed strategic sealift throughout the Atlantic region. Efficiently managed annual sealift exercise of $13 million.
- Coordinated with military and commercial shipping industry to successfully demonstrate intermodal transportation and significantly improved U.S. strategic deployment capabilities.

Senior Staff Officer, Logistics Squadron One, 1994-1997
- Directed executive staff of 35 employees. Responsible for training and evaluating ships' operational readiness and engineering.
- Hands-on engineering training experience with various class of Navy ships.

Executive Officer, 1991-1993
- Directed the planning, scheduling, and tracking of day-to-day operations for a large ship with five departments and 300 personnel.
- Guided and trained ship's crew on the proper use of Personnel Qualification System and Maintenance Materiel Management.

Main Propulsion Assistant, 1987-1990
- Planned and executed a $10 million shipyard overhaul for the main propulsion department.
- Effectively led the maintenance and training efforts that resulted in highly successful Light Off Exams and Operational Propulsion Plant Exams.

Engineer Officer, USS Cushing, 1985-1987
- Planned and executed strategic sealift throughout the Atlantic region. Efficiently managed annual sealift exercise of $13 million.
- Coordinated with military and commercial shipping industry to successfully demonstrate intermodal engineering.

Junior Officer Development Assignments, 1980-1984

EDUCATION

M.S., Organizational Effectiveness, University of Southern California, 1998
Naval Postgraduate School, Monterey, CA, 1991

SPECIAL QUALIFICATIONS

- Top Secret Security Clearance
- Surface Warfare Officer

Transportation Management

PATRICK M. SIMMONS
2913 West Broad St.
Fairfax, VA 22313
(703) 888-3333
SimmonsP@erols.com

OBJECTIVE

Transportation Management position where long-haul transportation experience can be fully utilized to the benefit of a national trucking company.

QUALIFICATIONS SUMMARY

TRANSPORTATION
- Directed the daily planning, coordination, and supervision of a 177-person transportation unit.

OPERATIONS
- Efficiently managed a 100-vehicle fleet, whose value exceeded $5 million, with no measurable losses.
- Planned, coordinated, and controlled the pickup and delivery of over 3 tons of cargo on time and under stressful conditions.
- Managed hazardous cargo certification requirements, vehicle maintenance, and safety deadlines with ease.

MANAGEMENT
- Supervised staffs of from 5 to 177 personnel involved in various transportation activities. Effective management resulted in successful accomplishment of projects within budgetary and time constraints.
- Focus on team building and unit esprit increased staff retention rates from 30% to 60% over a two-year period.
- Evaluated individual and team performance, providing positive reinforcement and constant encouragement.

TRAINING
- Revised curriculum of transportation training program, improving the student pass rate by 20%.
- Delivered educational presentations for audiences ranging from 10 to 200; consistently rated as "excellent" guest lecturer.

EMPLOYMENT HISTORY

Transportation Director, Fort Eustis, VA, 1995-Present
Transportation Staff Officer, Fort Bragg, NC, 1991-1994
Transportation Officer, Fort Eustis, VA, 1988-1990
Student, Fort Eustis, VA, 1987

EDUCATION & TRAINING

M.A., Transportation Management, University of Southern California, 1994
B.S., Statistics, University of Maryland, 1987

Warehouse Supervisor

Available: February 20XX

DANA PHILLIPS
2813 Lincoln Lane
Madison, CT 02521
W: (206) 918-7623 / H: (206) 231-8710
PhillipsD@aol.com

OBJECTIVE

Position in inventory management for a large department store where skills and experience in warehouse operations can be used to improve efficiency and profitability.

QUALIFICATIONS SUMMARY

- Skilled inventory stocking specialist with over 6 years experience.
- Disciplined, dedicated supply professional trained in proper procedures for shipping, receiving, storing, and issuing stock.
- Extensive experience handling medicine, food, and other perishable supplies.
- Knowledgeable about stock control and accounting procedures.
- Effective in team or individual-based settings.

EMPLOYMENT HISTORY

Stock Control Specialist, **9th District, Cleveland, OH, 1998-Present**

Locate and catalog supply items in a timely manner using a computer-based tracking system. Improved stock verification procedures, resulting in no discrepancies found over a two-year period. Load, unload, and move stock using forklifts and hand trucks. Maintain accurate records on incoming and outgoing stock, which comprises over 1,000 line items.

Stock Control Clerk, **Support Center, Elizabeth City, NJ, 1994-1997**

Designed innovative system to better organize storage space for incoming stock of 5,500 line items. Closely followed established procedures for shipping, receiving, storing, and issuing stock. Verified quantity and description of stock received against bills of lading, ensuring 100% accuracy. Maintained accurate records of quantities on hand. Received commendation medal for results achieved.

EDUCATION & TRAINING

A.A., Business Administration, Ohio State, 1999
Materials Management Course, Fort Lee, VA, 1995
Army Basic Training, Fort Lee, VA, 1994

7

Electronic Resumes and Your Job Search

AS TECHNOLOGY CONTINUES TO ADVANCE AT LIGHTNING speed, job seekers and corporations will make ever increasing use of the Internet and other electronic communication mediums. For you, the job seeker, distribution media such as electronic mail and the World Wide Web offer a tremendous opportunity to efficiently advertise your skills and qualifications to prospective employers worldwide. As corporations increasingly rely on such technology to find qualified candidates, you must understand how to use electronic media to gain maximum advantage. In this chapter we explain how to create and distribute an electronic resume in its myriad forms to prospective employers.

Enter the Information Age

Recent advances in telecommunications and information technology have significantly impacted our everyday lives. With the advent of the Internet and its prolific World Wide Web (WWW), we can now inexpensively engage in job hunting activities that span the globe in a matter of seconds rather than days, weeks, or months. This ability to quickly, easily, and cheaply transmit one's employment qualifications anywhere worldwide has important ramifications. First, it has expanded the pool of employment candidates vying for open positions. No longer is an employer constrained to advertising in a local newspaper or magazine. Now employers can broadcast the opportunity to a much larger audience using a company web site or Internet job site. With this enhanced exposure comes increased competition for available jobs.

The increased reliance by companies on electronic media like the WWW requires that you, the job seeker, understand this technology and be comfortable using it. Fortunately, the technology is not difficult to learn and the tools you need to effectively advertise your skills and qualifications are readily available. We'll give you all the ammunition you will need—it's up to you to execute. Shall we begin?

Essential Equipment

To participate in today's electronic job market, you will need access to four items—a computer, a modem, a word processing program, and a printer. If you don't have this equipment at home, don't despair. There are several free or low cost alternatives available to you as a transitioning service member. We suggest starting at your local military transition assistance office (ACAP, Family Service Center, Career Resource Management Center, or Family Support Center). Most will have the necessary equipment in their facility. If this equipment is not available or you are no longer authorized access, visit a local office services store like Kinkos, which will allow you to use such equipment for a minimal fee. With regard to word processing software, the two most widely used packages are Microsoft Word™ and WordPerfect™. Either can be used to transform your conventional resume, whether in improved chronological or combination format, into an electronic resume. Later in the chapter we describe how to accomplish this transformation. If you need help in using the word processing software, we suggest asking a friend or a military career counselor for assistance.

Conventional vs. Electronic Resumes

Before we compare traditional and electronic resumes, it's important to have a basic understanding of each. As previously discussed in Chapter 6, a conventional resume follows a traditional resume format, the most common being improved chronological, or combination. An electronic resume, as its name implies, is a resume that's in electronic form. It's an electronic document. As we discuss below, an electronic resume can take several different forms. However, whether a resume is in a conventional or electronic form, the purpose is the same—to accurately and succinctly convey your skills, abilities, and interests to prospective employers in a manner that will motivate them to learn more about you through a personal interview.

The comparison between conventional and electronic resumes varies depending upon the form of the electronic resume. We'll assume for the time being that the electronic resume currently exists as an ASCII text file. When in this form, the conventional and electronic resumes are similar in structure, both containing the core subcategories of header, work history, professional accomplishments, and education. The two types of resumes differ primarily in how one's work history/accomplishments are presented. In the conventional resume, most sentences or phrases start with an action verb. In the ASCII formatted electronic resume, the focus is on the selective use of keywords. Additional differences are discussed later when we discuss ASCII text resumes in depth.

When compared in this context, the four major advantages electronic resumes have over conventional resumes follow:

1. **Speed:** Whereas sending a conventional resume through a mail service such as the U.S. Postal Service will take one or more days, an electronic resume can be sent almost anywhere worldwide in a matter of seconds. Information technology enables the employer to quickly scan hundreds of resumes for those job applicants whose skills and qualifications match the company's job openings.

2. **Cost:** Assuming you have access to the Internet and the computer equipment listed above, the cost of sending an electronic resume is minimal. If you have a personal Internet account through an Internet service provider, your monthly Internet access costs will be in the vicinity of $10 to $20; transmitting a resume to an Internet site is usually free. Military transition sites do not charge for transmitting a resume as an electronic mail message or attachment over the Internet.

3. **Extended Presence:** Because of the global array of interconnected networks that exist today, you can send your electronic resume almost anywhere worldwide. Once received at an Internet web site, hiring managers, regardless of physical location, can access your resume over an extended period.

4. **Ease of Access:** Because the resume information is stored in electronic form, hiring managers or recruiters can use specially designed search software to identify those candidates whose resume matches one or

more search criteria. Then with the high quality resume tracking systems available today, hiring managers can easily retrieve the entire resume at their desktop for viewing or printing.

Electronic Mediums

There are several mediums for creating and distributing electronic resumes. Here we discuss four types of electronic resumes, starting with the scanning of a printed resume and ending with a high-tech multimedia resume. In the subsections that follow, we review the chronology of the electronic resume and show how improvements in information technology are continually making the job search "matching" process ever more efficient.

Scanning

Beginning in the mid-1980s, a popular method for creating an electronic resume was to scan a conventional resume in paper form into an electronic file. In the late 1980s, OCR (optical character recognition) software was introduced. After the printed text was scanned, the file would be passed through OCR software, which would attempt to interpret the printed text and convert it into a word processable file. To increase the likelihood of the OCR software working as intended, the resume writer was strongly encouraged to modify his or her resume to enhance readability. These changes would include:

- removal of special (non-ASCII) characters, such as italics and bold
- use of a plain font like Helvetica
- use of a larger font size such as 12 or 14 point
- deletion of boxes or shading
- use of high quality paper conducive to scanning
- re-writing one's work history and professional accomplishments using keywords

The resume format would continue to contain the same subcategories found in conventional resume formats. For resumes that were to be scanned into a job bank database, the "Objective" subcategory was often replaced with a "Keyword Preface," which was chock-full of keywords in the form of nouns or noun-centric phrases.

Once the resume information was successfully stored in the database, specially written software programs would be used to search for key words of interest to prospective employers. Such an approach had the appeal of using computer technology to efficiently search large numbers of resumes in a matter of seconds. However, there were obvious drawbacks. Most significant was the limited matching ability of this technology since it was based almost exclusively on the use of simple keyword matches. Nonetheless, some companies were able to build successful businesses as "job banks" that stored and retrieved scanned resumes for employers. However, with the explosion of the World Wide Web in the mid-1990s, interest in offline resume database services using scanned resumes has waned considerably. One should not deduce, however, that companies no longer scan resumes—many do. In fact, given the high volume of solicited and unsolicited resumes received by many medium- to large-sized companies, numerous HR departments use OCR software to scan resumes in order to better manage the resume screening, storage, and retrieval processes. Since you may not know whether or not your resume will be scanned, it's safer to assume that it will, especially if you are applying for a job that pays less than $50,000 a year. Therefore, you should prepare your resume so it can be scanned to your advantage. The following rules-of-thumb should assist you in creating such a resume.

ASCII Text Files

With the advent of user-friendly word processing software and the increased use of electronic mail (thanks in large part to the reduced cost and ease-of-use of the Internet), a popular distribution method in the early 1990s was to send an electronic resume in ASCII text format. The conversion of a conventionally formatted resume into an ASCII text file is a relatively simple process. We assume that you have all the necessary computer equipment described earlier and have created your own conventional resume using word processing software. Since you already have the conventional resume in electronic form, i.e., as a Microsoft Word or WordPerfect file, the steps in transforming your resume into an ASCII text file are relatively straightforward:

1. **Open your current conventional resume using your word processing software.** Using the "File" pull-down menu and "Save As" option, save the file as a standard DOS text file under a different name, e.g., *resume.txt*. Recent versions of both Microsoft Word and WordPerfect give allow you to save a file in ASCII format. The analogous word processing programs for Macintosh computers work the same way.

2. **Strip the resume of those special characters not supported by the ASCII character set, i.e., bold, italics, lines, shading, boxing, etc.** Use characters such as an "*" or ">" to set off your work history or professional accomplishments entries. If you are uncertain as to which characters are included in the ASCII character set, simply look at your keyboard. Any of the keys you can press (except for the function keys) are part of the ASCII character set.

3. **Make good use of white space.** As with a conventional resume, it's important that your resume not appear cluttered. To help achieve this effect, use paragraphs. Remember to move text using the space bar rather than tabs, which will disappear when your file is saved in text format.

4. **Limit the number of characters per line to 60.** By pressing the Enter or Return key instead of allowing the characters to wrap to the next line, you can cause the line to break where desired. In so doing you will ensure that the ASCII resume looks good when received at the other end.

5. **As with the conventional resume, we recommend limiting the length of the resume to two pages.** Given that the resume may be viewed electronically, it's important also that the resume break by page where intended. You may need to do some experimentation to achieve the desired effect.

The ultimate success of the resume in ASCII text file rests not in its format but in its substance. The proper selection of keywords to describe your work accomplishments and skills is particularly important. To enhance your probability for success, you must build on your networking and research activities to select keywords that are common to your desired industry and appropriate for your background. An aesthetically pleasing electronic resume that uses industry common words that accurately reflect your background will give you the competitive edge.

When you have finished developing your ASCII text resume file, we recommend sending it to a friend and asking him or her to review it for content and confirm it retained its format. Such testing is the only foolproof method of guaranteeing you have correctly formatted the ASCII file for transmission. Once you have proven that the electronic resume file displays as intended, you can send it to a prospective employer via electronic mail. Remember, however, to precede your resume with an electronic cover letter just as you would if sending the resume via regular mail. (We talk more about the cover letter in the next chapter.) In addition to sending the prospective employer the electronic resume, we also recommend sending your conventional resume on bond paper through the postal service. While it may take a couple days to reach the hiring manager, you will be reminding him or her of your interest in the position and providing a more attractively formatted resume for review.

The two versions of the resume (Samuel Adams) presented on pages 180-181 show how a conventional resume (page 180) can be transformed into an resume in ASCII text format (page 181). While the conventional resume is more aesthetically pleasing, the ASCII resume contains the same substantive information.

In addition to the rules-of-thumb for developing and distributing ASCII formatted resumes, the following "Do's" and "Don'ts" are relevant to electronic resumes:

Electronic Resume "Do's"

- **Do** use 12 to 14 point monospaced fonts, such as Arial, Bookman, Courier, Helvetica, or Times.
- **Do** limit the electronic resume length to 1-2 pages.
- **Do** put the most important information first.
- **Do** use industry-common keywords.
- **Do** use synonyms where appropriate.
- **Do** left align headings and indent and align the remainder of the text.
- **Do** set off major sections by capitalizing.
- **Do** include your name on the second page.
- **Do** keep individual lines to 60 characters or less to accommodate differences in screen width.
- **Do** experiment with asterisks, hyphens, and other characters appearing on your keyboard for optimal appearance.
- **Do** use high quality, lightly colored paper, if the resume is to be scanned.

Electronic Resume "Don'ts"

- **Don't** fold the resume. Send it in a 9" x 12" envelope.
- **Don't** use action verbs to emphasize experience and capabilities.

SAMUEL ADAMS
2913 West Broad St.
Fairfax, VA 22313
H: (703) 888-3333 W: (202) 123-4567
AdamsS@erols.com

OBJECTIVE   Supervisory position where aviation maintenance experience can be used to improve the effectiveness and quality of a commercial airline's maintenance operations.

QUALIFICATIONS SUMMARY

MAINTENANCE
- Extensive maintenance experience on a variety of jet aircraft, including the B-1, C-117, and C-130.
- Innovative problem solver who developed efficient methods for ensuring aircraft were maintained at peak levels. Recommended cost cutting measures that saved the Air Force $1.5 million over a 3-year period.
- Developed maintenance checklists and enforced compliance, resulting in a near perfect safety record for all assigned aircraft.

MANAGEMENT
- Evaluated performance of 15 maintenance technicians on a daily basis.
- Developed customized maintenance training program, which resulted in a 98% pass rate for staff under my supervision.
- Executed action-oriented plans, ensuring assigned missions were accomplished on time and within budget.

COMMUNICATION
- Effectively communicated aircraft maintenance tasks to fellow teammates.
- Briefed senior leaders on the readiness status of aircraft.
- Developed innovative plans for repairing defective components.
- Taught aviation maintenance courses to newly assigned staff.

EMPLOYMENT HISTORY

Assistant Director, Maintenance, 79th Tactical Air Wing, Hanscom AFB, 1998-Present
Manager, Aircraft Maintenance, 339th Fighter Squadron, Nellis AFB, NV, 1994-1997
Staff Non-Commissioned Officer, Andrews AFB, MD, 1991-1993
Leader Development Positions, 1980-1990

EDUCATION & TRAINING

A.S. Aircraft Maintenance, Community College of the Air Force, 1997
Aircraft Maintenance Training, Nellis AFB, NV, 1994
Basic Training, Randolph AFB, TX, 1980

SAMUEL ADAMS
2913 West Broad St.
Fairfax, VA 22313
H: (703) 888-3333; W: (202) 123-4567

AdamsS@erols.com

OBJECTIVE

Supervisory position where aviation maintenance experience can be used to
improve the effectiveness and quality of an airline's maintenance operations.

QUALIFICATIONS SUMMARY

MAINTENANCE
> Extensive maintenance experience in a variety of jet aircraft, including the B-1,
C-117, and C-130.
> Innovative problem solver who developed efficient methods for ensuring aircraft
were maintained at peak levels. Recommended cost cutting measures that saved the
Air Force $1.5 million over a 3-year period.
> Developed maintenance checklists and enforced compliance, resulting in a near
perfect safety record for all assigned aircraft.

MANAGEMENT
> Evaluated performance of 15 maintenance technicians on a daily basis.
> Developed customized maintenance training program, which resulted in a 98%
pass rate for staff under my supervision.
> Executed action-oriented plans, ensuring assigned missions were accomplished
on time and within budget.

COMMUNICATION
> Effectively communicated aircraft maintenance tasks to fellow teammates.
> Briefed senior leaders on the readiness status of aircraft. Developed innovative
plans for repairing defective components.
> Taught aviation maintenance courses to newly assigned staff.

EMPLOYMENT HISTORY

Assistant Director, Maintenance, 79th Tactical Air Wing, Hanscom AGB, 1998-
Present
Manager, Aircraft Maintenance, 339th Fighter Squadron, Nellis AFB, NV, 1994-
1997
Staff Non-Commissioned Officer, Andrews AFB, MD, 1991-1994
Leader Development Positions, 1980-1990

EDUCATION & TRAINING

A.S. Aircraft Maintenance, Community College of the Air Force, 1997
Aircraft Maintenance Training, Nellis AFB, NV, 1991
Basic Training, Randolph AFB, TX, 1980

- **Don't** stretch the truth when trying to match your capabilities with industry-common buzzwords
- **Don't** underline, italicize, or shade words.
- **Don't** misspell words.
- **Don't** use fancy fonts.
- **Don't** use boxes.
- **Don't** use columns.
- **Don't** waste space with personal data or a reference statement.

Development of an effective, ASCII-based electronic resume is not difficult. Simply convey your qualifications using keywords common to the industry and structure your resume so that it highlights your strengths. If you follow this guidance and the formatting rules above, we're confident your resume will look good when received by the company or its hiring manager.

Electronic Mail Attachment

Up to this point we've discussed sending the resume to a prospective employer as an electronic mail message. Another option is to send your resume as an attachment to your electronic mail message. When sending a word processed resume file in this manner, you are actually sending a binary file. All this means is that your resume file has been formatted in a particular way, such as in Microsoft's Word or Corel's WordPerfect.

When you send your resume as an attached binary file, the distinction between the conventional resume and electronic resume disappears—it's the same file. However, when you send your resume as an attached file, you risk the recipient not being able to open it for two reasons. First, he or she may not have compatible word processing software and hence cannot open the file. Second, he may use a different on-line services network (for example, you may send the resume using America Online, and he may attempt to open it using a different online service or a different Internet Service Provider and have difficulty reading the file because of file encoding/decoding complexities. One way to avoid this problem is to ask the recipient ahead of time whether he has the ability to read a particular file format. However, this approach might be inappropriate or not feasible. Bottom line—even in this technologically sophisticated age, there are still many conditions that can preclude a seamless transmission of an attached file. We suggest sending both the ASCII formatted resume in the body of the electronic mail message and attach the conventional file, preferably using Microsoft Word. In addition, we recommend sending the hiring manager your conventional resume on bond paper using regular mail. Such redundancy will keep your employment candidacy at the forefront of the prospective employer's mind.

Internet/WWW

An increasingly popular place to distribute your resume these days is on the World Wide Web. While the transmission of your resume via electronic mail most likely uses the Internet, the distribution method described here differs in that you enter the contents of your resume electronically into an Internet/ WWW site job database while connected online. There are two basic alternatives—entering your resume information directly into a particular company's online database or entering your resume information into commercial online employment databases, such as Monster.com, HotJobs.com, Headhunter.net, or CareerWeb.com.

Let's start by focusing on the company alternative. With regard to sending your electronic resume to a particular company, you can naturally send it to them using the distribution methods discussed above, i.e., ASCII text file or electronic mail attachment. Another option not discussed above, though less common, is to send your electronic resume to them on disk. However, many companies now offer (and prefer) a more "high-tech" alternative that enables you to enter your resume information directly into their candidate database while connected to their website through a series of interactive HTML forms, which guide you through the process. While it may sound complicated, in actuality the process is quite simple. What makes this option so appealing to individual companies is that resume information entered in this manner can be easily and rapidly searched across multiple criteria by hiring managers sitting at their desks. Hence, if a company hiring manager was looking for someone with a B.S. degree in Operations Research from Penn State with a graduation year of between 1990 and 1995, the system would display the resumes of only those candidates who met all three conditions. Such a sophisticated approach represents a significant advancement over earlier days when a company would often pay an outside firm to find all candidates whose resume "hit" on a particular keyword or phrase. Now individual companies can perform this function "in-house" at a fraction of the cost and with better results.

Important to note, many large defense contractors like SAIC, EDS, Northrop Grumman, General Dynamics, and Lockheed Martin are increasingly using their own web sites to facilitate the input and later retrieval of employment candidates' resumes. All you must do is know their Internet address, link to their employment page, and follow the instructions for entering your resume information. If you don't know the Internet address (technically known as the URL, or Uniform Resource Locator), simply use a search engine such as Google (*www.google.com*), iWon (*www.iwon.com*), Yahoo! (*www.yahoo.com*), Excite (*www.excite.com*), or AltaVista (*www.altavista.com*) and "surf the web" for the company name of interest. You will most likely find a link to the company's home page. Once there, make sure you add the website to your personal list of URLs using your browser's "Bookmark" feature.

While many companies have websites with links to their employment page, others rely on large, online career centers, such as **Monster.com** (*www.monster.com*), **HotJobs** (*www.hotjobs.com*), **CareerWeb** (*www.cweb.com*), **Headhunter** (*www.headhunter.net*), **CareerBuilder** (*www.careerbuilder.com*), and **America's Job Bank** (*www.ajb.com*), for recruiting personnel. Using these online services, more and more employers post job announcements and search online resume databases for candidates with particular education, skill, and experience profiles. A few sites, such as **FlipDog** (*www.flipdog.com*), troll the Internet for job listings found on the websites of thousands of employers (FlipDog covers more than 50,000 employers). Another site, **Employment911.com** (*www.employment911.com*), trolls 35 employment sites, such as Monster.com, for job postings.

Each day thousands of hiring managers access these online databases in search of candidates meeting their criteria. There is normally no cost to you, the individual job seeker. However, companies almost always pay a fee to gain access to these sites. Consequently, we strongly encourage you to visit their websites and learn more about their services. For a comprehensive listing of career-related websites, see the following books which are available through Impact Publications (see order form at the end of this book):

- *100 Top Internet Job Sites* (Kristina M. Ackley)
- *America's Top Internet Job Sites* (Ron and Caryl Krannich)
- *CareerXroads 2001* (Gerry Crispin and Mark Mehler)
- *Career Exploration on the Internet* (Ferguson)
- *Cyberspace Job Search Kit* (Fred E. Jandt and Mary B. Nemich)
- *Job Searching Online For Dummies* (Pam Dixon)
- *The Guide to Internet Job Searching* (Margaret Riley)

Transitioning military personnel should visit several websites specifically designed to deal with their employment needs, such as *www.greentogray.com*, *www.bluetogray.com*, *www.taonline*, *www.destinygroup.com*, *www.vetjobs.*

com, *www.hire-quality.com*, and *www.military hire.com*. Most of these sites allow you to post your resume, apply for jobs online, and research various military-friendly companies. We include these websites, along with several other employment sites, in the final section of this chapter.

Multi-Media Resume

The final and most advanced resume format is the multimedia resume. Such a resume format requires knowledge of a special computer language called HTML (HyperText Markup Language), the base language of the Internet's World Wide Web. While not overly complex, HTML is foreign to most job seekers and will take some time to learn should you elect to do so. To assist you in converting your current electronic resume into HTML form, there are several software utilities on the market. For example, Microsoft Corporation offers "Internet Assistant," which converts a resume in Microsoft Word format to HTML. Another well known package is titled *Front Page*. Through HTML you can add interest and zest to your resume by including pictures, photos, graphics, sounds, etc. But do you really want to do so? Probably not. Unless you are in search of a high-tech, software-related job, we would discourage you from enriching your multimedia resume to such a degree. For those who are pursuing such a position, we recommend a well designed HTML document that uses only text to describe your interests and qualifications. You can still include "hot links" to a more detailed textual description of some aspect of your background. Such a resume would demonstrate your above-average knowledge of the Internet and its usage.

Such a multimedia resume is normally distributed on the WWW as a personal home page. This means that you would require an Internet Service Provider capable of providing you with the technical facilities needed to host your resume at their Internet site. The cost for having such a high-tech rendition of your electronic resume varies by provider. We suggest looking in the Business or Technology section of your local newspaper for companies advertising such services. While the cost of Internet service varies, expect to pay between $10 and $25 per month. Often, the provider will give you a limited amount of storage space as part of this monthly fee. You could then use this space to store your personal home page, where it could be accessed by anyone worldwide.

If you should elect to create a "home page" and make it accessible via the WWW, we recommend including the Internet address on your paper resume. For example, your Internet address (URL) might appear as follows on your resume: *http://www.aol.com/~adamss.html*. It shows a prospective employer that you are probably Internet savvy. However, for most of our readers, we would not recommend investing the time or resources needed to develop a good looking multimedia resume. We include it here only as an option.

Privacy

Our high-technology world offers us many ways to reveal our employment interests, skills, and abilities to prospective employers worldwide. For people who are currently employed by a private sector firm but interested in seeking "greener pastures" elsewhere, privacy may be a major concern. The ramifications of having a current employer inadvertently discover you are seeking employment outside the firm could be ugly. What precautions should you consider under these circumstances? For starters, you would want to protect your identity by not publishing your name, address, phone numbers, employer's name, or easily recognizable screen address, e.g., JenkinsT@aol.com. Well then, how can anyone send a resume? Here are a few options to consider. First, you could use a Post Office box, which we earlier did not recommend for other reasons. Second, you could have your resume faxed to a commercial business like Mail Boxes Etc., which offers this service at a minimal fee (approximately $1 per page). Third, you could use an unrecognizable screen name or alias as your Internet address. CompuServe, for example, has for many years used numeric User IDs, though they recently introduced the use of alpha characters. If you are an America Online subscriber, you know that they have for many years used name-based User IDs. What you may not know is that they also offer an alias capability, which allows you to take on an unrecognizable name as another User ID at no additional charge. Fourth, you could go through a private placement service such as JOBTRAK (800-999-8725), which protects the confidentiality of currently employed job seekers.

Keep Electronic Resumes in Perspective

The electronic resume can take many forms and be distributed in multiple ways. As you explore the many options available to you, we advise you to take a conservative, yet forward-looking approach. As with the conventional, paper-based resume, make sure you do your homework up-front and carefully think through all the details required to make your electronic resume as powerful in content as your conventional resume. Remember, the intent of an electronic resume is the same as the paper resume—to motivate a prospective employer to learn more about you through a face-to-face interview.

Because of the more intricate nature of the electronic resume, we recommend that you take extra precautions when developing it. If you're creating an ASCII text resume, remember to follow the "Do's" and "Don'ts" on pages 179 and 182. Check to ensure that the keywords you have chosen accurately reflect your background and are terms common to the industry in which you are seeking employment. It's also important to check that your electronic resume retains its intended appearance when sent over the Internet. If you elect to send your resume in conventional form as an e-mail attachment, we suggest you consider calling the intended recipient ahead of time to check the compatibility of word processing software and Internet service provider. Microsoft Word seems to be the standard these days, but you don't know unless you first contact your recipient for information and permission to submit your resume as an attachment. Because e-mail transmission across different networks is not without some degree of risk, we also recommend sending the ASCII formatted resume in the text of the message. Such redundancy will be appreciated and is in your favor.

The Internet is and will continue to be an important venue for distributing your electronic resume. We encourage you to explore the many Internet sites that host employment databases and seek those sites most applicable to your qualifications and job interests. Always make sure to follow up by sending your electronic resume or entering the information online through the company's or on-line career service's employment web page. And should you be seeking a job in a high-tech field, don't forget to explore the potential advantages of posting a multimedia type resume on your own home page.

Key Websites You Should Visit

Numerous websites include useful information for transitioning military personnel. For example, ambitious sites such as **Military.com** (*www.military. com*) function as portals for capturing the attention and purchasing power of the military community. Casting a broad net, they focus on numerous issues relevant to the military community as a whole, from history, family, and finance to jobs, travel, shopping, relocation, and networking. These sites attempt to become one-stop-shops for military personnel and veterans. Other community-wide sites are primarily designed to capture the purchasing power of the military community, such as Ross Perot's **Salute.com** (*www.salute.com* – formerly known as *www.militaryhub.com*), **Maingate.com** (*www.maingate.*

com), and **Military-Net.com** (*www.military-net.com*). Many other military-specific sites primarily focus on job and career issues for transitioning military personnel and veterans. Most of these sites include information, advice, job listings, job banks, and resume databases:

Corporate Gray:	*www.greentogray.com*
	www.bluetogray.com
Transition Assistance Online:	*www.taonline.com*
Destiny Group:	*www.destinygroup.com*
Hire Quality:	*www.hire-quality.com*
Vet Jobs:	*www.vetjobs.com*
Military Hire:	*www.militaryhire.com*

Companies such as Destiny Group and VetJobs either operate the career section for community-wide sites (Destiny Group powers Military.com) or serve as career linkages to other sites (VetJobs with Military-Net; Destiny Group and Taonline with MilitaryPartners.com). Rich with advice and listings, these sites provide lots of opportunities to conduct an online job search.

However, do not limit your online job search just to these military sites. You should explore many of the large online commercial career sites. **Monster.com** (*www.monster.com*), for example, attracts many military personnel and veterans to its very active military message board ("Transition from Military to Civilian Work"). Monster.com also operates the largest commercial resume and employer database on the Internet. You can go directly to their military message board through either of these URLs:

> *http://community.monster.com/boards*
> *http://forums.monster.com/forum.asp?forum=122*

To access numerous military transition job search resources, including online excerpts from our Corporate Gray Series, go to this specialized Monster.com URL for the military:

> *http://content.monster.com/military*

Be sure to explore several major commercial websites where you can acquire job search advice, post your resume online, review job listings, and network for information and advice. Some of our favorite sites, which are relevant for transitioning military personnel, include:

Monster.com:	www.monster.com
CareerBuilder:	www.careerbuilder.com
	www.careerpath.com
NationJob:	www.nationjob.com
FlipDog:	www.flipdog.com
Hot Jobs:	www.hotjobs.com
Vault.com:	www.vault.com
VirtualResume:	www.virtualresume.com
Headhunter.net:	www.headhunter.net
	www.careermosaic.com
America's Job Bank:	www.ajb.org
CareerWeb:	www.careerweb.com
Career Journal:	www.careerjournal.com
Dice:	www.dice.com
Employment911.com:	www.employment911.com
WetFeet.com:	www.webfeet.com
PlanetRecruit:	www.planetrecruit.com
Career.com:	www.career.com
6FigureJobs.com:	www.6figurejobs.com
4Work:	www.4work.com
BestJobsUSA:	www.bestjobsusa.com
BrilliantPeople.com:	www.brilliantpeople.com
Career City:	www.careercity.com
JobOptions:	www.joboptions.com
JobTrak:	www.jobtrak.com
HireAbility:	www.hireability.com
HireStrategy:	www.hirestrategy.com
WashingtonJobs:	www.washingtonjobs.com
JobStar:	www.jobstar.org

If you are interested in auctioning your talents, especially on a freelance basis, check out these novel job auction sites:

Monster.com:	www.talentmarket.monster.com
FreeAgent:	www.freeagent.com
Bid4Geeks:	www.bid4geeks.com
Ants.com:	www.ants.com
eLance.com:	www.elance.com

While the Internet is a great place to post resumes, research jobs and employers, and network for information and advice, it also can be very seductive. Similar to shot-gunning your resume to hundreds of employers, using the Internet to post resumes and respond to electronic job listings may give you a false sense of making progress with your job search. Like a big black sinkhole, it can eat up valuable job search time. Our advice: Set aside "Internet time" for your job search, but don't become obsessed by converting most of your "job search time" to "Internet time."

As you incorporate the Internet into your job search, don't neglect some of the more traditional job search methods that continue to prove effective for transitioning military personnel. Above all, you need to talk with people by phone and in person about what appears on your resume – your objective, skills, and accomplishments. Networking with former friends, colleagues, and commanders continues to yield some of the best job search results. The Internet can assist you with several networking activities, such as finding individuals in your network and communicating your interests, skills, and qualifications by email. Just don't let it become your major approach to the job search.

It is truly an exciting time to be entering the job market. We wish you every success as you employ the tools and techniques discussed in this chapter to find the job that's right for you!

8

Essential Job Search
Letters For Success

WHILE MANY JOB SEEKERS BELIEVE THEIR RESUME IS the most important written product for getting a job, employers often report that a good cover letter is frequently more important to their hiring decisions than the resume. Indeed, cover letters and other types of job search letters can play a critical role in getting invited to a job interview and offered a job. Neglect these letters and you very well may neglect some of the most important elements in your job search.

The most important job search letters are cover, "T," approach, thank-you, and resume. Each can be subdivided into additional types of letters. Let's survey these letters before we examine the details of writing and distributing job search letters to complement and enhance your resume.

Cover Letters

The cover letter is a special type of job search letter. By definition, it always accompanies a resume and usually is targeted toward potential employers.

Employers regularly receive two types of cover letters—targeted and broadcast. Each letter literally provides "cover" for an enclosed resume.

Targeted Cover Letter

The targeted cover letter is the most commonly written job search letter. It is addressed to a specific person and in reference to a position which may or may not be vacant. It may be written in response to a classified ad or vacancy announcement or in reference to a job lead received from a referral.

A targeted cover letter should be specific and oriented toward the needs of the employer. The content of this letter should reflect as much knowledge of the employer and the position as possible. You should emphasize your skills that appear most compatible with the needs of the employer and the requirements of the position. You should tell the employer why he or she should take time to talk with you by telephone or meet you in person to further discuss your qualifications. Your letter should communicate both professional and personal qualities about you—that you are first and foremost a competent **and** likable individual.

> *A targeted cover letter should be oriented toward the needs of the employer. It should reflect as much knowledge of the employer and the position as possible.*

Always try to **address this letter to a specific person**, by name and title. A proper salutation should begin with Mr., Mrs., or Ms. If you are unclear whether you are writing to a male or female, because of the unisex nature of the first name or the use of initials only—Darrell Smith or L. C. Williams—use "Mr." or the full name—"Dear Darrell Smith" or "Dear L. C. Williams." Women should always be addressed as "Ms." unless you know for certain that "Mrs." or "Miss" is the appropriate and preferred salutation. However, many classified ads and vacancy announcements only include an address. Some may appear to be blind ads with limited information on the employer—P.O. Box 7999, Culver City, CA. If you are unable to determine to whom to address your letter, use one of two preferred choices:

1. "Dear Sir or Madam" or "Dear Sir/Madam." This is the formal, neutral, and most acceptable way of addressing an anonymous reader.

2. Eliminate this perfunctory salutation altogether and go directly from the return address to the first paragraph, leaving three spaces between the two sections. We prefer this "open" style since it directs your letter to the organization in the same manner in which the anonymous classified ad or vacancy announcement was addressed. Your opening sentence will indicate to whom the letter goes.

Whatever your choices, please do not address the individual as "Dear Gentleperson," "Dear Gentlepeople," "Dear Person," "Dear Sir," "Dear Future Employer," "Dear Friend," "Dear Company," "Dear Personnel Department," or "To Whom It May Concern." Employers are neither gentlepeople nor friends; a "sir" often turns out to be a female; you should not be so presumptuous to imply you'll be working there soon; and a company or department is not a person. Such salutations do nothing to elevate your status in the eyes of a potential employer. Several are negatives; most verge on being dumb! It's perfectly acceptable to follow the time-honored rule of *"When in doubt, leave it out."*

The targeted cover letter is designed to directly **connect** you to the needs of the employer. It is normally divided into three distinct paragraphs. In response to a classified ad or vacancy announcement, for example, the first paragraph of this letter should connect you to the advertised position by way of introduction. For openers, make your first sentence connect you directly to the employer's advertising efforts:

> I learned about your sales and marketing position in today's <u>Record-Courier</u>.

The remaining sentences should connect your skills and goals to the position and organization:

> I learned about your sales and marketing position in today's <u>Record-Courier</u>. I have seven years of progressive sales and marketing experience in pharmaceuticals, involving $3.5 million in annual sales. I'm interested in taking on new challenges with a highly respected and innovative pharmaceutical firm that values team performance and wishes to explore new markets.

Such an opening paragraph is short, to the point, grabs attention, and avoids the canned language and droning character of so many boring cover letters received by hiring personnel. Our letter emphasizes four key points:

- Where and when you learned about the position—you make a logical and legitimate connection to the employer. Also, employers like to know where candidates learn about the vacancy in order to determine the effectiveness of their advertising campaigns.

- You have specific skills and experience directly related to the employer's needs.

- You are interested in this position because you want to progress in your career rather than because of need (you're unemployed) or greed (you want more money). Your purpose is both employer- and career-centered rather than self-centered.

- Your style and tone is professional, personal, positive, upbeat, and value neutral. Most important, you appear "likable." You avoid making canned, self-serving, or flattering statements about yourself and the employer. The reader is probably impressed so far with your skills, interests, and knowledge of his firm. The reader's initial response is to learn more about you by reading the rest of the letter as well as reviewing the enclosed resume.

If you send a cover letter and resume in response to a referral, the only change in reference to our first original targeted cover letter involves the first sentence. In this case, you may or may not be responding to a specific position vacancy. An employer may be surveying existing talent to see what's available to the organization for possible personnel expansion. This is an example of how an employer may hire someone without ever advertising a vacancy—behavior in the so-called "hidden job market." He or she may want to let the market determine whether or not the organization is interested in adding new personnel. In this cover letter, the emphasis again is on making a legitimate connection to the employer. The tone is more personal:

> Jane Parsons, who spoke with you on Friday about my interests,
> suggested I contact you about my sales and marketing experience.
> She indicated you wished to see my resume.
>
> I have seven years of progressive sales and marketing experience in
> pharmaceuticals, involving $3.5 million in annual sales. I'm interested
> in taking on new challenges with a highly respected and innovative
> pharmaceutical firm that values team performance and wishes to
> explore new markets.

This is the best type of referral you can receive—an intermediary already introduced you to a potential employer who is requesting your resume. She has already legitimized your candidacy and screened your qualifications based on her own judgment and personal relationship with the employer. If she is highly respected by the employer for her judgment on personnel matters—or better still if the employer "owes her a favor"—you have an important foot in the door. At this point you need to reinforce her judgment with a well-crafted cover letter and resume immediately followed up with a phone call. In this case you need not mention a specific position being advertised since it may not actually be advertised. Include only the name of your referral as well as refer to those interests and skills you already know are compatible with the employer's interests. Keep in mind that the opening sentence—personal reference to your referral—is the most important element in this letter.

The remaining paragraphs in this type of targeted letter will follow the same form used for other kinds of cover letters—emphasize your relevant experience and skills, which are summarized in your resume, and call for action on your candidacy. We'll examine these other paragraphs later.

Broadcast Cover Letter

Broadcast cover letters are the ultimate exercise in delivering job search junk mail to employers. These letters are produced by job search dreamers. These are basically form letters sent to hundreds, perhaps thousands, of employers in the hope of being "discovered" by someone in need of your particular qualifications and experience. This is a favorite marketing method used by job search firms that charge individuals to help them find a job. It is their single most important indicator—however ineffective—that they are performing for their clients. The broadcast cover letter and resume prove to their clients that they are doing something for them in exchange for their fees: *"This week we sent 1,500 copies of your resume to our in-house list of employers."* Many paying clients actually believe they are getting their money's worth. Perhaps in a few days a job will be in the mail for them!

Many job hunters resort to sending such letters because the broadcast exercise involves motion. It gives them a feeling of doing something about their job search—they are actually contacting potential employers with their resume—without having to go through the process of making personal contacts through referrals and cold calls. Like most direct-mail schemes engaged in by the uninitiated, this is the lazy person's way to job search riches. Just find the names and addresses of several hundred potential employers, address the envelopes and affix postage, and then stuff them with your resume and cover letter. Presto! In a few days you expect phone calls from employers who just discovered your talents by opening their junk mail!

Let's speak the truth about going nowhere with this approach. Motion does not mean momentum. Anyone who thinks he or she can get a job by engaging in such a junk mail exercise is at best engaging in a self-fulfilling prophecy: it results in few if any responses and numerous rejections. If you want to experience rejections, or need to fill your weekly depression quota, just broadcast several hundred resumes and letters to employers. Wait a few weeks and you will most likely get the depressing news—no one is positive about you and your resume. At best you will receive a few polite form letters informing you that the employer will keep your resume on file:

> Thank you for sending us your resume. While we do not have a vacancy
> at present for someone with your qualifications, we will keep your resume
> on file for future reference.

If after receiving several such replies you conclude it's a tough job market out there, and no one is interested in your qualifications and experience, you're probably correct. Such an approach to communicating your qualifications to employers simply sets you up for failure. You probably don't need this type of compounding experience!

Let's speak the truth about going nowhere with this approach. Motion does not mean momentum.

This is not to say that this approach never works. Indeed, some people get job interviews from such broadcast letters and resumes. The reason they get interviews is not because of the quality of their resume, letter, or mailing list. It's because of dumb luck in playing the numbers game.

Direct mail operates like this. If you know what you are doing—have an excellent product targeted to a very receptive audience—you may receive a 2% positive response. Indeed, successful direct-mail campaigns use 2% as an indicator of success. On the other hand, if your product is less than exciting and is not well targeted on an audience, you can expect to receive less than 0.5% positive response. In some cases you may receive no response whatsoever. In fact, few direct-mail campaigns ever result in a 2% response rate!

You should never expect to receive more than a 1% positive response to your broadcast letters and resumes. Translated into real numbers, this means for every 100 unsolicited resumes you mail, you'll be lucky to get one interview. For every 1,000 resumes you mail, you may get 10 interviews. But you will be lucky if you even get a 1% positive response. Chances are your efforts will be rewarded with no invitations to interview.

The reason for such meager numbers is simple: you don't have a receptive audience for your mailing piece. Employers are busy and serious people who seek candidates when they have specific personnel needs. If they have no vacancies, why would they be interested in interviewing candidates or even replying to an unsolicited letter and resume for a nonexistent position? Such mail is a waste of their time. Writing responses to such mail costs them time and money. Employers simply don't interview people based upon a survey of their junk mail.

If you do get an interview from a broadcast letter, chances are you got lucky: your letter and resume arrived at the time an employer was actually looking for a candidate with your type of qualifications. This is your luck calling.

If you decide to engage in the broadcast exercise, please don't waste a great deal of time and money trying to produce the "perfect" mailing piece or acquiring a "hot" mailing list. It's wishful thinking that the quality of the mailing piece or your mailing list will somehow give you an "extra edge" in generating a higher response rate.

Simply write a short three-paragraph cover letter in which you generate interest in both you and your resume as well as demonstrate your enthusiasm, drive, honesty, goals, and performance orientation. The first two paragraphs introduce you to the employer by way of your experience, previous performance, and future goals. The final paragraph calls for action on the part of the receiver:

> I have seven years of progressive sales and marketing experience in pharmaceuticals. Last year alone I generated $3.5 million in annual sales—a 25% increase over the previous year. Next year I want to do at least $4.5 million.
>
> I'm interested in taking on new challenges with a firm that values team performance and is interested in exploring new markets. As you can see from my enclosed resume, I have extensive sales and marketing experience. For the past five years, I've exceeded my annual sales goals by 30%.
>
> If you have a need for someone with my experience, I would appreciate an opportunity to speak with you about how we might best work together in meeting your sales and marketing goals. I can be contacted during the day at 808-729-3290 and in the evening at 808-729-4751. My e-mail address is: RogerE@aol.com.

If this letter were received by an employer who had a specific need for an experienced and productive individual in pharmaceutical sales and marketing, chances are he or she would contact the writer. However, the chances are very slim that this letter would connect with an employer who just happened to have such an immediate and specific need. Therefore, this otherwise excellent letter is likely to result in numerous rejections because it has no audience on the day it arrives.

While it is always preferable to address your letter to a specific name and type each envelope rather than use computer-generated mailing labels, in the end it probably doesn't really make much difference if no position exists in reference to your letter and resume. It does make a difference if you are lucky to stumble upon a position through such a mailing effort. An employer either does or does not have a personnel need specifically coinciding with your qualifications and experience. The **content** of both your letter and resume is the most important element in this broadcast exercise. If an employer has a specific personnel need and your letter and resume indicate you fit those needs, you'll probably hear from the employer regardless of whether you have his or her correct name and title or if you used a computer-generated mailing label. The employer knows what you are doing regardless of any cosmetic pretenses to the contrary.

How effective this mailing piece becomes will depend on your luck. Whatever you do, don't expect to receive many positive responses. And be prepared for an avalanche of bad news—no one appears to want you! You will collect numerous rejections in the process. After you complete this direct-mail exercise, get back to what you should really be doing with your job search time—directly contacting potential employers through referral networks, cold-calling techniques, and in response to advertised vacancies. Cover letters targeted to employers with specific personnel needs will result in many more positive responses than the junk mail you generated. You will decrease your number of rejections with a higher number of acceptances.

The T-Letter – The Ultimate Weapon

Pioneered by Bernard Haldane Associates (*www.jobhunting.com*), one of the world's largest career management firms, the T-letter is the most powerful type of cover letter you can deploy in your job search. It targets your relevant skills, experience, and qualifications around an employer's specific job requirements. Organized in a two-column "T" format, with the employer's advertised requirements in a left column and your qualifications in a corresponding right column, it lists bullet by bullet the employer's requirements and your related qualifications. For example, you might respond to an advertisement for a Property Management position by targeting the employer's requirements with this type of letter. Be sure to carefully read and highlight the ad for specific required skills and experience, and then compose a letter that directly relates your skills and experience to those requirements. The most powerful type of letter in response to such an ad is the classic two-column T-letter:

As a Property Manager, I would bring to this job the following qualifications:

<u>Your Requirements</u>	<u>My Qualifications</u>
■ Enjoy working with people	■ Seven years of progressive experience in customer service.
	■ Regularly cited in annual performance appraisal for "excellent people skills."
	■ Serve as a volunteer to raise funds for the United Way.
■ Energetic personality	■ Recognized by current employer as a "go-getter" who maintains a high energy level, even in highly stressful situations.
	■ Enjoy new challenges and meeting new people.
■ Strong attention to detail	■ Five years experience as a quality control inspector. Improved the quality of inspections by 40% within first six months.
	■ Supervised housing inspection teams. Achieved a 97% rating for excellence.

You may or may not want to enclose a resume with this type of cover letter. If constructed properly, this T-letter can stand on its own as a combination letter-resume. Job seekers who write such letters report phenomenal results – a very high percentage of employers contact them for interviews. The reason for such a response is very simple. Over 90% of resumes and letters received by employers do not directly relate to their job requirements. The T-letter, by contrast, is 100% on target because it is custom-designed around required skills and experience and may include interesting examples of performance. Easy to

> *If you write only one type of letter, make sure it's a T-letter. It's the perfect medium for communicating military experience to civilian employers.*

read and centered on the specific needs of the employer, this letter quickly moves to the top of the pile where it receives more attention than most other resumes and letters. Well constructed T-letters result in numerous job interviews.

For more information on how to write innovative T-letters, including numerous examples of effective T-letters used by hundreds of clients seeking high paying professional positions, see *Haldane's Best Cover Letters For Professionals* (Impact Publications). Indeed, if you learn to write only one type of letter or resume, make sure it's a T-letter. This type of letter really works. It's the perfect medium for communicating your military experience to civilian employers who may otherwise have difficulty translating military positions, experience, and language that appear on your resume.

Approach Letters

Approach letters are some of the most important letters you should write during your job search. The purpose of these letters is to approach individuals for job search information, advice, and referrals. They play a central role in your prospecting and networking activities. You write them because you need information on alternative jobs, the job market, organizations, potential employers, and job vacancies. You need this information because the job market is highly decentralized and chaotic, and because you want to uncover job leads before others learn about them. Approach letters help you bring some degree of coherence and structure to your job search by organizing the job market around your interests, skills, and experience.

Approach letters are largely responsible for opening doors for informational interviews—one of the most critical interviews in your job search. Approach letters help give you access to important job information and potential employers. Failure to write these letters is likely to weaken your overall job search campaign.

One of the most important differences between approach letters and cover letters is that an approach letter should **never** be accompanied by a resume. The reason is simple: an enclosed resume implies you are looking for a job from the individual who receives your letter. You put responsibility on this individual to either give you a job or help you find one. Few individuals want such responsibility or are eager to become your job search helper. This pushy and presumptuous approach violates the most important principle of the approach letter—these letters are designed for gaining access to critical job search information, advice, and referrals. Such a letter should never imply that you are looking for a job with or through this individual. Only during an informational interview, preferably **after** you receive such information, advice, and referrals, should you share your resume with your letter recipient.

Time and again job searchers make the mistake of writing an approach letter but enclosing their resume. Such ill-conceived actions generate contradictory messages. While they may produce an outstanding approach letter, they in effect kill it by attaching a resume. The letter says they are only asking for information, advice, and referrals, but the enclosed resume implies they are actually looking for a job from the letter recipient. Job seekers who do this are unethical or dishonest. This puts the recipients on the spot and makes them feel uncomfortable.

You may want to write two different types of approach letters for different situations: referral and cold turkey. The **referral approach letter** is written to someone based on a referral or a connection with someone else. A friend or acquaintance, for example, recommends that you contact a particular individual for job search information and advice:

> Why don't you contact John Staples? He really knows what's going on. I'm sure he'd be happy to give you advice on what he knows about the pharmaceutical industry in this area. Tell him I recommended you give him a call.

This type of referral is **the** basis for building and expanding networks for conducting informational interviews that eventually lead to job interviews and offers. It's the type of referral you want to elicit again and again in the process of expanding your job search network into the offices of potential employers. When you receive such a referral, you have one of two choices for developing the connection.

First, depending on the situation and the individual's position, you may want to immediately initiate the contact by telephone. The use of the telephone is efficient; it gets the job done quickly. However, it is not always the most effective way of initiating a contact. The individual may be very busy and thus unable to take your call, or he may be in the middle of some important business that should not be interrupted by someone like you. When you telephone a stranger, you may face immediate resistance to any attempt to use his valuable time or schedule an informational interview.

Second, you may want to write a referral approach letter which can be sent as email or as a posted letter. While not as efficient as a telephone call, this letter is likely to be more effective. It prepares the individual for your telephone call. Such a letter enables you to be in complete control of the one-way communication; you should be better able to craft an effective message that will lead to a productive telephone call and informational interview.

This type of approach letter should immediately open with a personal statement that nicely connects you to the reader via your referral and a bit of honest flattery. Start with something like this:

> John Staples suggested that I contact you regarding the local pharma-
> ceutical industry. He said you know the business better than anyone else.

> When I spoke with Mary Thompson today, she highly recommended you as
> a source of information on the local pharmaceutical industry.

Such statements include two positives that should result in a favorable impression on the receiver: You've already been screened by the referral for making this contact, and this individual is recognized as an expert in the eyes of others who are important to him who, in turn, pass this recognition on to others.

The next two paragraphs should indicate your interests, motivations, and background in reference to the purpose of making this contact. It should clearly communicate your intentions for making this contact and for using the individual's time. You might say something like this:

> After several successful years in pharmaceutical sales and marketing in
> Boston, I've decided to relocate to the Midwest where I can be closer to my
> family. However, having moved to the East nearly 15 years ago, I've
> discovered I'm somewhat of a stranger to the industry in this area.

> I would very much appreciate any information and advice you might be
> able to share with me on the nature of the pharmaceutical industry in the
> greater Chicago Metro area. I have several questions I'm hoping to find
> answers to in the coming weeks. Perhaps, as John said, you could fill me in
> on the who, what, and where of the local industry.

Throughout this letter, as well as in your telephone conversation or in a face-to-face meeting, you should **never** indicate that you are looking for a job through this individual. You are only seeking information and advice. If this contact results in referrals that lead to job interviews and offers, that's great. But you are explicitly initiating this contact because you need more information and advice at this stage of your job search. This individual, in effect, becomes your personal advisor—not your future employer. Individuals who use the approach letter for the purpose of getting a job through the recipient abuse this form of communication. Their actions are exploitive, and they tend to become undesirable nuisances few people want to hire. Worst still, they give networking and informational interviewing bad names.

Whatever you do, make sure you are completely honest when you approach referral contacts for information and advice. You will get better cooperation and information as well as be seen as a thoughtful individual who should be promoted through referrals and networking. Therefore, the second and third paragraphs of your letter should indicate your true intentions in initiating this contact.

Your final paragraph should consist of an action statement which indicates what you will do next:

> I'll give you a call Tuesday afternoon to see if your schedule would permit some time to discuss my interests in the local pharmaceutical industry. I appreciate your time and look forward to talking with you in a few days.

You—not the letter recipient—must take **follow-up action** on this letter. You should never end such a letter with an action statement requesting the recipient to contact you (*"I look forward to hearing from you"* or *"Please give me a call if your schedule would permit us to meet"*). If you do, you're unlikely to receive a reply. It's incumbent upon you to further initiate the contact with a telephone call. Assuming you sent the letter by regular first-class mail or transmitted it by email, try to leave at least four days between when you sent the letter and when you make the telephone call. If you use special next-day delivery services, make your call on the same delivery day, preferably between 2pm and 4pm.

This action statement prepares the contact for your telephone call and subsequent conversation or meeting. He or she will most likely give you some time. However, please note that this action statement is also a thoughtful conclusion that does not specify the nature of your future contact nor is it overly aggressive or presumptuous (*"I'll schedule a meeting"*). The open-ended statement *"to see if your schedule would permit some time"* could result in either a telephone interview or a face-to-face meeting. In many cases a telephone interview will suffice. The individual may have a limited amount of information that is best shared in a 5-10 minute telephone call. In other cases, a face-to-face half-hour to one-hour informational interview would be more appropriate. By choosing such a closing action statement, you leave the time, place, and medium of the interview open to discussion.

The **cold-turkey approach letter** is written for the same purpose but without a personal contact. In this case you literally approach a stranger with no prior contacts. In contrast to the referral approach letter, in this situation you do not have instant credibility attendant with a personal connect. While cold-turkey contacts can be difficult to initiate, they can play an important role in your job search campaign.

Since you do not have a personal contact to introduce you to the letter recipient, you need to begin your letter with an appropriate "cold call" opener that logically connects you to the reader. Try to make your connection as warm, personal, and professional as possible. Avoid excessive flattery or boastful statements that are likely to make your motives suspect and thus turn off the reader. It's always helpful to inject in this letter a personal observation that gently strokes the ego of the reader. If, for example, you read a newspaper article about the individual's work, or if he just received an award or promotion, you might introduce yourself in this letter in any of the following ways:

> I read with great interest about your work with _____. Congratulations on a job well done. During the past twelve years I've been involved in similar work.

> Congratulations on receiving the annual community award. Your efforts have certainly helped revitalize our downtown area. My interests in urban development began nearly ten years ago when I was studying urban planning at St. Louis University.

> Congratulations on your recent promotion to Vice President of Allied Materials. I've been one of your admirers for the past five years, following your many community and professional activities. Your work in expanding Allied Materials' markets to Japan and China especially interests me because of my previous work in Asia.

Other openers might begin with some of the following lead-in phrases which help connect you to the reader:

> I am writing to you because of your position as . . .

> Because of your experience in . . .

> We have a common interest in . . .

> Since we are both alumni of Texas A&M, I thought . . .

> As a fellow member of Delta Sigma Alpha sorority, I wanted to congratulate you on your recent election to . . .

Whatever opener you choose, make sure you focus on making a **logical connection** that is both personal and professional. Inject some personality in this letter. After all, you want this stranger to take an immediate interest in you. Try to communicate that you are a likable, enthusiastic, honest, and competent person worth talking to or even meeting. The very first sentence should grab the reader's attention.

A strong opener in a cold-turkey approach letter can be nearly as effective as the personal contact opener in the referral approach letter.

The remaining paragraphs of the cold-turkey referral letter will be structured similarly to the referral approach letter—indicate your interests, motivations, and background in reference to your purpose in making this contact. Clearly communicate your intentions for making this contact and for using the individual's time. Again, be perfectly honest and tactful in what you say, but avoid making honest but stupid statements, such as *"I really don't know what's going to happen to me in the next three months."* Be sure to close with an indication of action—you will call on a particular date to see if the person's schedule would permit some time to discuss your interests.

If you incorporate these two types of approach letters in your job search, you will quickly discover they are the most powerful forms of communication in your job search arsenal. They must be written and targeted toward individuals who have information, advice, and referrals relevant to your job search interests. They are the bricks-and-mortar for building networks that generate informational interviews that lead to job interviews and offers. Resumes and telephone calls are no substitute for these referral letters. A resume **never** accompanies these letters, and a telephone call only follows **after** the recipient has received and read your approach letter. If you write these letters according to our suggested structure and content, and follow up with the telephone call, you will receive a great deal of useful job search information, advice, and referrals. You will learn about the structure of the job market, identify key players who can help you, and inject a healthy dose of reality into a job search that may otherwise be guided by myths and wishful thinking.

If for any reason you still feel compelled to sneak a resume in the envelope or as an email attachment with one of these approach letters, you will quickly discover few recipients want to see or talk with you. The enclosed or attached resume immediately transforms what was potentially an effective approach letter into an ineffective cover letter for a job application—something that is inappropriate in this situation. As we've already seen, an effective cover letter has a different purpose as well as follows other writing, distribution, and follow-up principles.

Thank-You Letters

Thank-you letters are some of the most effective communications in a job search. They demonstrate an important **social grace** that says something about you as an individual—your personality and how you probably relate to others. They communicate one of the most important characteristics sought in potential employees—**thoughtfulness**.

Better still, since few individuals write thank-you letters, those who do write them are **remembered** by letter recipients. And one thing you definitely want to happen again and again during your job search is to be remembered by individuals who can provide you with useful information, advice, and referrals as well as invite you to job interviews and extend to you job offers. Being remembered as a thoughtful person with the proper social graces will give you an edge over other job seekers who fail to write thank-you letters. Whatever you do, make sure you regularly send thank-you letters in response to individuals who assist you in your job search.

Many job seekers discover the most important letters they ever wrote were thank-you letters. These letters can have several positive outcomes:

- **Contacts turn into more contacts and job interviews:** A job seeker sends a thank-you letter to someone who recommended she contact a former college roommate; impressed with the thoughtfulness of the job seeker and feeling somewhat responsible for helping her make the right contacts, the individual continues providing additional referrals, which eventually lead to two job interviews.

- **Job interview turns into a job offer:** A job seeker completes a job interview. Within 24 hours, he writes a nice thank-you in which he expresses his gratitude for having an opportunity to interview for the position as well as reiterates his interest in working for the employer. This individual is subsequently offered the job. The employer later tells him it was his thoughtful thank-you letter that gave him the edge over two other equally qualified candidates who never bothered to follow up the interview.

- **A job rejection later turns into a job offer:** After interviewing for a position, a job seeker receives a standard rejection letter from an employer indicating the job was offered to another individual. Rather than get angry and end communications with the employer, the job seeker sends a nice thank-you letter in which she notes her disappointment in not being selected and then thanks him for the opportunity to interview for the position. She also reiterates her continuing interest in working for the organization. The employer remembers this individual. Rather than let her get away, he decides to create a new position for her.

- **A job offer turns into an immediate positive relationship:** Upon receiving a job offer, the new employee sends a nice thank-you letter in which he expresses his appreciation for the confidence expressed by the employer. He also reassures the employer that he will be as productive as expected. This letter is well received by the employer who is looking forward to working closely with such a thoughtful new employee. Indeed, he becomes a mentor and sponsor who immediately gives the employee some plum assignments that help him fast-track his career within the organization.

- **Termination results in strong recommendations and a future job offer:** An employee, seeking to advance her career with a larger organization, receives a job offer from a competing firm. In submitting her formal letter of resignation, she also sends a personal thank-you letter to her former employer. She sincerely expresses her gratitude for having the opportunity work with him and attributes much of her success to his mentoring. This letter further confirms his conclusion about this former employee—he's losing a valuable asset. While he cannot offer her a similar or better career opportunity in this organization, he will keep her in mind if things change. And things do change two years later when he makes a major career move to a much larger organization. One of the first things he does as Vice-President is to begin shaping his own personal staff. He immediately contacts her to see if she would be interested in working with him. She's interested and soon joins her former employer in making another major career move.

In these cases it was the job seekers' thank-you letters, rather than their cover letters and resumes, that got them job interviews and offers.

As indicated in the above scenarios, thank-you letters should be written in the following situations:

- **After receiving information, advice, or a referral from a contact:** You should always express your gratitude in writing to individuals who provide you with job search assistance. Not only is this a nice thing to do, it also is functional for a successful job search. Individuals who feel they are appreciated will most likely remember you and be willing to further assist you with your job search and recommend you to others.

- **Immediately after interviewing for a job:** Whether it be a telephone or face-to-face interview, always write a nice thank-you letter within 12 hours of completing the interview. This letter should express your gratitude for having an opportunity to interview for the job. Be sure to reiterate your interest in the job and stress your possible contributions to the employer's operations. The letter should emphasize your major strengths in relationship to the employer's needs. All other things being equal, this letter may give you an "extra edge" over other candidates. It may well become your most effective job search letter!

- **Withdrawing from further consideration:** At some point during the recruitment process, you may decide to withdraw from further consideration. Perhaps you decided to take another job, you're now more satisfied with your present job, or the position no longer interests you. For whatever reason, you should write a short thank-you letter in which you withdraw from consideration. Explain in positive terms why you are no longer interested in pursuing an application with the organization. Thank them for their time and consideration.

- **After receiving a rejection:** Even if you receive a rejection, it's a good idea to write a thank-you letter. How many employers ever receive such a letter from what ostensibly should be a disappointed job seeker? This unique letter is likely to be remembered—which is what you want to accomplish in this situation. Being remembered may result in referrals to other employers or perhaps a job interview and offer at some later date.

- **After receiving a job offer:** However well they think they hire, employers still are uncertain about the outcome of their hiring decisions until new employees perform in their organization. Why not put their initial anxieties at ease and get off on the right foot by writing a nice thank-you letter? In this letter express your appreciation for having received the confidence and trust of the employer. Reiterate what you told the employer during the job interview(s) about your goals and expected performance. Conclude with a reaffirmation of your starting date as well as a statement about how much you look forward to becoming a productive member of the team. Such a thoughtful letter will be well received by the employer. It could well accelerate your progress within the organization beyond the norm.

- **Upon leaving a job:** Whether you leave your job voluntarily or are forced by circumstances to terminate, try to leave a positive part of you behind by writing a thank-you letter. Burning bridges behind you through face-to-face confrontation or a vindictive, get-even letter may later catch up with you, especially if you anger someone in the process who may later be in a position to affect your career. If you quit to take a job with another organization, thank your employer for the time you spent with the organization and the opportunities given to you to acquire valuable experience and skills. If you terminated under difficult circumstances—organizational cutbacks or a nasty firing—try to leave on as positive a note as possible. Employers in such situations would rather have you out of sight and mind. Assure them there are no hard feelings, and you wish them the best as you would hope they would wish you the same. Stress the positives of your relationship with both the employer and the organization. Remember, your future employer may call your previous employer for information on your past performance. If you leave a stressful situation on a positive note, chances are your previous employer will give you the benefit of the doubt and stress only your positives to others. He may even commit a few "sins of omission" that only you and he know about: *"She really worked well with her co-workers and was one of our best analysts"* does not tell the whole story which may be that you couldn't get along with your boss, and vice versa. After having made peace with each other through the medium of the thank-you letter, what would your former employer have to gain by telling the whole story to others about your work with him? Your thank-you letter should at least neutralize the situation and at best turn a negative situation into a positive for your career. Indeed, he may well become one of your supporters—for other jobs with other employers, that is!

Examples of each type of letter, written according to our principles of effective thank-you letters, appear at the end of this chapter and are identified accordingly.

Thank-you letters should always be written in a timely manner. Make it a practice to sit down and write these letters within 12 hours of the situation that prompts this letter. It should be mailed immediately so that it reaches the recipient within three to four days. If you wait longer, the letter will have less impact on the situation. Indeed, in the case of the interview thank-you letter, if an employer is making a final hiring decision among three candidates, your letter should arrive as soon as possible to have a chance to affect the outcome.

Whether you handwrite or type this letter may not make a great deal of difference in terms of outcomes, but your choice says something about your professional style and mentality. Many people claim handwritten thank-you letters are more powerful than typed letters. We doubt such claims and have yet to see any credible data on the subject other than personal preferences and questionable logic. It is true that handwritten thank-you letters communicate a certain personal element that cannot be expressed in typewritten letters. If you choose to handwrite this letter, make sure you have attractive handwriting. Your handwriting form and style could be a negative.

The problem with handwritten letters is that they can express a certain nonprofessional, amateurish style. They also may raise questions about your motivations and manipulative style. They turn off some readers who expect a business letter, rather than an expression of social graces, in reference to a business situation. Furthermore, some readers may consider the handwritten letter an attempt at psychological manipulation—they know what you're trying to do by handwriting a letter. That's what real estate and car salespeople are taught to do in their training seminars! When in doubt, it's best to type this letter in a neat, clean, and professional manner. If typewritten, such a personal letter also will express your professional style and respond to the expectations appropriate for the situation. It tells the reader that you know proper business etiquette, you know this is a business situation, you are equipped to respond, and you attempt to demonstrate your best professional effort.

Resume Letters

A resume letter is a special type of approach letter that substitutes for a formal resume. Merging the cover letter and resume into a single document, this type of letter is written when it is appropriate to target your qualifications in a format other than a separate cover letter and resume. It's most often used to approach employers with information on your experience and skills in the hope that they will have vacancies for someone with your qualifications.

Since it outlines your experience and skills, the resume letter is designed to get job interviews with employers. It, in effect, asks for a job interview rather than information, advice, or referrals for expanding your job search.

Similar to the cold-turkey approach letter, the resume letter should open with a logical connection between you and the employer. The second paragraph, however, is what defines this as a resume letter. This paragraph should summarize your major experience and skills in relation to the employer's needs. In fact, you may want to take this section directly from the "Areas of Effectiveness," "Experience," or "Work History" section appearing on your resume. For ease of reading, it's best to bullet each item, preferably including three to five items similar to the examples found at the end of this chapter. The final paragraph should call for action—you taking the initiative to call the recipient at a specific time for the purpose of scheduling a possible interview.

You should try to keep this letter to a single page. Remember, it is neither a cover letter nor a resume, but a combination of both which has a specific purpose—you are trying to invite yourself to a job interview. Since this type of letter tends to put employers on the spot—here's another "cold-caller"—it will probably generate few positive responses and numerous rejections. However well written this letter may be, few employers are prepared to give job interviews based on such a letter. Chances are most employers will not have vacancies available at the time you send this letter. What they may be able to do is give you referrals to other employers who may have vacancies—but only if you follow up this letter with a phone call. In the end, your resume letter may become an important prospecting letter for uncovering job leads.

COVER LETTER
Response to Advertised Position

724 Grand Avenue
St. Louis, MO 62345

July 15, 20__

Jeff Morris
Director of Personnel
GREATER CHICAGO BANK
245 LaSalle Street
Chicago, IL 60000

Dear Mr. Morris:

The accompanying résumé is in response to your listing in yesterday's <u>Chicago Tribune</u> for a loan officer.

I am especially interested in this position because my experience as an Army finance officer has prepared me for understanding the budget issues associated with large organizations as well as the financial needs of a diverse array of individuals. I wish to use this experience with a growing and community-conscious bank such as yours.

I would appreciate an opportunity to meet with you to discuss how my experience will best meet your needs. My ideas on how to improve small business financing may be of particular interest to you. I will call your office on the morning of July 21 to inquire if a meeting can be scheduled at a convenient time.

I look forward to meeting you.

Sincerely yours,

Maurine Davis

Maurine Davis

COVER LETTER
Referral

2101 Terrace Street
Sacramento, CA 97342

May 3, 20____

Terry Ford
Vice President
Fulton Engineering Corporation
1254 Madison Street
Sacramento, CA 97340

Dear Mr. Ford:

John Bird, the Director of Data Systems at Ottings Engineering Company, informed me that you are looking for someone to direct your new management information system.

I enclose my resume for your consideration. During the past 10 years I have designed and developed a variety of information systems for the U.S. Air Force. I have worked at both the operational and managerial levels and know how to develop systems appropriate for different types of organizations.

I would appreciate an opportunity to visit with you and examine your operations. Perhaps I could provide you with a needs assessment prior to an interview. I will call you next week to make arrangements for a visit.

I look forward to speaking with you next week.

Sincerely,

Steven Paris

Steven Paris

T-LETTER
Response to Advertised Position

431 Wilson Street
Columbus, OH 53211

November 17, 20___

Mary Tilman
Director of Training
SITMORE ENTERPRISES
822 Liberty Street
Philadelphia, PA 17175

Dear Ms. Tilman:

I noticed with interest your ad in *Training Resources* for an experienced Management Trainer. I would bring to this position these qualifications:

Your Needs	My Qualifications
■ Five years training experience.	■ Seven years of progressive experience as a management trainer in a variety of organizational settings.
■ Strong writing and presentation skills.	■ Annually produce 6-8 training manuals and conduct more than 30 3-day training sessions on a variety of supervisory skills for entry-level to senior-level managers.
■ Ability to supervise a group of training professionals	■ Annually supervise 7 trainers who conduct more than 300 programs in 18 U.S. and European locations.

The enclosed resume further summarizes my qualifications. I would appreciate an opportunity to speak with you about this position. I'll call your office next Thursday morning to answer any question you may have about my candidacy.

Sincerely,

David Watson

David Watson

APPROACH LETTER
Referral

2931 Gadwall Place
Virginia Beach, VA 23462

November 3, 20____

Doris Leffert, Director
Architectural Design Office
ABC ENGINEERING COMPANY
213 Landmore Street
Cleveland, OH 44444

Dear Ms. Leffert:

Captain David Johns suggested that I write to you in regards to my interests in architectural drafting. He thought you would be a good person to give me some career advice.

I am interested in an architectural drafting position with a firm specializing in commercial construction. As a trained draftsman for the U.S. Navy, I have six years of progressive experience in all facets of construction, from pouring concrete to developing plans for $15 million in residential construction. I am particularly interested in improving construction design and building operations of shopping complexes.

Captain Johns mentioned you as one of the leading experts in this growing field. Would it be possible for us to meet briefly? Over the next few months I will be conducting a job search. I am certain your counsel would assist me as I begin looking for new opportunities.

I will call your office next week to see if your schedule permits such a meeting.

Sincerely,

Barry West

Barry West

APPROACH LETTER
Cold Turkey

881 Potomac Street
Quantico, VA 22222

August 9, 20_____

Judy Zukaris, Director
NORTHEAST ASSOCIATION
    FOR SENIOR CITIZENS
1267 Connecticut Avenue
Washington, DC 20000

Dear Ms. Zukaris:

I have been impressed with your work with the elderly. Your organization takes a community perspective in trying to integrate the concerns of the elderly with those of other community groups. Perhaps other organizations will soon follow your lead.

I am anxious to meet you and learn more about your work. While serving in the U.S. Marine Corps, I used my off-duty hours as a volunteer working with senior citizens in my local community. From this experience I decided to pursue a career working with community organizations and the elderly.

However, before I pursue my interest further, I need to talk to people with experience in gerontology. In particular, I would like to know more about careers with the elderly as well as how my background might best be used in the field of gerontology.

I am hoping you can assist me in this matter. I would like to meet with you briefly to discuss several of my concerns. I will call next week to see if your schedule permits such a meeting.

I look forward to meeting you.

Sincerely,

Darrell Rutherford

Darrell Rutherford

THANK-YOU LETTER
Referral

3211 Fairview Blvd.
Ft. Lauderdale, FL 30000

June 16, 20____

Albert Bates
123 Riggs Drive
Miami, FL 30301

Dear Mr. Bates:

Thank you so much for putting me in contact with Jane Burton at Fordham Manufacturing Company.

I spoke with her today about my interests in technical training. She was most gracious with her time and provided me with a great deal of useful information on job opportunities in the Miami area. She even made some valuable suggestions for strengthening my resume and gave me a few names of individuals who might be interested in my qualifications.

I'll send you a copy of my resume once I revise it. Please feel free to make any comments or suggestions as well as share it with others who might be interested in my background.

Again, thank you for the Jane Burton contact. She spoke very highly of you and your work with the United Fund.

Sincerely,

Clark Owens

Clark Owens

THANK-YOU LETTER
After Informational Interview

2234 Taylor Drive
Cincinnati, OH 43333

January 5, 20 ____

Michael Marris, Director
OHIO FINANCE CORPORATION
1145 Davis Street
Columbus, OH 43380

Dear Mr. Marris:

Your advice was most helpful in clarifying my questions on careers in finance.
I am now reworking my resume and have included many of your thoughtful
suggestions. I will send you a copy next week.

Thank you so much for taking time from your busy schedule to see me. I will
keep in contact and follow through on your suggestion to see Janet Olson about
opportunities with the Cleveland-Akron Finance Company.

Sincerely,

Perry Wilson

Perry Wilson

THANK-YOU LETTER
Post Job Interview

421 Center Street
Denver, CO 82171

September 7, 20 _____

Fred Thomas
Director, Personnel Department
Coastal Products Incorporated
7229 Lakewood Drive
Denver, CO 82170

Dear Mr. Thomas:

Thank you again for the opportunity to interview for the marketing position. I appreciated your hospitality and enjoyed meeting you and members of your staff.

The interview convinced me of how compatible my background, interests, and skills are with the goals of Coastal Products Incorporated. As discussed, I am a fast learner with a strong propensity for sales. During my off-duty time in the military, I was very successful in selling long distance telecommunications services. This work required developing a marketing strategy and carefully following through with implementation. Combined with my military background in Asian and Pacific affairs and my fluency in Chinese, I am confident my skills and experience would increase market share for Coastal Products Incorporated in the rapidly expanding Pacific Rim market.

For more information on the new product promotion program I mentioned, call Steve Barry in the evening at 333/411-2351. I talked to Steve this morning and mentioned your interest in this program.

I look forward to meeting you and your staff again.

Sincerely,

Mark Harris

Mark Harris

THANK-YOU LETTER
Responding to Rejection

2491 Clarkson Drive
Springfield, MA 01281

March 21, 20_____

Jeffrey Lane
Vice President for Sales
SERVICE ENTERPRISES
221 Vermont Street
Washington, DC 20011

Dear Mr. Lane:

Thank you for giving me the opportunity to interview for the Customer
Services Representative position. I appreciate your consideration and interest
in me. I learned a great deal from our meetings.

Although I am disappointed in not being selected for your current vacancy, I
want you to know that I appreciated the courtesy and professionalism shown to
me during the entire selection process. I enjoyed meeting you, John Roberts,
and other members of your sales staff. My meetings confirmed that Service
Enterprises would be an exciting place to work and build a career.

I want to reiterate my strong interest in working for you. Please keep me in
mind should another position become available in the near future.

Again, thank you for the opportunity to interview. Best wishes to you and your
staff.

Yours truly,

Barbara Miller

Barbara Miller

THANK-YOU LETTER
Withdrawing From Consideration

921 Peters Street
Williamsburg, VA 23512

February 9, 20_____

Dr. Thomas C. Bostelli, President
Northern States University
2500 University Drive
Greenfield, MA 03241

Dear Dr. Bostelli:

It was indeed a pleasure meeting with you and your staff last week to discuss your need for a Director of Public and Government Relations. Our time together was most enjoyable and informative.

As I discussed with you during our meetings, I believe one purpose of preliminary interviews is to explore areas of mutual interest and to assess the fit between the individual and the position. After careful consideration, I have decided to withdraw from consideration for the position.

My decision is based upon several factors. First, the emphasis on fund raising is certainly needed, but I would prefer more balance in my work activities. Second, the position would require more travel than I am willing to accept with my other responsibilities. Third, professional opportunities for my wife would be very limited in northwest Massachusetts.

I want to thank you for interviewing me and giving me the opportunity to learn about your needs. You have a fine staff and faculty, and I would have enjoyed working with them.

Best wishes in your search.

Sincerely,

Edward Rollins

Edward Rollins

THANK-YOU LETTER
Accepting Job Offer

190 Wilson Blvd.
San Francisco, CA 94826

April 25, 20____

Martin Franks
Vice President
PACIFIC COAST AIRLINES
781 McDonnell Street
San Francisco, CA 94829

Dear Mr. Franks:

I am pleased to accept your offer, and I am looking forward to joining you and your staff next month.

The customer relations position is ideally suited to my background and interests. I assure you I will give you my best effort in making this an effective position within your company.

I understand I will begin work on July 1. If, in the meantime, I need to complete any paper work or take care of any other matters, please contact me at 377-4029.

I enjoyed meeting with you and your staff and appreciated the professional manner in which the hiring was conducted.

Sincerely,

Jennifer Nash

Jennifer Nash

THANK-YOU LETTER
Terminating Employment

914 Sixth Avenue
Pittsburgh, PA 43211

November 11, 20____

Kevin Wallace
Chief Engineer
PITTSBURGH CONSTRUCTION COMPANY
2111 Hillsborough Road
Pittsburgh, PA 43210

Dear Kevin,

I am writing to inform you that I will be leaving Pittsburgh Construction Company on December 12 to accept another position.

As you know, I have developed an interest in architectural drafting which combines my drafting skills with my artistic interests. While I was vacationing in Houston recently, a relative approached me about an opening for someone with my background with a large architecture and engineering firm. I investigated the possibility and, consequently, received an offer. After careful consideration, I decided to accept the offer and relocate to Houston. I will be working with Brown and Little Company.

I have thoroughly enjoyed working with you over the past two years, and deeply appreciate your fine supervision and support. You have taught me a great deal about drafting, and I want to thank you for providing me with the opportunity to work here. It has been a very positive experience for me both personally and professionally.

I wanted to give you more than the customary two weeks notice so you would have time to find my replacement. I made the decision to relocate yesterday and decided to inform you immediately.

Best wishes.

Sincerely,

Garry Slater

Garry Slater

RESUME LETTER

773 Main Street
Williamsburg, VA 23572

November 12, 20____

Barbara Thompson, President
SRM ASSOCIATES
421 91st Street
New York, NY 11910

Dear Ms. Thompson:

I just completed reading the article in <u>Business Today</u> on SRM Associates. Your innovative approach to recruiting minorities is of particular interest to me because of my background in public relations and minority recruitment.

I am interested in learning more about your work as well as the possibilities of joining your firm. My qualifications include:

- research and writing on minority recruitment in the military
- administered a major minority representation program for DoD
- published several professional articles on career development for minorities
- organized and led public relations, press, and minority conferences
- M.A. in Journalism and B.A. in English

I will be in New York City during the week of December 10. Perhaps your schedule would permit us to meet briefly to discuss our mutual interests. I will call your office next week to see if such a meeting can be arranged.

I appreciate your consideration.

Sincerely yours,

Chris Taylor

Chris Taylor

RESUME LETTER

3331 Taylor Road
Baltimore, MD 20000

April 4, 20____

Carol Watson
TRC CORPORATION
719 Olson Road
Rockville, MD 21101

Dear Ms. Watson:

TRC Corporation is one of the most dynamic computer companies in the nation. Its model employee training and development program makes it the type of organization I am interested in joining.

I am seeking a training position with a computer firm which would use my administrative, communication, and planning abilities to develop effective training and counseling programs. My experience includes:

Administration: Supervised instructors and counselors. Coordinated job vacancy and training information for military businesses and schools.

Communication: Conducted over 100 workshops on interpersonal skills, stress management, and career planning. Frequent guest speaker to various agencies and associations. Experienced writer of training manuals and public relations materials.

Planning: Planned and developed counseling programs for over 5,000 employees. Reorganized interviewing and screening processes and developed program of individualized and group counseling.

I am also completing my M.A. in industrial psychology with an emphasis on developing training and counseling programs for technical personnel.

Could we meet to discuss your program as well as how my experience might relate to your needs? I will call your office on Tuesday morning, April 12, to arrange a convenient time.

I especially want to show you a model employee counseling and career development program I recently developed. Perhaps you may find it useful for your work with TRC.

Sincerely,

Harold Haines

Harold Haines

9

Letter Organization
and Evaluation

SSUMING YOUR LETTER IS IMPRESSIVE ENOUGH TO PASS the five to ten second reading test, what you say and how you say it will largely determine if the reader will take desired actions. The power of your paper must move the reader to action. You can best do this by observing the rules of effective letter organization and content.

Common Mistakes

Individuals who receive hundreds of letters from job seekers report similar problems with most letters they read. These problems can be corrected by following a few simple organization and content rules. Letters that don't pass the five to ten second test tend to include several of these errors:

- **Looks unprofessional in form, structure, and design:** Many letters neglect the basic rules of form, structure, and design for writing effective letters. They look amateurish rather than reflect the professional competence of the writer. They don't demonstrate the writer's best professional effort.

- **Addressed to the wrong person or sent to the wrong place.** Many letter writers still forget to include proper contact information or send their letters to the wrong people and places. Make sure your letter includes a complete return address and a telephone number you can be reached at during the day. Also, closely check the name and address of your letter recipient.

■ **Does not relate to the reader's knowledge, interests, work, or needs.** Many letter writers fail to research the needs of their audience and target them accordingly. They simply waste employers' valuable time. If you respond to an ad or vacancy announcement, make sure you address the requirements specified for submitting your letter and resume.

■ **Includes spelling, grammatical, and punctuation errors.** The worst mistakes you can make in a letter are spelling, grammatical, or punctuation errors. These are unforgiving errors that clearly communicate your incompetence. Such mistakes demonstrate you are either careless or semi-illiterate—both deadly to a job search!

■ **Uses awkward language and the passive voice.** Carefully watch your use of language and try to mainly use the active voice. The active voice gives your writing more energy. Good, crisp, interesting, and pleasing language is something few readers experience in reading letters.

■ **Overly aggressive, assertive, boastful, hyped, and obnoxious in tone.** Employers receive many letters from individuals who try to impress them with what is essentially obnoxious language. They think that telling an employer they are the "hottest thing since sliced bread" will get them an interview. These letters even appear in some books that claim they are examples of "outstanding letters"! We have yet to encounter employers who are impressed by such letters. They tend to be low-class letters that follow the principles of low-class advertising.

■ **Self-centered rather than job- or employer-centered.** Too many job applicants still focus on what they want **from** employers (position, salary, benefits) rather than what they can do **for** employers (be productive, solve problems, contribute to organization, give benefits). Make sure your letters are oriented toward employers' needs. Tell them about the **benefits** you will give them. If you start referring to "you" rather than "I" in your letters, you will force yourself to be more employer-centered.

- **Poorly organized, difficult to follow, or wanders aimlessly.** Many letter writers still fail to plan the logic, sequence, and flow of their letters. They often begin with one idea, wander off to another idea, continue on to yet another disconnected idea, and then end the letter abruptly with no regard for transitions. Readers often must examine the letter two or three times to figure out what the writer wants. Such poor writing is inexcusable. If you can't say something in an organized and coherent manner, don't waste other people's time with your drivel!

- **Unclear what they are writing about or what they want.** Is there a goal or purpose to this letter? Many letters still lack a clear purpose or goal. Writers assume the reader will somehow figure out what they are writing about! Make sure your letter has a clear purpose. This should be revealed in the first paragraph.

- **Says little about the individual's interests, skills, accomplishments, or what he or she expects to achieve in the future.** Your job search letters should tell letter recipients what it is you can do for them. Unfortunately, many letter writers fail to communicate their strengths and benefits to potential employers.

- **Fails to include adequate contact information.** Be sure to include your complete address, including zip code, and a day-time and/or evening telephone number. Do not use a P.O. Box number.

- **Dull, boring, and uninspired.** Employers are looking for individuals who have enthusiasm, energy, and fire. However, most letters they receive give little indication of these critical characteristics. Try to use language that expresses your enthusiasm, energy, and fire. At least start with the active voice!

- **Too long.** Busy people don't have time to read long letters. Chances are you can say just as much, and more effectively, in a short letter. If you're writing a cover letter that accompanies an enclosed resume, be sure you do not repeat the same information that already appears on your resume. Follow the principle of "less is best."

- **Poorly typed.** We still receive letters from people who use a typewriter with dirty keys and worn ribbons. They often make typing errors and then try to correct them with erasures, chalk tape, or correction fluids. The result is an amateurish looking letter that reflects poorly on the professional style and competence of the letter writer. If you write a job search letter, make sure it reflects your **best** professional effort.

- **Produced on cheap and unattractive paper.** Professional correspondence should be produced on good quality paper. However, many letter writers cut corners and go with poor quality paper. Don't be cheap. Good quality paper only costs a few cents more than the cheap product, and it's easy to find at your local stationery or print shop. It more than pays for itself.

- **Lacks information on appropriate follow-up actions.** In addition to indicating the writer's purpose, the letter should include information on what actions should or will be taken next. This information normally appears in the last paragraph.

In other words, many letters aren't just poorly written; they make poor impressions on readers. Letters that avoid these errors tend to be read and responded to. Make sure your letters are free of such errors!

Principles of Good Advertising

Several principles of effective advertising can be adapted to business writing and the job search. Indeed, the advertising analogy is most appropriate for a job search since both deal with how to best communicate benefits to potential buyers and users. These principles should assist you in developing your creative capacity to get what you want through letter writing.

Job search letters should be written according to the key principles of good advertising copy. They should include the following principles:

- **Catch the reader's attention:** While advertising copy primarily captures attention through a visual (headline, photo, illustration), a job search letter can do the same. It should project an overall quality appearance and an opening sentence or paragraph that immediately grabs the reader's attention. Like any good presentation, an attention-grabbing opening can be a question, startling statement, quotation, an example or illustration, humorous anecdote, a suspenseful observation, or a compliment to the reader. You must do this at the very beginning of your letter—not near the end which may never get read or where the reader's attention span has dissipated. You should always present your most important points first.

- **Persuade the reader about you, the product:** Good advertising copy involves the reader in the product by stressing **value and benefits**. It tells why the reader should acquire the product. A good job search letter should do the same—the product is you and the letter should stress the specific benefits the reader will receive for contacting you. The benefits you should offer are your skills and accomplishments as they relate to the reader's present and future needs. Therefore, you must know something about your reader's needs before you can offer the proper mix of benefits.

- **Convince the reader with more evidence:** Good advertising copy presents facts about the product that relate to its benefits. An effective job search letter should also present evidence of the writer's benefits. Statements of specific accomplishments and examples of productivity are the strongest such evidence.

- **Move the reader to take action (acquire the product):** Effective advertising copy concludes with a call to take action to acquire the product. This usually involves a convenient order form or a toll-free telephone number. To stress the benefits of the product without moving the reader to take action would be a waste of time and money. When writing job search letters, you should conclude with a call to action. This is the ultimate power of paper. You want the reader to do something he or she ordinarily would not do—pick up the telephone to contact you, or write you a positive letter that leads to job search information, advice, and referrals as well as job interviews and offers. But we know few letters are so powerful as to move the reader to take initiative in contacting the letter writer. Simply put, the benefits are not as clear in a job search letter as they are in selling a product through advertising copy. Therefore, your call to action should mention that **you** will contact the reader by telephone at a certain time.

Form, style, content, production, and distribution all play important roles in communicating these persuasive elements in your letters.

Planning and Organizing

It goes without saying that you need to plan and organize your writing. By all means do not copy or edit a letter you think may be a good example of an effective job search letter. "Canned" letters tend to be too formal. Worst of all, they look and sound canned and thus they lack credibility.

Your letters should represent **you**—your personality, your credibility, your style, and your purpose. Start by asking yourself these questions **before** organizing and writing your letters:

- What is the **purpose** of this letter?

- What are the **needs** of my audience?

- What is a good opening sentence or paragraph for grabbing the **attention** of my audience?

- How can I maintain the **interest** of my audience?

- How can I best end the letter so that my audience will be **persuaded** to contact me?

- How much **time** should I spend revising and proofreading the letter?

- Will this letter represent my **best professional effort**?

After writing your letter, review these questions again. But this time convert them into a checklist for evaluating the potential effectiveness of your letter:

- Is the **purpose** of this letter clear?

- Does the letter clearly target the **needs** of my audience?

- Does the opening sentence or paragraph grab the **attention** of my audience?

- Does the letter state specific **benefits** for the reader?

- Does the letter sustain the **interest** of my audience?

- Will the letter **persuade** the reader to contact me?

- Have I spent enough **time** revising and proofreading the letter?

- Does the letter represent my **best professional effort**?

Always keep in mind what you want your audience to do in reference to your job search:

- Pay attention to your message.

- Remember you.

- Take specific actions you want taken.

Content Rules

The body of the letter should clearly communicate your message. How well you structure this section of the letter will largely determine how much impact it will have on your reader.

The basic principles of effective communication are especially applicable to the body of your letter. In general you should:

1. **Have a clear purpose in writing your letter:** First ask yourself "What message do I want to convey to my reader? What do I want him or her to do after reading my letter?" Your message should be directly related to some desirable action or outcome.

2. **Plan and organize each section:** Each paragraph should be related to your overall purpose as well as to each other. The message should be logical and flow in sequential order. Start with a detailed outline of your message.

3. **Put your most important ideas first:** Since readers' attention decreases in direct relation to the length of a message, always state your most important points first.

4. **Keep your paragraphs short and your sentences simple:** Your reader is most likely a busy person who does not have time to read and interpret long and complex letters. The shorter the letter the better. Plain simple English is always preferred to complex usages which require the reader to re-read and decode your language. Three to four paragraphs, each three to five lines in length, should be sufficient. Keep sentences to no more than 25 words. Avoid including too many ideas in a single sentence.

5. **Your opening sentence should get the attention of the reader:** Your first sentence is the most important one. It should have a similar function as an advertisement—get the interest and involvement of your audience. Avoid the standard canned openers by making your sentence unique.

6. **Your opening paragraph should clearly communicate your purpose:** Get directly to the point in as short a space as possible. Remember, this is a business letter. Your reader wants to know why he should spend time reading your letter. Your first sentence should tell why and begin motivating him or her to take actions you desire.

7. **Your letter should convince the reader to take action:** Most letters function to inform and/or to persuade. In either case, they should lead to some action. Incorporate the four principles of good advertising in your letter writing:

   - Catch the reader's attention.
   - Persuade the reader about you or your product—establish your credibility.
   - Convince the reader with more evidence and benefits.
   - Move the reader to acquire the service or product.

8. **Follow of rules of good grammar, spelling, and punctuation:** Grammatical, spelling, and punctuation errors communicate a lack of competence and professionalism. Always check and re-check for such errors by (1) proofreading the letter yourself at least twice, and (2) asking someone else to proofread it also.

9. **Communicate your unique style:** Try to avoid standard or "canned" business language which is found in numerous how-to books on business writing and sample letters. Such language tends to be too formalistic and boring. Some examples go to the other extreme in presenting excessively aggressive and obnoxious letters which would turn off any normal employer. Write as if you were talking to a reader in a natural conversational tone. Be honest and straightforward in your message. Use your imagination in making your letter interesting. Put your personality into this letter. Try to demonstrate your energy and enthusiasm through your writing tone. For example, what type of impression does this letter leave on a reader?

> I'm writing in response to your recent ad for an assistant manager at your Great Falls Super store.
>
> Please find enclosed a copy of my resume which outlines my experience in relationship to this position.
>
> Thank you for your consideration.

While this letter is short and to the point, it doesn't grab the reader's attention, sustain interest, nor lead to action. It screams "b-o-r-i-n-g!" It sounds like hundreds of canned letters employers receive each day. Why not try writing with more personality and energy? Consider this more energetic and action-oriented alternative:

> Last year I increased profits by 15 percent at Star Drugs. It was a tremendous challenge, but the secret was simple—conduct the company's first management review which resulted in reorganizing the pharmaceutical and video sections. We eliminated two full-time employees and dramatically improved customer service.
>
> I'm now interested in taking on a similar challenge with another company interested in improving its productivity. When I saw your ad in Sunday's <u>Toledo Star</u>, I thought we might share a mutual interest.
>
> If you're interested in learning more about my experience, let's talk soon on how we might work together. I'll call you Thursday afternoon to answer any questions. In the meantime, please look over my enclosed resume.

Which letter do you think will grab the attention of the employer and lead to some action? The first letter is both standard and boring. The second letter, equally true, incorporates most principles of effective letter writing—and advertising!

10. **Be personable by referring to "you" more than "I" or "we":** Your letters should communicate that you are other-centered rather than self-centered. You communicate your awareness and concern for the individual by frequently referring to "you."

11. **Try to be positive in what you say:** Avoid negative words and tones in your letters. Such words as "can't," "didn't," "shouldn't," and "won't" can be eliminated in favor of a more positive way of stating a negative. For example, instead of writing:

> I don't have the required five years experience nor have I taken the certification test.

Try putting your message in a more positive tone by using positive content:

> I have several years of experience and will be taking the certification test next month.

12. **Follow the basic ABC's of good writing:** These consist of <u>A</u>lways <u>B</u>eing:

- Clear
- Correct
- Complete
- Concise
- Courteous

- Considerate
- Creative
- Cheerful
- Careful

Inclusions and Omissions

What should be included and omitted in your cover letters? This question depends on your purpose and your audience. If you are responding to a vacancy announcement or a classified ad, you need to address the stated requirements for submitting an application. This usually involves a resume and sometimes information on your "salary requirements."

Use the following general guidelines when trying to decide what to include or omit in your letters:

THINGS YOU SHOULD INCLUDE:

- Positive information that supports your candidacy.

- Information on your skills, abilities, strengths, accomplishments, interests, and goals.

- Examples of your productivity and performance.

- Benefits you can offer the reader.

- A daytime contact telephone number.

THINGS YOU SHOULD OMIT:

- Any extraneous information unrelated to the position, the employer's needs, or your skills.

- Any negative references to a former employer, your weaknesses, or the employer's organization and position.

- Boastful statements or proposed solutions to employer's problems.

- Salary requirements or history.

- References.

- Personal information such as height, weight, marital status, hobbies—information that should not appear on a resume.

One major question concerning many job applicants is whether or not to include salary information in their letter. Our general rule is to omit such information in letters; never volunteer salary information unless asked for it since this is the last question you want to deal with **after** you have demonstrated your value in job interviews. However, it is not always possible to avoid the salary question. In certain situations you must address this question in your letter. Job ads or vacancy announcements, for example, often request a statement about your salary requirements or salary history. If you don't respond, you may be eliminated from consideration. Be careful in how you respond to this requirement. When asked, state a **salary range** rather than a specific salary figure. If, for example, you currently make $40,000 a year but you expect to make $50,000 in your next job, you might state your salary expectation is *"in the range of $48,000 to $54,000."* When stating your salary history, make sure to include your *total compensation package*—not just your monthly salary figure.

The basic rule for including information in cover letters is to include only positive information that stresses your skills and abilities in reference to the employer's needs. Never, never, never volunteer your weaknesses or negatives. These are subjects which may be discussed during a job interview, but you should never put them in writing.

The biggest problem facing most job seekers is keeping focused on their goal. The job search is an intensely ego-involved activity that often goes astray due to a combination of wishful thinking and bouts of depression attendant with rejections. If you keep focused on your goals, what you include or omit in your cover letters will come naturally. You will know what should be communicated to employers as your qualifications.

Evaluation

Evaluate the quality of the organization and content of your letters by responding to the following evaluation criteria. Circle the numbers to the right that best describe your letter.

Characteristic

		Yes	No
1.	Immediately grabs the reader's attention.	1	3
2.	Presents most important ideas first.	1	3
3.	Expressed concisely.	1	3
4.	Relates to the reader's interests and needs.	1	3
5.	Persuades the reader to take action.	1	3
6.	Free of spelling, grammatical, and punctuation errors.	1	3

7. Incorporates the active voice.   1   3

8. Avoids negative words and tones; uses
    positive language throughout.   1   3

9. Expresses the "unique you."   1   3

10. Employer-centered rather than self-centered.   1   3

11. Stresses benefits the reader is likely to
    receive from the letter writer.   1   3

12. Demonstrates a clear purpose.   1   3

13. Sentences and paragraphs flow logically.   1   3

14. Includes complete contact information
    (no P.O. Box numbers).   1   3

15. Expresses enthusiasm, energy, and fire.   1   3

16. Follows the ABC's of good writing.   1   3

TOTAL   _____

Add the circled numbers to arrive at your composite score. If you incorporate the principles identified in this chapter into the organization and content of your writing, your letter should score a perfect "16."

10

Creating Your Resume Database

THE FOLLOWING WORKSHEETS ARE DESIGNED TO HELP you systematically generate a complete database on yourself for writing each resume section. We recommend completing the forms **before** writing your resume.

Generate the Right Data On Yourself

You will be in the strongest position to write each resume section after you document, analyze, and synthesize different types of data on yourself based on these forms. Each form will assist you in specifying your accomplishments and generating the proper resume language. Since your experience/education may exceed the number of worksheets provided here, make several copies of these worksheets if necessary to complete the exercises.

Try to complete each form as thoroughly as possible. While you will not include all the information on your resume, you will at least have a rich database from which to write each resume section. Our general rule is to go for volume—generate as much detailed information on yourself as possible. Condense it later when writing and editing each resume section.

The final worksheet focuses on detailing your **achievements**. In many respects, this may be the most important worksheet of all. After you complete the other worksheets, try to identify your seven most important achievements. The language generated here will be important to both writing your resume and handling the critical job interview. You should be well prepared to clearly communicate your qualifications to potential employers!

Employment Experience Worksheet

1. Name of employer: _____

2. Address: _____

   _____

3. Inclusive dates of employment: From _____ to _____.

                                            month/year   month/year

4. Type of organization: _____

5. Size of organization/approximate number of employees: _____

6. Approximate annual sales volume or annual budget: _____

7. Position held: _____

8. Earnings per month/year: (not to appear on resume) _____

9. Responsibilities/duties: _____

   _____

   _____

   _____

10. Achievements or significant contributions: _____

    _____

    _____

    _____

    _____

11. Demonstrated skills and abilities: _____

    _____

    _____

12. Reason(s) for leaving: _____

    _____

Educational Data

1. Institution: _____

2. Address: _____

   _____

3. Inclusive dates: From _____ to _____.

   month/year   month/year

4. Degree or years completed: _____

5. Major(s): _____ Minor(s): _____

6. Education highlights: _____

   _____

   _____

7. Student activities: _____

   _____

   _____

8. Demonstrated abilities and skills: _____

   _____

   _____

9. Significant contributions/achievements: _____

   _____

   _____

10. Special training courses: _____

    _____

    _____

11. G.P.A.: _____ (on _____ index)

Community/Civic/
Volunteer Experience

1. Name and address of organization/group: _____

_____

_____

2. Inclusive dates: From _____ to _____.

                        month/year   month/year

3. Offices held/nature of involvement: _____

_____

_____

_____

_____

_____

4. Significant contributions/achievements/projects: _____

_____

_____

_____

_____

_____

5. Demonstrated skills and abilities: _____

_____

_____

_____

_____

_____

Additional Information

1. Professional memberships and status:

   a. _____

   b. _____

   c. _____

   d. _____

   e. _____

   f. _____

2. Licenses/certifications:

   a. _____

   b. _____

   c. _____

   d. _____

3. Expected salary range: $ _____ to $ _____ (do not include on resume)

4. Acceptable amount of on-the-job travel: _____ days per month.

5. Areas of acceptable relocation:

   a. _____ c. _____

   b. _____ d. _____

6. Date of availability: _____

7. Contacting present employer:

   a. Is he or she aware of your prospective job change? _____

   b. May he or she be contacted at this time? _____

8. References: (name, address, telephone number—not to appear on resume)

   a. _____ b. _____

       _____   _____

       _____   _____

c. _____   d. _____

_____   _____

_____   _____

9. Foreign languages and degree of competency:

a. _____

b. _____

10. Interests and activities: hobbies, avocations, pursuits

a. _____

b. _____

c. _____

d. _____

Circle letter of ones which support your objective.

11. Foreign travel:

Country	Purpose	Dates
a. _____	_____	_____
b. _____	_____	_____
c. _____	_____	_____
d. _____	_____	_____
e. _____	_____	_____

12. Special awards/recognition:

a. _____

b. _____

c. _____

d. _____

13. Special abilities/skills/talents/accomplishments:

a. _____

b. _____

c. _____

d. _____

Detail Your Achievements

Definition: An "Achievement" is anything you enjoyed doing, believe you did well, and felt a sense of satisfaction, pride, or accomplishment in doing.

ACHIEVEMENT # ____: _____

_____

1. How did I initially become involved? _____

_____

_____

_____

_____

2. What did I do? _____

_____

_____

_____

_____

3. How did I do it? _____

_____

_____

_____

_____

4. What was especially enjoyable about doing it? _____

_____

_____

_____

_____

Detail Your Achievements

Definition: An "Achievement" is anything you enjoyed doing, believe you did well, and felt a sense of satisfaction, pride, or accomplishment in doing.

ACHIEVEMENT # ____: _____

_____

1. How did I initially become involved? _____

_____

_____

_____

_____

2. What did I do? _____

_____

_____

_____

_____

3. How did I do it? _____

_____

_____

_____

_____

4. What was especially enjoyable about doing it? _____

_____

_____

_____

_____

Detail Your Achievements

Definition: An "Achievement" is anything you enjoyed doing, believe you did well, and felt a sense of satisfaction, pride, or accomplishment in doing.

ACHIEVEMENT # _____: _____

_____

1. How did I initially become involved? _____

_____

_____

_____

_____

2. What did I do? _____

_____

_____

_____

_____

3. How did I do it? _____

_____

_____

_____

_____

4. What was especially enjoyable about doing it? _____

_____

_____

_____

_____

The Authors

CARL S. SAVINO, a retired Army Major (USAR), is a recognized leader in the field of military-to-civilian career transitions. After completing active service as an Army officer, Carl worked as a consultant for Booz-Allen & Hamilton and later the Hay Group. In 1996, Carl founded Competitive Edge Services, a company dedicated to connecting transitioning and former military with firms looking to hire them. His popular "Corporate Gray Job Fairs for Military Personnel" (*www.corporate-gray.com*) are held at various locations across the country. Carl is co-author of four military career transition books— *From Army Green to Corporate Gray*, *From Navy Blue to Corporate Gray*, *From Air Force Blue to Corporate Gray*, and *Military Resumes and Cover Letters*. He holds a bachelor's degree in Engineering from the U.S. Military Academy at West Point and advanced degrees from George Washington University and the University of Pennsylvania. He can be contacted through the publisher: *savino@impactpublications.com*.

RONALD L. KRANNICH, Ph.D., is one of America's leading career and travel specialists. Co-author with Carl Savino of four career transition books for military personnel, he also is the principal author of over 50 books, including such career bestsellers as *Change Your Job Change Your Life*, *High Impact Resumes and Letters*, *Dynamite Resumes*, *Dynamite Salary Negotiations*, *Jobs for People Who Love to Travel*, *International Jobs Directory*, *Find a Federal Job Fast*, and *The Best Jobs for the 21st Century*. In the field of travel, he is author of *Travel Planning on the Internet* and 14 volumes in the popular Impact Guides travel-shopping series. Much of his work can be found on two newly launched websites: *www.winningthejob.com* and *www.ishoparoundtheworld.com.* Ron is president of Development Concepts Incorporated, a training, consulting, and publishing firm in Virginia. He is a former Peace Corps Volunteer, high school teacher, university professor, and Fulbright Scholar who received his undergraduate and graduate degrees from Northern Illinois University. He can be contacted through the publisher: *krannich@impactpublications.com.*

Contributors

We wish to thank several individuals and organizations for their contributions to this book. Many transitioning members of the military volunteered sample resumes as well as offered feedback on their resume and letter writing experiences. We especially want to acknowledge the contributions of four TAMP managers and counselors who shared examples of resumes: Winston Coye, Ron Lancaster, Fred Van Leeuwen, and Marie Lashapelle. The following employment specialists, who regularly work with transitioning military personnel, also provided resume examples that appear in this book. They represent some of the best professional employment services available, from writing resumes to placing candidates. If you need assistance, we highly recommend contacting these career professionals and firms:

HIRE QUALITY
3166 N. Lincoln Avenue, Suite 402
Chicago, IL 60657
Tel. 1-800-414-4733
Fax 773-281-6993
Email: *hqchic@hire-quality.com*
Website: *www.hire-quality.com*
Specializes in recruitment and placement of former military personnel, both Officers and Enlisted.

David Henderson
HM3
11745 Longshore Way E.
Naples, FL 34119
Tel. 941-594-1790
Fax 971-594-7789
Email: *davehm3@aol.com*
Author of *Job Search: Marketing Your Military Experience*
(Stackpole Books, see order form on page 256)

Wendy S. Enelow, CPRW, JCTC, CCM
CAREER MASTERS INSTITUTE
119 Old Stable Road
Lynchburg, VA 24503
Tel. 804-386-3100
Fax 804-386-3200
Email: *wendyenelow@cminstitute.com*
Website: *www.cminstitute.com*
One of America's leading experts in resume writing and career coaching for executive-level candidates. Author of *100 Winning Resumes for $100,000+ Jobs*, *201 Winning Cover Letters for $100,000+ Jobs*, *1500+ KeyWords for $100,000+ Jobs*, *Winning Interviews for $100,000+ Jobs*, *Resume Winners From the Pros* (Impact Publications, see order form on pages 253-258). Wendy is currently president of Career Masters Institute, a professional training and development association of career service providers worldwide. She serves as a featured guest speaker nationwide.

Career Resources

THE FOLLOWING CAREER RESOURCES, SOME OF WHICH were mentioned in previous chapters, are available directly from Impact Publications. Complete the following form or list the titles, include postage (see formula at the end), enclose payment, and send your order to:

IMPACT PUBLICATIONS
9104 Manassas Drive, Suite N
Manassas Park, VA 20111-5211
1-800-361-1055 (orders only)
Tel. 703/361-7300 or Fax 703/335-9486
E-mail address: *orders@impactpublications.com*
Quick & easy online ordering: ***www.impactpublications.com***

Orders from individuals must be prepaid by check, moneyorder, Visa, MasterCard, or American Express. We accept telephone and fax orders.

Qty.	TITLES	Price	TOTAL
Current Title			
_____	Military Resumes and Cover Letters	$19.95	_____
Resumes			
_____	100 Winning Resumes For $100,000+ Jobs	24.95	_____
_____	101 Best Resumes	10.95	_____

_____	1500+ KeyWords For $100,000+ Jobs	14.95	_____
_____	Adams Resumes Almanac & Disk	19.95	_____
_____	America's Top Resumes For America's Top Jobs	19.95	_____
_____	Asher's Bible of Executive Resumes	29.95	_____
_____	Best Resumes For $75,000+ Executive Jobs	14.95	_____
_____	Better Resumes in Three Easy Steps	12.95	_____
_____	Blue Collar Resumes	11.99	_____
_____	Complete Idiot's Guide to Writing the Perfect Resume	16.95	_____
_____	Dynamite Resumes	14.95	_____
_____	Encyclopedia of Job-Winning Resumes	16.95	_____
_____	Gallery of Best Resumes	16.95	_____
_____	Gallery of Best Resumes For Two-Year Degree Grads	14.95	_____
_____	Global Resume and CV Guide	17.95	_____
_____	Haldane's Best Resumes For Professionals	15.95	_____
_____	Heart and Soul Resumes	15.95	_____
_____	High Impact Resumes & Letters	19.95	_____
_____	Internet Resumes	14.95	_____
_____	Military Resumes and Cover Letters	19.95	_____
_____	Overnight Resume	12.95	_____
_____	Portfolio Power	14.95	_____
_____	Ready-to-Go Resumes	29.95	_____
_____	Resume Catalog	15.95	_____
_____	Resume Shortcuts	14.95	_____
_____	Resume Winners From the Pros	17.95	_____
_____	Resumes For Dummies	14.99	_____
_____	Resumes For the Over-50 Job Hunter	14.95	_____
_____	Resumes For Re-Entry	10.95	_____
_____	Resumes in Cyberspace	14.95	_____
_____	Resumes That Knock 'Em Dead	14.95	_____
_____	Savvy Resume Writer	10.95	_____
_____	Sure-Hire Resumes	14.95	_____

Cover Letters

_____	175 High-Impact Cover Letters	10.95	_____
_____	201 Dynamite Job Search Letters	19.95	_____
_____	201 Killer Cover Letters	16.95	_____
_____	201 Winning Cover Letters For $100,000+ Jobs	24.95	_____
_____	Adams Cover Letter Almanac & Disk	19.95	_____
_____	Complete Idiot's Guide to the Perfect Cover Letter	14.95	_____
_____	Cover Letters For Dummies	14.99	_____
_____	Cover Letters That Knock 'Em Dead	10.95	_____
_____	Dynamite Cover Letters	14.95	_____
_____	Haldane's Best Cover Letters For Professionals	15.95	_____

Salary Negotiations and Databases

_____	American Almanac of Jobs and Salaries	20.00	_____
_____	American Salaries and Wages Survey	120.00	_____

_____ Better Than Money	18.95	_____
_____ Dynamite Salary Negotiations	15.95	_____
_____ Get More Money On Your Next Job	14.95	_____
_____ Get a Raise in 7 Days	14.95	_____
_____ Jobs Rated Almanac	16.95	_____
_____ Negotiate Your Job Offer	14.95	_____
_____ Occupational Outlook Handbook	23.95	_____
_____ Unofficial Guide to Earning What You Deserve	15.95	_____

Key Directories

_____ American Salaries and Wages Survey	120.00	_____
_____ Business Phone Book USA 2001	175.00	_____
_____ Careers Encyclopedia	39.95	_____
_____ Complete Guide to Occupational Exploration	39.95	_____
_____ Consultants & Consulting Organizations Directory	620.00	_____
_____ Dictionary of Occupational Titles	47.95	_____
_____ Directory of Executive Recruiters 2001	47.95	_____
_____ Encyclopedia of Associations 2001 (all 3 volumes)	1345.00	_____
_____ Encyclopedia of Associations 2001 (National only)	520.00	_____
_____ Encyclopedia of Careers & Vocational Guidance	149.95	_____
_____ Enhanced Guide For Occupational Exploration	34.95	_____
_____ Enhanced Occupational Outlook Handbook	34.95	_____
_____ Job Hunter's Sourcebook	95.00	_____
_____ National Job Hotline Directory	16.95	_____
_____ National Trade & Professional Associations 2001	129.95	_____
_____ Occupational Outlook Handbook	23.95	_____
_____ O*NET Dictionary of Occupational Titles	49.95	_____
_____ Professional Careers Sourcebook	105.00	_____
_____ Vocational Careers Sourcebook	105.00	_____

Recruitment and Retention

_____ 101 Hiring Mistakes Employers Make & How to Avoid Them	14.95	_____
_____ Anger and Conflict in the Workplace	15.95	_____
_____ The Best 100 Web Sites for HR Professionals	13.95	_____
_____ The Difficult Hire	14.95	_____
_____ The Employer's Guide to Recruiting on the Internet	24.95	_____
_____ Recruit and Retain the Best	14.95	_____

Job Search Strategies and Tactics

_____ Career Change	14.95	_____
_____ Career Intelligence	15.95	_____
_____ Change Your Job, Change Your Life	17.95	_____
_____ Complete Idiot's Guide to Getting the Job You Want	24.95	_____
_____ Five Secrets to Finding a Job	12.95	_____
_____ Get a Job You Love!	19.95	_____

_____ Headhunters Revealed! Career Secrets for
Choosing and Using Professional Recruiters   14.95 _____
_____ How to Succeed Without a Career Path   13.95 _____
_____ Is It Too Late to Run Away and Join the Circus   14.95 _____
_____ Job Hunting For the Utterly Confused   14.95 _____
_____ Job Search: Marketing Your Military Experience 16.95 _____
_____ Knock 'Em Dead   12.95 _____
_____ Me, Myself, and I, Inc   17.95 _____
_____ No One Is Unemployable   29.95 _____
_____ The Pathfinder   14.00 _____
_____ Reinventing Your Career   9.99 _____
_____ Strategic Job Jumping   13.00 _____
_____ What Color Is Your Parachute?   16.95 _____
_____ Zen and the Art of Making a Living   17.95 _____

Best Jobs and Employers

_____ 50 Coolest Jobs in Sports   15.95 _____
_____ 100 Great Jobs and How to Get Them   17.95 _____
_____ Best Jobs For the 21st Century   19.95 _____
_____ Cool Careers For Dummies   16.99 _____
_____ Great Jobs Ahead   11.95 _____
_____ Sunshine Jobs   16.95 _____
_____ The Top 100   19.95 _____

Electronic Job Search

_____ 100 Top Internet Job Sites   12.95 _____
_____ Adams Electronic Job Search Almanac   10.95 _____
_____ Career Exploration on the Internet   24.95 _____
_____ CareerXroads 2001   26.95 _____
_____ Cyberspace Resume Kit   16.95 _____
_____ Electronic Resumes   19.95 _____
_____ Guide to Internet Job Search   14.95 _____
_____ Heart and Soul Internet Job Search   16.95 _____
_____ Internet Jobs Kit (software)   29.99 _____
_____ Internet Resumes   14.95 _____
_____ Job Searching Online For Dummies, With CD-ROM 24.99 _____
_____ Resumes in Cyberspace   14.95 _____

$100,000+ Jobs

_____ The $100,000 Club   25.00 _____
_____ 100 Winning Resumes For $100,000+ Jobs   24.95 _____
_____ 201 Winning Cover Letters For $100,000+ Jobs 24.95 _____
_____ 1500+ KeyWords For $100,000+ Jobs   14.95 _____
_____ New Rites of Passage at $100,000+   29.95 _____
_____ Six-Figure Consulting   17.95 _____
_____ Winning Interviews For $100,000+ Jobs   17.95 _____

Finding Great Jobs

_____	101 Ways to Power Up Your Job Search	12.95 _____
_____	Adams Executive Recruiters Almanac	16.95 _____
_____	Careers For College Majors	32.95 _____
_____	College Grad Job Hunter	14.95 _____
_____	Get Ahead! Stay Ahead!	12.95 _____
_____	Get What You Deserve!	23.00 _____
_____	Great Jobs For Liberal Arts Majors	11.95 _____
_____	Perfect Pitch	13.99 _____
_____	Professional's Job Finder	18.95 _____
_____	What Do I Say Next?	12.95 _____
_____	What Employers Really Want.	14.95 _____
_____	Work Happy Live Healthy	14.95 _____
_____	World Almanac Job Finder's Guide	24.95 _____

Assessment

_____	Career Satisfaction and Success	14.95 _____
_____	Career Tests	12.95 _____
_____	Dictionary of Holland Occupational Codes	45.00 _____
_____	Discover the Best Jobs For You	15.95 _____
_____	Discover What You're Best At	12.00 _____
_____	Do What You Are	16.95 _____
_____	Finding Your Perfect Work	16.95 _____
_____	Gifts Differing	14.95 _____
_____	I Could Do Anything If Only I Knew What It Was	19.95 _____
_____	Making Vocational Choices	29.95 _____
_____	Real People, Real Jobs	15.95 _____
_____	Richard Bolles Self-Assessment Tool Kit	21.95 _____
_____	Type Talk	11.95 _____
_____	WORKTypes	12.99 _____

Inspiration & Empowerment

_____	100 Ways to Motivate Yourself	15.99 _____
_____	Awaken the Giant Within	12.00 _____
_____	Doing Work You Love	14.95 _____
_____	Emotional Intelligence	13.95 _____
_____	If Life Is a Game, These Are the Rules	15.00 _____
_____	Power of Purpose	20.00 _____
_____	Seven Habits of Highly Effective People	14.00 _____

Networking

_____	Dig Your Well Before You're Thirsty	24.95 _____
_____	Dynamite Networking For Dynamite Jobs	15.95 _____
_____	Dynamite Telesearch	12.95 _____
_____	Effective Networking	10.95 _____
_____	Golden Rule of Schmoozing	12.95 _____

_____ Great Connections	19.95	_____
_____ How to Work a Room	14.99	_____
_____ Networking For Everyone	16.95	_____
_____ People Power	14.95	_____
_____ Power Networking	14.95	_____
_____ Power Schmoozing	12.95	_____
_____ The Savvy Networker	14.95	_____

Etiquette and Image

_____ Dressing Smart For the New Millennium	15.95	_____
_____ Executive Etiquette in the New Workplace	14.95	_____
_____ John Molloy's Dress For Success	13.99	_____
_____ New Professional Image	12.95	_____
_____ New Women's Dress For Success	12.99	_____
_____ Power Etiquette	14.95	_____
_____ Red Socks Don't Work	14.95	_____
_____ Winning Image	17.95	_____
_____ You've Only Got 3 Seconds	22.95	_____

Interview & Communication Skills

_____ 101 Dynamite Answers to Interview Questions	12.95	_____
_____ 101 Dynamite Questions to Ask At Your Job Interview	13.95	_____
_____ 101 Secrets of Highly Effective Speakers	14.95	_____
_____ Complete Idiot's Guide to the Perfect Job Interview	14.95	_____
_____ Complete Q & A Job Interview Book	14.95	_____
_____ Proof of Performance	17.95	_____
_____ Haldane's Best Answers to Tough Interview Questions	15.95	_____
_____ Information Interviewing	10.95	_____
_____ Interview For Success	15.95	_____
_____ Interview Power	12.95	_____
_____ Job Interviews For Dummies	14.99	_____
_____ Killer Interviews	10.95	_____
_____ Savvy Interviewer	10.95	_____
_____ Winning Interviews For $100,000+ Jobs	17.95	_____

Government, Security, & Law Enforcement Jobs

_____ Alternative Careers in Secret Operations	17.95	_____
_____ Barron's Guide to Law Enforcement Careers	13.95	_____
_____ Complete Guide to Public Employment	19.95	_____
_____ Directory of Federal Jobs and Employers	21.95	_____
_____ Federal Applications That Get Results	23.95	_____
_____ Federal Jobs in Law Enforcement	14.95	_____
_____ Government Job Finder	16.95	_____
_____ Jobs For Lawyers	14.95	_____
_____ Paralegal Career Guide	24.95	_____
_____ Quick & Easy Federal Application Kit (software)	49.95	_____

International & Travel

_____	Careers in International Affairs	17.95	_____
_____	Global Resume and CV Guide	17.95	_____
_____	Great Jobs Abroad	14.95	_____
_____	How to Get a Job in Europe	21.95	_____
_____	International Jobs	16.00	_____
_____	International Jobs Directory	19.95	_____
_____	Jobs For People Who Love to Travel	15.95	_____
_____	Jobs in Paradise	16.00	_____
_____	Jobs In Russia & the Newly Independent States	15.95	_____
_____	Living, Studying, and Working in France	16.00	_____
_____	Living, Studying, and Working in Italy	16.00	_____
_____	Work Worldwide	14.95	_____

Nonprofit Sector

_____	100 Best Nonprofits to Work For	16.95	_____
_____	From Making a Profit to Making a Difference	15.95	_____
_____	Jobs and Careers With Nonprofit Organizations	17.95	_____
_____	Non-Profits and Education Job Finder	16.95	_____

SUBTOTAL _____

Virginia residents add 4½% sales tax _____

POSTAGE/HANDLING ($5 for first
product and 8% of SUBTOTAL over $30) $5.00

8% of SUBTOTAL over $30 ------------------------------------- _____

TOTAL ENCLOSED ------------------------------------- _____

NAME _____

ADDRESS _____

_____

_____

❏ I enclose check/moneyorder for $ _____ made payable to
IMPACT PUBLICATIONS.

❏ Please charge $ _____ to my credit card:
   ❏ Visa   ❏ MasterCard   ❏ American Express   ❏ Discover

Card # _____
Expiration date: _____/_____
Signature _____

The Click and Easy™ Online Resource Centers –

Books, videos, software, training materials, articles, and advice for job seekers, employers, HR professionals, schools, and libraries

Visit us online for all your career and travel needs:

www.impactpublications.com
(career superstore and Impact Publications)

————

www.winningthejob.com
(career articles and advice)

————

www.contentforcareers.com
(syndicated career content for job seekers,
employees, and Intranets)

————

www.greentogray.com
www.bluetogray.com
(military transition databases and content)

————

www.ishoparoundtheworld.com
(unique international travel-shopping center)